South Union

A Novel of the Civil War

Rick Kelsheimer

ISBN: 1478100389
ISBN 13: 9781478100386

Also by Rick Kelsheimer

The Hanging of Betsey Reed
A Wabash River Tragedy of the Illinois Frontier

Wa-Ba-Shik-Ki
Conquest of the Wabash

The Adventures of Wabash Jake

The Lost Slab

www.rickkelsheimer.com

For Judie Kelsheimer

Chapter 1

It was a cool spring evening as we sat on the front porch of the log cabin and watched the sun disappear behind the wall of budding maples. Ma was in her rocking chair with Bub on her lap while humming a familiar mountain lullaby. She patted his back in rhythm with the creaking rocker until he finally gave up and went to sleep. Bub was as good natured as a four year old brother could be. He rarely raised a fuss and woke up every morning with an ear to ear grin on his face. Ma claimed that he was an angel sent from Heaven, on account "that no boy was ever born so purdy." Pa always complained that she babied him too much, but looked the other way most of the time in order to keep the peace.

My other brother, Jaybird, was busy teasing an old mother cat. He crowed like a banty rooster every time the calico took a playful swipe at the piece of string dangling in front of her nose. Jaybird, on the other hand, was as ornery as any seven year old brother could be. He seemed to be on a perpetual search to find new ways to get into trouble and was quite successful in his endeavors. He had a shock of unruly blonde hair that turned white under the summer sun, bright blue eyes and a disarming smile, which often was his only defense against a trip to the wood shed. Even though he was three years younger than me, Jaybird considered himself to be my equal in all matters; mentally and physically. Every now and then, whenever he got a little too big for his britches, Pa would allow me to knock him down a peg or two. Ma used to cry every time we'd fight, but Pa said it was necessary for a boy to know his place in life. He said it was all part of growin' up. I don't know if it ever did any good. You could knock Jaybird to the ground a hundred times and he'd get up every single time; ready for more. All it did was tucker us both out. Maybe that was Pa's reasoning whenever he wanted a little peace and quiet. I don't know why Jaybird and I seemed to fight all the time. It just came natural to us; just like Jacob and Esau in *The Scriptures*. I suppose we were just two brothers scuffling over the pecking order.

There was no fighting that night, not even a cross word. Pioneer life was hard in southern Illinois, but that evening everything seemed perfect. Sister Rose had just finished washing the dishes and took a seat next to me on the porch step. She rested her head on my shoulder and looked out at the barn as a milk cow grazed on new spring bluegrass. Rose was actually my maternal aunt. She came to live with us when Grandma and Grandpa Brooks took ill with the yellow fever and died in the spring of 1853. I was only three at the time and it seemed silly to call a seven year old girl Aunt Rose. I favored the idea of having an older sister, so I started calling her "Sister Rose." She liked the name and said it made her feel like part of the family. Rose was a beautiful auburn-haired girl with emerald green eyes, but suffered from an uneasy shyness that overwhelmed her whenever she was around anyone other than our immediate family. It was hard to understand why a girl so full of love toward other folks could be so scared about meeting people. She made up for her shyness with kindness and toiled like a servant, always making sure everything got done around the cabin. Ma struggled greatly while bringing Bub into the world and was never the same as she was before. It would have been a much harder life without Sister Rose.

Pa filled his pipe with tobacco and gazed toward a field that might be dry enough to plow in a couple of days if the rains held off. "It sure would be good to get the crop in early this year," he said. "Especially this year." He looked to the northwest when he heard the distant rumble of thunder. He shook his head and mumbled something about the irony of Providence. A few minutes later when the thunder seemed to be getting closer he smiled. "I reckon we'll plow when *The Almighty* sees fit."

Hardship and tragedy were a part of everyday life, but Samuel Farmer was always the same. Pa seemed to take everything in stride. He was as big as a mountain, slow to anger and even handed with everyone he met. Nothing ever seemed to bother him. He made us feel like nothing could hurt us as long as he was around.

There were storm clouds brewing that night. The storm was coming fast. No doubt about it. A bolt of lightning shot across the sky. I counted to seven before the boom rattled the cabin like a blast from a cannon. Bub fussed a little, but soon quieted down after Ma covered him in her threadbare shawl. A wisp of wind stirred up a dust devil in the barnyard, sending the last pullet into the hen house to roost for the evening. Everyone had survived the winter and the promise of spring was always a time of hope and optimism on a pioneer farm in southern Illinois. Like clockwork, I listened to Pa speak the same words every spring. "This year's crop would be the finest ever" and "Maybe there'll be enough left over to buy Ma and Sister Rose a new dress and a pair of shoes for the boys." Anything was possible in the springtime. However, the storm was closer than any of us realized.

The ominous black clouds blotted out the last of the sun in the western sky. Goosebumps popped up on my arms as the wind let loose with all its strength and fury. The sweet aroma of spring rain arrived seconds before the deluge. A powerful gust chased the mother cat under the porch and the barn door flew open, allowing the yearling colt to run out into the weather. "Everybody get inside!" Pa shouted. "Will—you come with me!"

We plodded out into the storm as the barnyard promptly turned into a swamp. Pa grabbed a rope and told me to work the colt close enough for him to throw the loop around his neck. The little roan was mean to begin with, but the lightning bolts and claps of thunder turned him into a four-legged demon with little regard for my well being.

I went to the right, but instead of the horse going to the left, he rose up and tried to crush my skull with his front hooves. I dove out of his way and crawled through the fence rails to safety.

"Quit foolin' around, boy!" Pa's voiced roared above the wind and thunder. "Walk him over to the corner. You've got to show that blasted critter who's boss!"

I looked into the wild eyes of the colt and realized he had no intention of doing me any favors. I looked over at Pa and saw the look of "don't disappoint me" on his face. If the colt kicked me, and I managed to live through the ordeal; my wounds would eventually heal. The ramifications of disappointing Pa was a fate I deemed to be worse than death.

I waited until the colt landed on his front legs and then made my move. I closed my eyes, screamed like a wildcat and ran as fast as I could at the animal. He was beginning to rear back as I slammed my shoulder into his chest. I went flying into the mud, but he decided to run in the opposite direction toward the corner of the fence. Pa had him where he wanted, but there was still room for him to escape the trap. I picked myself up and ran at him once again. This time the colt knew what was coming and decide to fight back. He took two steps backwards and prepared to wallop me good, but Pa got the rope over his head before he could strike. Pa snapped the horse's head back in the opposite direction and he submitted unconditionally to his authority.

Pa led the colt back into the barn while I followed two steps behind. He got him settled back into the stall and tossed in a sheaf of hay to settle his nerves while I closed the barn door behind us.

I thought I was in trouble when Pa turned around and glared at me until I saw the hint of a smile on his weathered face. "Son, you look like a mud-puppy. What exactly was you doin' out there?"

"You told me to show him that I was the boss," I explained.

"I didn't want you to show him any fear, not wrassle the poor critter to death."

"I'm sorry, Pa. I didn't know what else to do."

"That's alright son," he chuckled. "At least you showed some gumption. That's somethin' to be proud of."

"Thanks, Pa."

"You might not be a thankin' me when your Ma gets a look at your clothes."

"Maybe I should stand in the rain a bit and let 'em soak for a spell," I suggested.

"Best not," he replied. "Ma would take me to task for not having enough sense to get you out of the rain." He laughed and ran his heavy hand through my hair. Pa rarely showed any affection, so it was an occasion to remember. "But you better step out of them muddy clothes on the porch before steppin' indoors, just to be on the safe side."

We were just about to brave the elements and make the dash for the cabin when a lone silhouette of a man on horseback appeared on the road from New Hebron. "What kind of fool would be out in weather like this?" Pa asked.

"Maybe his horse got loose too?" I answered.

He ignored me and studied the rider as he neared the house. He was almost upon us when Pa recognized the swayback plug and motioned for the rider to come into the shelter of the barn.

Bill Maxwell jumped out of the saddle and hit the ground with a muddy splash. "Mind if I ride out the weather in your barn, Mr. Farmer?"

"Nonsense, Bill!" Pa replied. "We ain't rich, but I'm no man to treat a guest like he was an animal. See to your critter and come inside."

"Much obliged, sir."

Pa tossed his saddle over a rail to dry and sent me on ahead to have Ma brew some fresh coffee. With all the excitement, I forgot to heed Pa's warning and ran into the cabin while still wearing my muddy clothes. Ma immediately chased me back outside with the business end of her straw broom and made me strip down to my drawers before delivering the news that we had company.

Visitors were few and far between on the farm during the winter, so it was a special occasion, even if it was only a neighborhood traveler coming in out of the rain. Ma put some coffee on hot coals to boil while Sister Rose set out a plate of cornbread and molasses. I sat by the fireplace and tried to dry off while Jaybird took a seat at the head of the table to make sure he'd be in the middle of everything.

Bill Maxwell, the oldest of John Maxwell's seven boys, was soaked to the bone by the time he walked through the door. He left his hat and coat on the porch and took the seat of honor after Pa shooed Jaybird out of the chair. He was tall and rail thin. His sand-colored hair and beard dripped water onto the table until Ma fetched a blanket for him to dry himself.

"You best be getting out of those clothes." Ma said "You'll catch yourself a death of a cold."

"Thank you, Ma'am, But I'll be heading back out as soon as the rain slows down." He paused and took a healthy swallow of coffee. "I've got to get home with the news."

"What news would that be, Bill?" she asked.

"The *Johnny Rebs* opened fire at Fort Sumter in Charleston Harbor yesterday!" He spoke in a manner that made you think they had fired at him personally. "It's War!"

"Are you sure?" Pa asked.

"The word came across the telegraph in Robinson this morning. Honest Abe is gonna' teach those secesh boys a lesson that they'll never forget. I hear he's callin' for seventy-five thousand volunteers. The boys will be standin' in line to join up. Archie, Joe and I already decided we'd sign up if it came to this."

"Three brothers off to war!" Ma cried. "Have you no regard for your poor mother?"

Pa lit his pipe and took a puff before speaking. "Now Ma, it ain't none of your affairs. A man's got to do what he feels is right, but I can't help but worry that you'll be leaving your Pa a little short handed."

"The four younger boys can put in the crop. It can't take more than a few weeks to whip them *rebs*, so we should be back in time for the harvest." We all watched as he slathered a hunk of cornbread with molasses. "Besides, Pa is a stubborn abolitionist. He says slavery is a blight on the country and it needs to be squashed like a bug before *The Almighty* sends judgment on us all."

Pa scratched his chin whiskers and shook his head. "I can't say that I disagree with your pa, but most folks around here has got kin in the South. It's a sad day when a brother sets off to kill his own brother."

Bill shrugged his shoulders and stuffed his mouth full of cornbread.

The storm roared on for another couple of hours before tapering off to a steady drizzle. Bill Maxwell thanked Ma for the hospitality, shook Pa's hand and left into the rainy night. Ma tucked Jaybird into the trundle bed with Bub while Sister Rose tended to the fire. Pa sat at the table and smoked his pipe in silence while staring at the fire. After the brothers were down for the night, Ma took a seat in her rocker and went to rockin' at a feverish pace.

My heart was racing with excitement. I wanted to ask a hundred questions about war, but I knew better than to interrupt Pa when he was thinking. Pa was a deep thinker and didn't take kindly to questions when he was figurin' out problems.

Ma was just as dangerous when she got fretful about things. "That poor woman," she cried. I could tell by the speed at which she was rocking that she was mighty worked up. "Three sons handed over to *Ol' Scratch*, himself."

I decided that discretion was the better part of valor and crawled up to my mattress in the loft. I closed my eyes and tried to name off the secesh states. I pretended I was old enough to sign up to fight. I'd show those *Johnny Rebs* a thing or two. War was simple when you were a ten year old boy. Within minutes I began to dream about the glory of battles in faraway southern places.

The day was April 13, 1861. *The Ides of April.* That's when everything changed forever. That's the day when the storm came to South Union.

—— ⁓ ——

Chapter 2

During the next few months, the war was mostly fought with words as far as South Union was concerned. Half of the neighbors wanted to preserve the Union and sided with Abe Lincoln. The other half sympathized with the rebels and said the federal government didn't have any business messing with the southern way of life.

Even though Pa and Ma were born in the South; neither one of them believed that a person had the right to own another person. Pa never considered himself an abolitionist. He said it was best for the family to not take sides because most of the immediate neighbors supported the secessionists. This course of action, however, was the toughest road to follow as both sides took aim at a man who tried to straddle the fence. He turned his cheek whenever a neighbor made a salty comment, but when a local Copperhead called him a coward, Pa came down from the fence and relieved the man of his two front teeth. From that day forward, our family stood firmly with Honest Abe and the Union.

The Maxwell brothers, along with a dozen others from the surrounding farms, joined the 21st Illinois Infantry in Mattoon under Ulysses S. Grant. We heard that they spent thirty days learning how to march and then headed off for Missouri. Since it took so long to learn how to walk in a straight line, I was concerned what would happen if they actually ran up against some rebel troops who knew what they were doing. Some of the neighborhood men said that one well-armed Yankee soldier from Illinois could whip ten of the secesh, so I didn't worry much.

While the men were on their way to Mattoon; Marshall Burris, Whit Mumphrey and the Goff brothers from Port Jackson met up with some boys from the Dark Bend and headed south to fight for the Confederates. Pa always said Marshall Burris wasn't much better that a horse thief so I wasn't surprised when he turned out to be a Reb.

Tempers began to flare as the neighborhood grew further apart with each passing day. Fisticuffs became common place. A Democrat couldn't pass a Republican without insulting his heritage or condemning that 'nigger in sheep's clothing,' Abe Lincoln. Any man who considered himself a patriot felt duty bound to defend the honor of his family and commander in chief.

Pa was slow to anger and never allowed himself to be dragged into a war of words. "It takes two to argue and if you hold your tongue, the other feller will give up yappin' and sooner or later go away." Pa always treated people fairly and never provoked anyone about their political views. Besides that, he was as strong as a bull and could scare you to death with his scowl. Sam Farmer was an intimidating man and managed to avoid confrontation with the local Democrats. Unfortunately, the same could not be said about his two eldest sons.

Every week after the *Sunday Meeting* at the log church house, while the women were preparing the community meal and the men were discussing the war; all of the boys would get together and play soldier. At first it was all good natured fun, but as folks declared allegiance on both sides of the struggle, so did the boys. Gradually, the numbers tilted in favor of the boys wearing grey and butternut. Jaybird and I lined up with the union boys and realized that we were outnumbered two to one. Apparently, the boys on the other side came to the same conclusion. Burl Stubbs, the biggest and meanest boy in the neighborhood, walked to the middle of the yard and drew a line in the dirt with his bare foot. "I dare any one of you Yankee pot lickers to step across this here line!" He put his hands on his hips and unfurled a devilish grin that highlighted the fact that he was missing his two front teeth. "I double black dog dare ya!"

Just like the Philistine, Goliath, Burl Stubbs had called out the righteous to a fight.

I was aware of how David took care of the giant with a sling-shot and I didn't take kindly to being labeled as a *pot licker*, but Burl was as big as an outhouse and didn't smell much better neither. As a matter of principle, I felt obligated to defend the honor of the Union, but I couldn't force my feet to carry me into battle. When I looked down the line, I saw that my brothers in arms had come to the same conclusion.

Burl seemed pleased that nobody accepted his challenge. He turned to face his *Johnny-Reb* cronies. "I told you they ain't nothing but a pack of Yankee yellow-bellies."

All of the boys in the other line laughed and joined in with the name calling and insults.

I could feel a fire brewing in my stomach and was doing my best to control my temper when I noticed Jaybird breaking rank and marching toward Burl with his fists balled and words coming out of his mouth that weren't fit to be spoken on a Sunday. "I ain't scared of you, Burl Stubbs!" Jaybird declared as he charged at his target.

Suddenly, I was faced with a whole new set of circumstances. My honor would be questioned if I let my younger brother do my fighting for me, but Pa would surely take me to the wood-shed for fighting at the Sunday meeting. On the other hand, a trip to the wood shed would be mandatory if I stood by and let Burl Stubbs whip up on Jaybird without coming to his defense. Either way, I was going to end up on the wrong side of Pa's stick. I decided to stand up for my honor along with the honor of the Union Army.

Burl sidestepped Jaybird's frontal assault and knocked him to the ground without exerting himself. He turned and was ready to stomp his boot into Jaybird's ribs, when I reached the overgrown bully. I jumped on Burl's back and held on with my left hand while punching the back of his head with my right. Burl bucked like an unbroken stallion, but I managed to get in three good licks, before he threw me to the dirt.

Burl had fire in his eyes as he ran straight at me. I tried to crawl out of the way just as he left his feet in an attempt to flatten me like a human anvil. I saw that I wasn't going to make it, so I rolled into a ball. He groaned as he landed on my knee with a sickening thud before ending up on his back in the dirt. I got ready to take advantage of his weakened state, but immediately stopped when I saw the look in his eyes. His face was bright red and he couldn't catch his breath. I had never seen anybody die before, but I was convinced that Burl was on his way to the *Pearly Gates*. He desperately tried to draw air into his lungs without success. I couldn't believe what was happening. I didn't know what to do. I looked around and saw I wasn't alone. The remainder of the boys seemed just as helpless.

Suddenly the fear of ending up at the wrong end of Pa's belt was the least of my worries. What if I killed him? They lynched murderers in Honey Creek Township! I could almost feel the noose tightening around my neck.

It was at that moment that Reverend Parker noticed the activity and came running. He took one look at the situation and diagnosed the problem immediately. "This boy's got the wind knocked out of him. One of you boys, go get his folks!" Toady Kincaid raced back to the maple grove where the men were congregating, while Reverend Parker started to work on Burl. He picked him up by the front of his trousers and told him to simmer down.

"I...can't...breathe..." Burl gasped. He started to struggle, but stopped when *the Reverend* slapped his face with the back of his hand.

"Be quiet and let the air come back to your lungs," said *the Reverend*.

Burl did as he was told and within a few seconds the color started to return to his face. He gulped in a deep helping of air and then started to breathe normally again. He seemed to be calming down until he saw his pa running towards him and then he began bawling like a newly weaned calf. The closer his pa got, the louder he cried.

I felt like running, but knew it would only make things worse for me. I probably should have been thinking about what I needed to say in order to save the top layer of skin beneath my britches, but I couldn't take my eyes off of the bawling bully. Suddenly, an overwhelming sense of pride swept over me. I puffed out my chest and felt like I was David after he slew the Philistine. I could tell that the other boys, on both sides of the skirmish, looked at me in awe. Without the aid of sling or stone, I stood victorious over my giant fallen foe.

Unfortunately, while I was basking in the light of my victorious glory, Burl regained the use of his tongue and index finger and they were both pointing at me. "He did it, Pa! Will Farmer sucker punched me and then he kicked me when I was down on the ground!"

"That's a lie!" I shouted with the conviction of Daniel Webster. "You know that you started the fight! You called us a bunch of Yankee pot lickers!"

"That don't give you the right to sucker punch my boy," growled Virgil Stubbs as he headed in my direction. "I'm gonna teach you a lesson you ain't never gonna forget."

In the twinkling of an eye, I went from a conquering hero to the intended victim of a grown man that made his son, Burl, look small and insignificant. I breathed a sigh of relief when Reverend Parker stepped in front of him in the name of *Christian love and harmony*. My reprieve was short lived when he knocked the preacher to the ground and continued his charge in my direction. A man who would strike a man of the cloth wouldn't hesitate to beat the tar out of a boy of my stature and age. I wanted to run, but my Pa's words were entrenched in my mind. "Always respect your elders!" That's what I intended to do, but when I looked into the blood red eyes that seemed ready to pop out of Virgil Stubbs's sockets, I realized that he was prepared to render some substantial retribution to my body. I decided to forgo any elderly respect and run for my life. Unfortunately, my hesitation was my downfall. I only made two steps before I felt the meaty paw of Virgil Stubbs grab a handful of my hair and simultaneously felt my feet losing contact with the ground.

"Where do you think you're goin', boy?" he roared. His breath was so putrid; it almost made me forget the pain of my scalp being pulled away from my head. "You think it's alright to fight dirty—you little sombitch! I'll show you dirty." He pulled me close, took a better handhold of my hair and started twirling me around like a rag doll. After the completion of my third full orbit, the hair and my head parted company while making a hideous ripping noise. I went flying through the air and slammed into a rough barked hickory tree. The top of my head was stinging and I felt a sharp pain in my back. When I opened my eyes, through the wobbly galaxy of stars, I saw Virgil Stubbs once again stomping a beeline in my direction with a bloody shock of my hair still in his hand. I had been scalped without the use of an Indian's knife! I tried to escape but only managed a single step before he had a hold of my tattered mane once again. I was preparing myself for my second helping of the inevitable whirlwind tour, when the crack of a rifle shot echoed from somewhere behind me.

"Let go of the boy," sternly ordered the familiar voice of my father.

Stubbs lowered my feet back to the ground but refused to relinquish his hold on my hair. "Your cowardly boy nearly killed my son with a sucker punch!" Stubbs shouted defiantly. "I'm just givin' him a taste of his own medicine."

"I said let the boy go, Stubbs!" Pa repeated as he quickly reloaded his rifle.

"Or what?" he taunted. "You gonna shoot me? You don't have the guts. You Yankee cowards are all talk. That's why Jeff Davis is gonna win this war before the end of the year."

"Last chance, Stubbs. Let the boy go." Pa pointed his rifle at my captor.

As Virgil Stubbs was contemplating what to do, I could feel his grip tighten on my hair. His breath was heavy and deliberate in the same manner a horse breathes just before he tries to kick in your brains. I closed my eyes and braced myself for whatever he had in store for me.

Much to my relief, he sighed and let loose of my hair. Before I could scamper away, he kicked me in the seat, sending me face first onto the ground. I rolled over and wiped the dust from my eyes just in time to see a well-chewed chaw of tobacco flying in my direction. I was fast, but not fast enough. I was instantly covered in the most rancid regurgitated mix of liquid and silage that ever came out of the mouth of man or beast. "I guess my boy was right about you, son," Stubbs taunted. "You ain't nothin' but a damn Yankee pot licker, but I can see you get your manners honest. At least you didn't need to hide behind a gun." He turned toward Pa and shouted: "Why don't you put that rifle down, Sam Farmer, and deal with me man to man?"

"I'll not be scrappin' with you at *Sunday Meeting*, Stubbs, but I will shoot you if you lay another hand on my son."

I remained motionless on the ground as everyone watched with trepidation as an eerie silence fell over the congregation. You could practically hear the gears grinding in Virgil Stubbs's brain as he calculated his next move. He could see that Pa was serious, so he apparently decided covering me in a second helping of tobacco spit was a tolerable compromise. The second dose wasn't any better than the first. I got up and ran to Sister Rose who was standing behind Pa.

Rose peeled off her apron and did her best to wipe away the filthy stench, while Virgil Stubbs berated Pa with words not fit for a saloon, let alone a worship service. When Reverend Parker intervened and told Stubbs that he had learned from the other boys that Burl had indeed started the fight with Jaybird, it only added more wood to the fire. Stubbs knocked the preacher to the ground for a second time and expanded the target of his wrath to Reverend Parker and his *Yankee-lovin'* church and then to Abe Lincoln, hisself, and the whole damn Yankee nation. "I hope all you Yankees rot in Hell! Every last one of you!" He walked back to the spot of my victory and grabbed Burl by the scruff of his neck and headed for their wagon. After his wife joined him, they rode away while Virgil Stubbs hurled his final volley. "You can't sit on the fence forever, Sam Farmer! You're gonna have to pick a side in this war! When you do...me and my Enfield will be waitin' for you!"

—⚬—

Chapter 3

Pa never uttered a word all the way home and neither did the rest of the family. He was never one to make a scene in front of others, so the fact he had aimed a rifle at a man on my behalf didn't bode well for me. Justified as I felt for my actions, I was the cause of his embarrassment and knew that retribution was on the immediate horizon.

Ma wrapped her arms around Bub in a manner that said *'you cannot touch this one—Sam Farmer. I might not be able to stop you from doing what you will with the other boys, but you will not touch my baby!'* Not that he would have done anything to him anyway. As usual, Bub was innocent. Pa, if anything, was fair. He would only whip a boy if he was convinced that the boy deserved it. At that moment, there was not a shred of doubt that his mind was already made up. My fate had been sealed. The manner and severity of the punishment was all that was left to decide.

I figured it would either be the belt or the switch. Those were Pa's weapons of choice when it came to executing the sentence. There were advantages and disadvantages to both approaches of corporal punishment. The belt always hurt more at the time of delivery. The stinging sensation from the wide strip of leather was sharp and severe and more than likely you were forced to sleep on your front side for a night or two. After that, you could go about your business as usual without any lingering reminder of your misbehavior. The switch, however, was a horse of a different color. It required you to go through the act of picking your own poison. Pa would send you down to the creek behind the house with either a hatchet or a knife with instructions to cut your own rod of reproof. If you cut something that Pa felt was too feeble to learn a proper lesson, he would send you down a second time to choose a bigger sapling. He would then explain that the whipping would be twice as intense as it would have been if you had chosen wisely in the first place. If he wasn't happy with your second choice, he simply went to the buggy whip. The buggy whip would put a burr in your saddle for up to ten days, so you didn't want to go down that path either. The only solution was to choose an acceptable piece of wood on the first try. The problem with that was that you were forced to err on the side of "too big." A big stick didn't sting like the belt, but the dull throbbing pain could be with you for weeks. The worst part of choosing a switch was the trip to the creek and back. Just the thought of Pa's heavy handed justice made it impossible to hold back the tears before he even touched you, which led to the problem that tears required a couple extra swats for acting like a baby. With all things being equal, I preferred the belt because it was over quickly and you didn't have to agonize in anticipation of the actual event.

But this long ride home in the back of a wagon seemed worse than the traditional trip to the creek. The silence was deafening. On one hand, the trip seemed to be taking forever, which prolonged the agony of knowing what would happen when we finally reached home. On the other hand, the horses weren't moving slow enough, because each step they trotted was a step closer to the moment of my judgment.

Jaybird, however, didn't seem to be bothered a bit by what was about to transpire. Because of his predisposition for finding trouble, an appointment with the belt or switch was as commonplace for him as a Saturday night bath or saying grace over dinner. It was just a part of his everyday life and he accepted it as such. He sat alone in the back of the wagon and tossed stones at birds in the trees as we passed by them. He smiled and giggled as a squirrel warned us to stay away from his stash of nuts and acorns. Jaybird looked at the world as his own private playground, which was provided solely for the purpose of his amusement. He was put on this Earth to laugh and have fun and he wasn't about to let a few swats on the backside change that. It was a skill that I had always envied, but was never able to possess.

It was obvious Sister Rose also recognized that it wasn't going to go well for me. She wrapped her arm around me and held my hand as I rested my head on her shoulder. She knew better than to speak, so she squeezed my hand every few seconds as if sending me a secret code, telling me to be strong.

Rose and I had grown close over the past few years. Ma had never been the same since Bub was born. It took weeks for her to get out of bed and when she did, she didn't have the energy or gumption that she used to have. Rose and I were forced to take over most of her chores and in the process Rose had become part sister, part mother and part best friend to me. We shared our secret thoughts and swore an oath to always protect each other in times of trouble. I suppose what she was feeling for me at that moment was similar to what Ma was feeling for Bub.

I suddenly felt guilty because Jaybird didn't have someone feeling sorry for him. Not that he desired any sympathy; he didn't. Jaybird was as tough as a penny nail and most assuredly would not shed a single tear during the whipping. Yet whether he wanted one or not, a seven year old boy should have someone to champion his cause in such a dire situation. When he turned and winked at me as if to say everything was going to be alright, I felt honor bound to do what I could on his behalf.

It was always a risky situation to speak during a time when my opinion was not requested, but I decided to take a chance anyway. It was less than a half mile to our cabin and I wanted Pa to have a chance to ponder over what I was about to say. "Jaybird had no real part in the fight, Pa," I almost choked on the words as soon as they left my mouth. "I just thought you ought to know that he did nothin' to deserve a lickin'. Everything was my doing and all of the consequences should fall to me."

I thought it had been quiet before, but even the horses seemed to hold their breath as if to listen to what Pa would say. When he didn't respond, I figured I had just tightened the noose around my neck. I don't know what I expected him to say, but his refusal to say anything was worse than a tongue lashing. He kept his hands tight on the reins and never looked back to acknowledge that he had even heard a single word. Rose squeezed my hand even tighter to make sure I didn't make matters worse by speaking again. Even Jaybird looked uneasy with the current state of affairs. I could feel my heart beat in my throat as I contemplated what was in store for me at the end of the road.

As soon as the horses came to a stop, Pa silently helped Ma down from the wagon. She bustled to the cabin with Bub in her arms without looking back. Jaybird hopped out of the wagon and skipped behind her. I figured my plea for clemency on his behalf had worked when Pa didn't call him back.

"Take care of the horses, Will," Pa said without emotion. "Meet me down by the creek when you are finished." He walked away from the wagon and disappeared on the trail that led to the stream.

I didn't know what to make of things. Pa, if anything, was consistent. Punishment had always taken priority over everything else. After all—how long does it take to whip a boy? He could have taken me directly to the barn and used the belt or put the horses away while I was cutting my switch. Something was going on in Pa's mind and I wasn't for sure if I wanted to find out what it was.

Sister Rose sensed the same thing and was reluctant to leave my side. She helped me put the horses in the barn and said she would speak to Pa on my behalf. "Everybody knows that Burl Stubbs is an overgrown bully," she said as she patted my hand. "I heard the other boys say you were just protecting Jaybird from getting hurt. I'm sure if your Pa understood what really happened…"

"I appreciate what you are trying to do," I told Rose, "but I think it will go better for everyone if I go down to the creek and take my medicine."

She kissed my cheek and reluctantly let loose of my hand. I heard her chanting a prayer of protection as I walked the winding path toward the creek. I figured it wasn't a bad idea after all and whispered a quick request to *The Almighty*, myself. I needed all of the help I could get.

When I finally reached the creek, Pa was sitting on a limestone ledge and seemed to be alone with his thoughts. I stopped a few feet away and waited silently to see what would happen.

I knew that he was aware that I was there, but he never said a word and never looked in my direction. Not that I was in a hurry to get whipped on, but the waiting seemed to be a worse fate. "The horses are in the barn, Pa." My voice trembled.

Still, nothing but silence. I almost decided to sneak away, but realized that would be considered a second offence so I stood there and waited for him to speak. It was five minutes at least before he uttered a word.

"Old man Stubbs was right, you know."

"About what?" I asked. All that came to mind was that Stubbs's said I was a coward, a Yankee pot licker and that I needed to be punished. I was curious as to which one of those statements Pa was referring.

"He said that everybody is going to have to choose sides in this war. I was hoping to sit it out without gettin' my hands dirty. Everybody said it would be over in a few weeks, and I suppose that I believed them. But from what I'm reading in the newspapers, it isn't going to leave us anytime soon. Abe Lincoln is calling for volunteers now, but if the Union Army don't start fightin' any better than they did at Bull Run, it won't be long before they will begin to conscript every able bodied man in the North."

"What does conscript mean?" I asked. I was willing to partake in any conversation that took us away from the subject of my crime and punishment.

"It means that the government forces men into the army to fight in a war," he replied.

"You don't think that Lincoln is going to have you conscripted, do you Pa?"

"I reckon he will eventually, but it is not my intention to let things progress that far."

"I don't understand what you mean."

"It's just like you boys playing soldier at the meeting today. You had to pick which side you were on, didn't you?"

"Yeah, I guess so."

"And when Burl Stubbs was about to hurt Jaybird, you stepped in for your brother, didn't you?"

"Yes."

"Why did you do that, son?"

"I guess I couldn't stand around and let that bully beat up on Jaybird. He didn't stand a chance against Burl." I was curious as to where this conversation was headed. I was in uncharted waters.

"You did it because it was the right thing to do, Will," he answered. "And that is how it is with this war. There is a right side and a wrong side and a man has to choose which side he is gonna stand on. That's what I meant when I said Virgil Stubbs was right."

It was the first time my Pa had ever talked to me like I was a grown-up. But I couldn't get past the fact that I had a whipping hanging over my head. "Does this mean you don't want me to cut a switch?"

"No, I do not," Pa answered. "Not that you don't deserve one; getting into a scuffle at church on the *Lord's Day*. But I wouldn't be much of a man if I punished you for choosing a side and fightin' for someone who couldn't defend themselves, when I wasn't willing to do the same thing."

I was relieved by my reprieve from the sting of the rod, but wasn't sure I wanted to know where Pa was going with our talk. "Pa, you did the same thing for me that I did for Jaybird when you pulled your gun on old man Stubbs. You ain't no fence sitter!"

"That is different," he answered. "Someday you will understand that, when you have young'uns of your own. There ain't a decent man alive who would let another man hurt one of his own. I'm talking about something else."

"I guess I don't understand what you mean." I removed my hat and scratched my head.

"I wouldn't expect you to, son. You have been raised in the North and ain't never seen a slave."

"I saw one cutting hair in the barber shop in New Hebron."

"You saw a negra in New Hebron," he corrected me, "but Ole Joe ain't no slave. He is as free as you and me. He has lived in these parts longer than I have. What I am talking about is a south of the Mason-Dixon line, bought and sold, cotton and tobacco picker for the master."

"Sorry, Pa." I immediately realized that I should have kept my mouth shut and just listened.

"I just need you to hear what I have to say," Pa had a serious and desperate tone to his voice. "Slavery is the reason your Grandpa moved the family out of Virginia. He couldn't stand the notion of a man owning another man. His Granddaddy fought with Washington at Yorktown and said that when we throw'd off the chains of tyranny from King George, we did it for all. When I was younger, I always thought that they were lofty words and really didn't know what they meant. We lived near the Cumberland Gap in Tennessee. Folks around there barely had enough money to feed themselves, let alone own any slaves. But once when I was about your age, I went to visit some kinfolk back east in Richmond and saw boys no older than me wearin' chains on their ankles on their way to market to be sold like hogs or cattle. Some had lash marks on their backs that were so bad, that there wasn't an inch of skin that wasn't scarred. I decided then and there, that I would never own a slave. I now realize that it ain't enough. The stench of this nation's sin has reached the Pearly Gates and Providence is rendering judgment on the land. Do you understand what I'm trying to say?"

"I think so," I answered. "This war is God's way of punishin' us because of slavery?"

"That's right, son, and it's up to every man to choose whether he is willin' to right this wrong."

"You aren't leavin' us to go fight, are you Pa?"

"I don't see that I have much of a choice in the matter," Pa explained. "This storm has been a long time comin' and if my generation doesn't fight this battle, you will be the one to pay the price a few years down the line. I wouldn't be much of a man if I allowed that to happen. "

"When are you leavin'?" I asked while realizing that ten whippings would have been preferable to this.

"I won't enlist until the harvest is in the barn and the animals are butchered, and there is enough food stuff to get through the winter. Your Grandma and Grandpa will be moving up here from Kentucky to watch over the farm, but most of the work will fall to you. It is a heap big sacrifice for everyone concerned, but I couldn't live with myself if I didn't do the right thing."

The realization of his words hit me like a brickbat and tears ran down my face as if I had been beaten with a dozen switches.

Pa motioned for me to sit next to him on the rock and he put his heavy arm around my shoulders. "I need you to cry every last tear out of your system now. Do you understand?"

I nodded yes.

"Because when we walk back to the cabin, I'll need you to act like a man for the family's sake. I know that you are mighty young for such a heavy burden, but I wouldn't ask you to carry it if I didn't think you were able."

"Does Ma know about this?" I asked.

"She knows that I've been wrasslin' with the notion, but she doesn't know that I've made up my mind. For now I need you to make this—our secret."

"Are you leavin' because of me fightin' with Burl Stubbs?"

"Heavens no, Will!" he replied. "This has been on my mind for quite a spell, but I do have to admit that your willingness to fight for your brother did put me to shame a little bit. Like I said before; Virgil Stubbs was right. I thought I could sit out this war on the fence. I was wrong. You fightin' with that bully just gave me the nudge I needed to do the right thing."

I don't know how long we sat there on that hot Sunday afternoon, but I do remember that my childhood changed dramatically on that day. I would never be so audacious to declare that I walked back to the cabin as a man, but the innocence of my youth was gone forever.

—m—

Chapter 4

The summer of 1861 seemed to pass quicker than any prior season. I helped Pa with the chores and tried my best to take hold of the lessons he was trying to pass on to me. It was important for me to learn all I could before he left for the war. It was also a strange time for me. Part of me longed to be the man that Pa wanted, while the other part was often drawn to the natural distractions of boyhood adventures. Swimmin' holes, cane poles, jumpin' frogs, turtles and snakes all called me away like a bee to wild flowers. Sometimes Pa was put out by my lack of commitment, but he usually allowed me to explore the backwoods along Honey Creek after my work was done.

Jaybird, along with my pet pig, Muddy, were always willing companions on my adventures in the woods. Bub was more than willing too, but once Ma learned that Pa was going to fight for the Union, she rarely let my little brother out of her sight.

Jaybird had won Muddy in a greased pig contest at the South Union Fourth of July celebration two summers earlier. There were at least two dozen boys entered in the competition that year. Capturing the porker guaranteed the winner a year's worth of bragging rights around the neighborhood.

Bus Gamble had donated a sturdy young gilt from his finest sow and got the honor of starting the action by ringing a cowbell. To even the odds on the side of the pig, some of the men had covered the animal with a healthy helping of axle grease and then let her wallow in a mud hole before turning her loose in the watered down pen. I entered the contest along with all of the boys my age with full intentions of winning, but every time anyone got close enough to grab a leg or get an arm around her belly, she managed to wiggle away. I personally had her in my arms on three separate occasions, but that muddy pig was just too slippery to hold. She had avoided capture by every boy in the neighborhood for almost a half hour before falling to an underdog. Even though he was only five years old and the smallest entrant in the contest, Jaybird managed to come out of the pile with the prize. Pa was proud and I was mad. I wanted that pig, but worse than that, I would have to listen to Jaybird crow about winning the pig for the rest of my life. But after the dust settled, things turned out as they were supposed to. By the end of the first day, Jaybird lost interest in taking care of the animal and traded her to me in exchange for a slingshot. I named her Muddy in honor of the contest.

I immediately realized that Muddy was smarter than the average hog and taught her to fetch a stick, roll over, and play dead. Even our dog, King, was envious. I went so far as to build her a separate pen to keep her away from the rest of the less educated pigs. I didn't think of Muddy as a pig and neither did she. Pa tolerated me keeping her as a pet, but warned me she would be butchered like the rest of the hogs if I didn't take care of her. With such dire consequences hanging over her head, I was careful to hold up my end of the bargain.

One hot afternoon, after scything an acre of pasture grass, Pa decided I had done enough and told me I could cool off in the creek before supper. He didn't have to offer twice. I ran back to the cabin as fast as I could and changed into my swimmin' clothes. Jaybird was more than ready for some excitement and was right behind me. Bub wanted to go with us, but Ma wasn't about to chance an accidental drowning of her baby and put her foot down. But Bub threw such a big fit that Ma finally relinquished and allowed him to go. However, she made us promise that we wouldn't swim in any hole that was more than knee deep.

I loved Bub and all, but a swimming hole that was less than knee deep was nothing but a mud puddle. I complained, but Ma said it was shallow water or no water at all. Therefore, I agreed to her terms and decided to leave before she changed her mind. I threw Bub on Muddy's back and we all headed for Honey Creek with sincere intentions of following all of the rules.

Bub became consumed in laughter as our pet porker trotted wildly behind us on the dirt path that snaked down the hill beneath a canopy of hardwood trees. In many ways, Muddy was better than riding a pony. She seemed to be aware that Bub was considered precious cargo and stayed clear of low hanging branches and sticker bushes. Even at top speed, she never went fast enough to break any bones even if he happened to fall. I wasn't sure if she considered us to be her own piglets or just playmates, but whichever it was, there wasn't a mean spirited bone in her round body. That is more than you can say for a lot of people or ponies that I know.

By the time we finally reached the creek bed, we were ready to get wet. Jaybird was upset that we had to walk past our usual swimming spot because it was too deep for our little brother. He whined that Bub wasn't worth the trouble. As soon as we found a shaded pool near a sandbar that seemed to stay within Ma's boundaries, Jaybird yanked hard on Muddy's corkscrew tail. Being unprepared for the dastardly sneak attack, she squealed in horror and jumped into the air like a frightened colt. Bub went flying into the late summer afternoon sky with eyes as wide as saucers! Fortunately the two feet of water and muddy creek bottom softened his face-first landing.

Muddy took off at a dead run upstream and Bub came out of the water with his eyes, nose and mouth full of wet Honey Creek clay. I breathed a sigh of relief when I realized he was still breathing. But as soon as he cleared the mud away from his mouth, he let loose with a scream that shook me to my core. It was so loud that anyone listening within a mile radius would think that we were killin' him. Who would have thought that a four year old would have lungs big enough to wake the dead? Dead is what we were gonna be if Ma saw Bub in his current condition.

Jaybird was also shaken by the end results of his shenanigan. We splashed water in his face and tried to wipe the mud away, but that only made him scream louder. I was looking around to see if Ma was coming when Jaybird got the notion to do something so outrageous that it actually worked. He reached down into the creek and came up with two handfuls of mud and plopped it directly atop his head. Bub looked confused and amused at the same time. When Jaybird repeated the act, Bub's cries were reduced to the occasional sob. When I joined in the mud bath, his sobs were replaced by a laughing fit. Bub reached down in the creek and added even more muddy mess on his noggin. After a few minutes passed with no sign of Ma, I knew we had dodged a bullet. Heaven help the boy who would harm a hair on the head of Sarah Farmer's baby boy. It wasn't long before the three of us were covered from head to toe in mud. Once Muddy had calmed down and forgiven Jaybird's chicanery, she reappeared and joined in the fun. Before long, she looked like a sow worthy of her name.

Time seemed to come to a standstill that afternoon. Every rock, stick, frog, turtle and minnow we came across became a new adventure. After the initial pig tail incident, not a cross word was exchanged.

Jaybird chased after a baby water snake until he met the snake's mama and then the roles were suddenly reversed. He fled upstream like a gumball thief on the lam. Bub and I laughed at him until we saw the size of the mama snake and were right on his heels. Apparently Muddy viewed the over-grown serpent as a potential meal rather than a threat and quickly made the baby snake an orphan. As we approached the scene of the crime with trepidation, we found Muddy lying contently on a sandbar with the remnants of snake tail hang-ing from the side of her mouth. She grunted in a manner that was most assuredly a chuckle. It was as if she was having a good laugh on our account and a fresh meat supper to boot.

The sun was getting low in the sky and I decided it was time to head for the cabin. Ma had a tendency to get upset when we were late for supper. We were almost to the path that led home when Jaybird found an empty turtle shell that was almost two feet in diameter. As far as I was concerned, it was a treasure worthy of the European kings I had read about in winter school. We plopped it on Bub's head like a helmet and watched him march around like a toy soldier. It was good for another laugh. When I repeated that we needed to start for the cabin, Jaybird found a use for the shell that was just too hard to resist.

He used the shell as a makeshift bucket and began splashing the water at a bare creek bank until it became a muddy mess. Once the consistency reached his approval, he climbed to the top of the steep banking and sat inside the shell.

"Ye—haaa!" Jaybird hollered as he pushed himself over the edge and plunged down the muddy slide to the creek below. He hit the water with a giant splash and tumbled head over heels and finally came to a stop twenty feet downstream.

Since we were already filthy, I didn't see how it could hurt if we tarried a few minutes longer. We took turns riding the shell down the mudslide until we were completely covered in muddy slop. After a while, we were so slippery the shell wasn't necessary. We went head first, feet first and hooked together like railroad cars. I was lost in the moment and by the time we heard Ma calling we were caked in ten layers of Honey Creek mud.

It was starting to get dark and we didn't want to spark her ire by being late, so we ran directly to the cabin with the intention of washing up at the well. Looking back, it was not a wise decision.

Ma and Pa were both sitting on the front porch when we first appeared. Ma started screaming in horror while Pa began laughing like a braying mule. Ma grabbed Bub by the arm and dragged him to the well. Bub fussed as Ma dumped a bucket of cold spring water over his head. She took a wash cloth from her apron and frantically began to wash the mud away from his face.

"Take off your britches," she growled.

Bub did as she ordered which caused her to cut loose with another scream.

"Leeches! Get over here Samuel!" she cried. "Lord have mercy! My baby is covered in leeches!"

Pa ran into the cabin and came out with a bag of salt. Jaybird and I started peelin' away our clothes and found we were covered in the black slimy blood suckers too.

"Don't touch them!" Pa yelled when I tried to yank one off.

He covered Bub in handfuls of salt and carefully picked every one of the toothy worms away from his scrawny body. By that time, both Bub and Ma were singing a duet of horror and agony. Once Pa was sure he had gotten the last one, he ordered them to go into the cabin while he went to work on Jaybird.

Sister Rose had been making soap behind the barn and came running when she heard the commotion. While Pa was pulling leeches off of Jaybird, she started peeling my clothes away and dousing me with water. I immediately started to cover myself in shame. It was one thing for Ma to see me in my birthday suit, but Rose was only a few years older than me. Leeches or not; it didn't seem right for a feller to be humiliated in such a way.

"T'aint nothin I haven't seen before, Little Brother," she said as she picked the first leech away from the back of my thigh. "It wasn't that long ago that I was a givin' you your Saturday night baths. I need to get these devil serpents off of you before the poison sets in."

I was about to argue with her, but I decided that a little shame was better than having poison from demonic serpents flowing though my body. I kept my eyes and mouth shut until she was finished.

Pa told us to keep washing up at the well while Rose took our mud covered clothes to the wash kettle and kindled a fire. Pa tentatively went into the cabin to check on Ma and Bub, and then returned with a pair of blankets for us.

"Better cover up before it gets dark," Pa told us. "It might be safer if you boys spent the night in the hayloft. At least until your Ma simmers down. I'll have Rose fetch some clothes with your supper."

"I'm sorry, Pa. I didn't know there were leeches in the creek."

"It's not your fault, boys," he assured us. "I found myself in a similar situation when I was your age and my Ma threw a fit too. A week from now, she'll be laughin' about this."

"It don't sound like she's laughin' now," Jaybird added.

"I said the laughs will be comin' next week. Right now— your Ma wants a pound of flesh from both of your backsides."

Jaybird bent over naked as his name and prepared for a swat.

"That ain't necessary," Pa laughed. "Just because your Ma wants a piece of your hide doesn't mean I have to take it."

"You mean you're gonna fib to Ma?" Jaybird asked.

"Don't be getting any ideas that it's proper to tell a lie, but in this case I think a trip to the woodshed ain't exactly necessary. Unless you boys are so guilt-riddled that you feel a whoopin' is called for."

"No sir!" We answered in chorus.

"Well then—I would say that we are in agreement. Sister Rose will be out with supper directly. I better go in and tend to your Ma." He took two steps toward the cabin, then turned around one last time. "Did you boys have a good time this afternoon?"

"The best!" I admitted.

A smile of understanding appeared on his face. "Sometimes—that's all that matters."

That night in the hayloft, Jaybird and I feasted on sow belly, beans, corn pone and gravy along with a couple of mugs of cool buttermilk, fresh from the springhouse. A half hour after dinner, Sister Rose brought us some biscuits and honey for dessert. It was such a cool night, we didn't even mind sleeping in the barn. Even with leeches and Ma's commotion; that day at the mud hole would go down as one of the best days of my life.

—m—

Chapter 5

Shortly before sundown, Pa and I were feeding the hogs when we saw them coming down the red dirt road. Pappy and Granny Farmer arrived on an old clapboard wagon carrying all of their earthly possessions. The wear and tear of the month-long journey had taken its toll as they struggled to stand up as soon as the knobbed-knee plug pulled the wagon to a stop. Pappy looked at me and shook his head. "This strappin young buck surely couldn't be Will Farmer?"

"It's me in the flesh, Pappy," I replied.

"Naw—it couldn't be," he cackled. "You were no bigger than a corn nubbin, last time I laid eyes on you."

"It's really me—I swear."

"Oh I know'd it was you, Will," he admitted. "You're the spitin' image of your Pa when he was your age. Why don't you climb up here and help me unload the wagon?"

I climbed up and started untying a maze of knots that held the pile of cargo in place. Beneath a linen tarp was a walnut pie cupboard, a rickety bed frame, a dresser, a set of dishes, five or six assorted kettles and pots, two broken down trunks with linens and blankets, a wash basin and pitcher along with a tattered feather mattress. "It ain't much to show for six decades of livin'," Pappy declared. "But what we got—we came by honest and we don't owe nothin' to neither man nor the devil hisself."

I hadn't seen my grandparents since we moved to South Union when I was four years old. They were much older than I remembered. Pappy's name was John Farmer. He was nearly six feet tall and as narrow as a bullwhip. His hair was snow-white and unruly. His weather-worn face proudly displayed the lines and scars that come with years of hardship on the American frontier. He always had a smile on his face and looked for any excuse to laugh out loud.

Granny Farmer, on the other hand—was all business. She was short and stout and spoke with the singsong voice of a nightingale. But as far as I could tell, most of her singing came in the form of telling everybody else what to do. Being the oldest of the brothers, I soon realized that I was destined to become her *step and fetch it* boy. She wore a threadbare gray bonnet and a butternut linsey dress with a half dozen patches purposefully placed to cover the holes. She howled like a panther when Pa lifted her out of the wagon and twirled her in the air before placing her gently on the ground. "Samuel Farmer—you are a scoundrel!" she scolded.

"Just wanted to dance with my favorite girl," Pa laughed. "Besides, you're light as a feather."

"Shame on you!" she fired back. "You know where liars go!"

"I was just joshing, old girl," he said. Pa looked down at the ground and pretended to be sorry.

Granny pursed her lips as long as she could before allowing a hint of a smile to break through. "Aww…come here and give your old Ma a kiss. I've missed you, Samuel."

"I've missed you too, Ma", he whispered, "It's been too long."

Granny started to tear up and buried her head on Pa's shoulder for a moment as we all watched silently. Finally Granny let go and whispered, "How's Sarah?"

"She's inside cookin' dinner," Pa replied. "Why don't you go see for yourself?"

"That's not what I asked," Granny's demeanor suddenly changed.

Pa sighed, then removed his hat and combed his fingers through his hair. "She's struggled mightily ever since Bub was born. She does the best she can."

"And now her husband is runnin' off to war. I do declare!"

"Ma, don't get all worked up," Pa protested. But it was too late. Granny had already worked up a full head of steam and was heading for the cabin.

Pa had me help him unload the wagon while he kept a worried eye fixed on the cabin door.

When I saw Sister Rose come running out with a sheepish look on her face, I began to worry. "Do you think we should go inside and see if anything is wrong?" I asked.

"I reckon it would be best to stay outside for a while and let them talk in peace," Pa replied. "They probably need to iron a few things out."

Ma and Granny hadn't seen each other in years, so I couldn't imagine what needed to be ironed out. "They ain't fightin' are they?" I asked.

Pa shrugged his shoulders and looked at Pappy as he removed the riggings from the swayback horse that had pulled the wagon from the Cumberland Country. "It's all about peckin' order in the hen house," Pappy explained.

"Peckin' order? I don't understand."

Pappy's smile exposed the gap where his front teeth used to be. "It's like this, son; your folks lived with us when they first got married and your Granny ruled the cabin with an iron fist. Your Ma didn't seem to mind all that much, but at the time she was still a young gal and didn't know no better. Once she got a little older and you came along, she got the itch to spread her wings and fly off on her own. That's when your folks moved here to the Wabash Country to start a new life. It gave your Ma a chance to run her own house. Your Granny had a hard time letting the chicks leave the nest and some things were said that ought not have been spoken. Granny loves your Ma like she was one of her own and wants to make things right. Now that we'll be movin' under your roof, Granny is worried that your Ma might be thinkin' she's gonna lose her spot on the top perch. She just wants her to know that we are here to help and that your Ma is still the queen bee of her own honey hole."

Despite all of the talk about chickens and bees, I understood enough to realize that Ma might not take kindly to having another woman in the kitchen; even if it was Granny. Despite Pappy's attempt to put my mind at ease, I had an uneasy feeling that somehow I was about to get caught in the middle of a female firestorm.

Five minutes later Ma walked out of the cabin and sat in her rocking chair on the front porch without speaking a single word. She didn't look happy, but she didn't look unhappy either. She was staring in my direction, but acted like I was as invisible as a ghost. She crossed her arms around herself and started rocking slowly while humming Bub's favorite lullaby. Bub heard the song and waddled over and held out his arms, but she didn't see him either. It was like she didn't see anything at all.

A few seconds later Granny appeared at the door with a fresh cup of coffee in hand and called for us to haul her belongings inside. She looked at Ma, then walked over and lovingly held her hand. "Don't worry about a thing, Sarah. I'll take care of everything and you can finally get the rest you need."

Ma didn't answer. She kept rocking and humming the lullaby until the sun started to sink behind the trees.

That was the day when Granny became the head chicken of our little henhouse.

—⚜—

Chapter 6

That night we sat around the table and listened to Pappy tell stories about crossing the Ohio River along with all of the news of the war in Tennessee. "Folks are split right down the middle on the subject of which side to get behind," Pappy explained. "Ain't nobody in the mountains got enough money to own any slaves, so they didn't see much reason to go to war over the matter. But once the fightin' started at Fort Sumter and Abe Lincoln called for 75,000 volunteers, the boys in Tennessee didn't take kindly to the thought of fightin' their kin. At first I thought most everybody would get along, but Champ Ferguson has a gang of murderers that he calls rangers and they are killin' anybody who sympathizes with the Union. It don't matter if they are eight or eighty. He'll slit any throat who speaks a kind word about a Yankee. He even killed a man on his death bed for cursing Jefferson Davis. He's the son of the devil, himself; that one is."

"I thought I read something about Champ Ferguson being tried for murder in the Vincennes Sun," Pa said. "I think it said something about his killing the sheriff with a sword."

Pappy nodded his head and took a long draught from his corncob pipe. "That would be when he killed Big Jim Reed.

Champ tied Big Jim to a tree and circled him and cut him a little bit with each pass until he bled to death. That's what started it all. As far as anybody knows, Jim Reed was the first soul that Ferguson ever killed. But now he's like the dog that killed a chicken and learns that he's got a taste for blood. There ain't enough chickens in the hen house to satisfy that dog's appetite. His best friend was a man named Frogg. When Frogg came down with the measles, ole Champ figured he had been up at the Union Camp in Monticello, Kentucky where half the camp was down with the disease. Frogg swore on the Bible that he wasn't a Yankee spy, but Champ shot him dead in his own bed anyway. Most folks in the mountains are sidin' with the Union, but bein' patriotic can get a feller killed with Champ Ferguson around."

"John Farmer! Don't be tellin' those stories in front of the children," Granny scolded. "You'll give them nightmares for sure."

"Just tellin' the truth, Mother," Pappy replied. "Ain't never any harm in tellin' the truth. Ain't that right, boy?" Pappy asked while patting Jaybird on top of his head.

"I always tell the truth," he answered.

"Uh-uhm!" Pa cleared his throat and cast a stern eye upon Jaybird.

"'cept when I forget," Jaybird corrected himself.

"Well—as long as you get it right most of the time, son—you're all right with me," Pappy cackled. "Some of the folks thought that by movin' across the border from Tennessee to Kentucky, they would be safe, but the Confederate guerillas make nightly raids into Clinton County. Some of the men resorted to sleeping in the fields so the raiders wouldn't catch them asleep in their beds. But Ferguson's men caught on to what they was doin' and started taking the women and children hostages. There just ain't nobody safe in the Cumberland Hills anymore."

"What kind of man leaves his family alone and helpless?" Ma yelped as she stood from the table and walked over to the fireplace.

"Now Sarah—you won't be alone," Pa assured her.

"That's right," Pappy chimed in. "Ain't no harm gonna come to you and the children as long as Granny and me is around. Besides there ain't no raiders up here in Illinois."

"Might not have any raiders, but there is a nest of Copperheads up here that are plenty dangerous enough," Ma argued. "The Union can survive without Samuel Farmer in uniform!"

"That will be enough, Sarah," Pa replied sternly. "I'm honor bound to do my duty. Besides if I don't volunteer, it will only be a matter of time before I'm conscripted."

"Your duty is to protect your family." Ma cried.

Pa started to answer, but thought better of it. An uneasy silence fell over the cabin. I wanted to say something funny, but Ma appeared to be on the cusp of having an episode—so I decided to keep my lips sealed.

Sister Rose nervously poured a fresh cup of tea for Granny, and refilled Pappy's coffee cup for the third time. "It's been months since I've tasted real coffee," Pappy said. "I think this may be the best I have ever tasted."

Rose smiled shyly and offered some to Ma, who shook her head no. "You haven't touched a thing," Rose complained. "You'll get sick if you don't eat, Sarah."

"I'll eat after the children go to bed," Ma whispered as she went back to her rocking chair. Bub, whose eyes had already began to droop, grabbed his blanket and climbed up on Ma's lap. Ma's eyes glistened in the glow of the candle light as she tried to hold back the tears.

Pa had a frown on his face and clenched his jaw before speaking. "Rose, take Jaybird and Bub up to the loft and get them settled in bed while Will washes the dishes."

Something was changing in Ma and I didn't like it one bit. She had always been the worrying type, but this was different. There was a bitterness in her voice that was never there before and it scared me. Rose had noticed it too, but was afraid to say anything in fear of getting her head bitten off. Ma could get fussy at times when things weren't done in a particular manner, but there was never any doubt about her unconditional love for her family. As of late, there hadn't been any love mixed in with the fussing. She still clung to Bub like a rag doll, but ignored the rest of us for hours of a time. Her disposition, to say the least, could be described as cantankerous. So when Pa ordered Bub and Jaybird upstairs, I figured he had tolerated enough guff and was about to tangle with Ma. Even Jaybird must have sensed it too, because he never went to bed without putting up a fight. Normally, I like being treated differently than my kid brothers, but in this instance, I would have rather been sent to the loft with the others.

I gathered the dishes and carried them to the wash tub on the front porch. I grabbed the old oak bucket and made my way to the well while looking up at the sky. It was an extra dark night and the yellow sliver of the moon was just rising on the eastern horizon. The stars twinkled like thousands of tiny candles. At ten years of age, I could look at the sky for hours. The sky was always different and yet it was always the same. I could always find the North Star along with the Big and Little Dippers, but the other stars seemed to come and go as they pleased. Some nights only a few stars came out and other nights there seemed to be more stars than there were numbers to count them. This night was one of those nights.

I lowered the bucket into the well and drew enough water so I wouldn't have to make a second trip. I dropped a few sprigs of soapwort and ashes into the tub and scraped the plates clean with an old corncob. I could hear voices coming from inside the cabin and none of them sounded happy. After carefully placing the dishes on a wooden block to dry, I went out by the barn and fell backward in a haystack. I covered my ears in the hay until the voices disappeared. I searched the sky until I found the Big Dipper. It was exactly where it was supposed to be. I began at the handle and started counting the stars between it and the treetops to the east. I lost count somewhere around seventy-five. I was just starting over when I felt Rose bounce in the hay next to me.

"Didn't you hear me callin' you?" she complained as she thumped my chest with the back of her knuckles.

"I buried my ears so I couldn't hear a thing," I said as I thumped her back in fun. "I figured it was safer to wait out here and look at the stars until things quieted down."

"I reckon that to be a good idea right about now. Sarah is riled up somethin' awful and Pa is trying to hold his tongue, but he ain't doin' too good of a job of it. Granny is tellin' both of em what she thinks while Pappy just sits there with a smile on his face."

"What are they fussin' about?" I asked.

"Same thing as they always fuss about. Your Ma and Granny don't want your Pa to go to war. Sister Sarah says the Lord has come to her in a dream and told her that if your Pa goes—he'll be dead within a year."

"Pa says the war is the Lord's judgment on the country because of the sin of slavery," I reminded her. "He says it is his Christian duty to fight against the *Johnny Rebs*."

"They both can't be right," she said. "The Lord wouldn't tell one of them one thing and the other something else."

"Reverend Parker says the Lord works in mysterious ways," I replied. "Maybe this is what he meant."

"I suspect that Sister Sarah is just scared about losing Pa. To be honest—I'm kind of scared myself," Rose admitted. "He's the only father I've ever known."

"Pa won't let any *Johnny Reb* get the better of him," I assured her.

"But aren't you scared too, Will?"

"Maybe a little," I admitted, "but Pa expects me to be the man of the house while he's away. He says I need to act brave even when I'm scared."

"What about Pappy?" she asked. "I thought he was supposed to be in charge while your pa is away."

"Naw…" I yawned. "Pa just wanted him to come up here and lend a hand if things got too tough."

"If you are the man of the house, why are you hiding in this haystack instead of partaking in the grown up conversation in the cabin?"

"Pa ain't left yet." I replied. "I'm waiting till he's gone before I take over."

Rose thumped me in the chest again.

"Ouch! Why did you do that?"

"I think somebody is too big for his britches," she laughed.

"You're just jealous because you'll have to answer to me." I teased.

"That will be the day, Will Farmer. Besides, I don't believe you'll be giving many orders with Granny around."

"I can't argue with you about that," I conceded.

Suddenly, the bright yellow flash of a shooting star danced across the sky. "Make a wish!" said Rose.

"You're supposed to wish on the first star of the night you see," I reminded her. "It doesn't work for shooting stars."

"It all works the same way," she huffed. "Just hush up and make a wish! But don't say what you wished for or it won't come true."

I wished for the Union to win the war before Pa had to leave. I would never admit it to Rose, but I feared for Pa's life too. Sometimes I wanted to be a man, but now that I knew the day was soon coming, I was beginning to have second thoughts. I was already beginning to miss my days of carefree mischief. I hoped that an early end of the war would postpone my ascent to growin' up for the time being.

Rose and I watched the sky for quite a while before she broke the silence. "Which star do you think God lives on?"

"He doesn't live on a star," I corrected her. "He lives up in the clouds with the angels."

"Reverend Parker says that *He* lives in Heaven among the stars." Rose spoke as if I had just missed a word on my spelling test. "Besides—where would *He* live on a sunny day when there aren't any clouds in the sky? Do you see any clouds in the sky tonight?"

I didn't have an answer for her. "I guess you got me on that one."

"Don't worry, Will," she giggled. "I won't tell anybody you don't know everything. Your secret is safe with me."

"You're makin' fun of me!"

"I'm just havin' a little sport with you," she assured me. "You know that I love you, little brother."

"You have a strange way of showin' it," I complained.

She rolled over and kissed me on the top of my head. She didn't have to say anything else.

"I love you too, Sister Rose."

We stayed in the haystack and watched the stars until the Big Dipper disappeared in the west and the Morning Star appeared in the east. Neither one of us spoke more than a dozen words for the rest of the evening. It was on that crystal clear night in the late summer of 1861 that Sister Rose and I made an unspoken bond to be there for each other, regardless of what the future had in store.

—w—

Chapter 7

There was a hint of frost on the pumpkins on that brisk morning when the neighbors got together for the annual hog killing. It was a time when everybody brought their livestock to Enoch Wheeler's farm and butchered enough meat to get through the cold Wabash winter. As the owner of the only pet pig in the neighborhood, it was also a nervous time for me as Muddy had now grown big enough to keep a family alive for a good part of the winter. I heard old lady Phillippe tell the Widow Tohill that it was a sin to not kill such a fine sow. Granny also heard what she had said and told her she should keep her mouth shut because a horsefly might mistake it for an empty barn. The two women scurried away in a huff, muttering something about *Tennessee trash*. Pa told me not to listen to the old biddys, but the fact that there were people that would just as soon see Muddy dead than alive gave me an uneasy feeling in the pit of my stomach.

Even though most farmers had the skill to butcher their own meat, there were several widows and older folks who couldn't. There were other people, who for one reason or another, didn't have the means to provide for themselves, or as Pappy would say; "didn't have a pot to piss in." They would show up and help in any way they could and in turn, would be given ample provisions for their smokehouses. It was a way for the community to make sure everyone had enough to get by. Nobody was ever turned away. There wasn't any shame in being poor. In South Union, there wasn't anybody who was what you would call wealthy. Some were better off than others, but that could change in a minute in *Egypt*. All it took was a drought, a bad crop or an infirmity to strike for a family to be devastated. So by making sure your neighbor had enough to eat, it gave you the peace of mind that others would be there to help you in bad times.

At sundown, after all of the work was done, the women served a feast of pork, sweet potatoes, green beans, corn pone with butter and molasses and apple pie. There were dozens of pitchers of cold buttermilk from the springhouse, and kettles steaming with fresh sassafras tea. Even though the women objected, there were also several jugs of corn squeezins for the men. As a matter of principle, not a single drop of the Blue Ruin was touched until all of the work was finished, but the gathering didn't officially end until the last jug was empty.

The hog killing was usually a time of celebration, but with the cloud of the war and the exodus of our southern-leaning neighbors, it felt more like a funeral. Many of the local men had enlisted and some had even seen action in Missouri. Pa had already signed his enlistment papers at the recruiting station in Robinson and was scheduled to report to Camp Butler in Springfield on New Year's Day.

The news of the Union troops being routed at a place in Virginia called Bull Run and the heroics of Stonewall Jackson was discouraging to those who thought that the war would be over in a few weeks. A few days later when we heard about General

Nathaniel Lyon being killed and his Army of the West losing the battle of Wilson's Creek to the Rebels in Missouri, folks started to realize how long and deadly the war was going to be.

As far as Pa was concerned, it only added to his resolve. He said it was his duty as a "God-fearin' Christian" to do his part to win the war. He became more and more agitated when folks said the war was about state's rights and preserving the Southern way of life. "This fight is about slavery and everybody knows it. Politicians might try to put a ribbon on it and call it something else, but that ain't nothin' but a mess of window dressin'. The Lord never created a slave and He never created a master, neither. You can pin that crime on man and *The Devil*, himself." Pa had turned from a man who rarely said a word in public, to a man who stepped on the soapbox whenever he got the chance. When *old man* Stubbs forced Pa to choose a side in the war, he jumped in the water with both feet. For all intents and purposes; Samuel Farmer had become a righteous abolitionist.

Ma, on the other hand, had grown so distressed about Pa's eminent departure that she refused to leave her rocking chair and stayed home in the cabin by herself. Granny offered to stay with her, but Ma said she would rather be alone and spend time with the Lord. Granny started to make a fuss, but Pa stepped in and said that some quiet time might do Ma some good. From the looks on the faces of the women at the dinner table that evening, it was evident many felt the same way as Ma. Everybody seemed to agree that the war needed to be fought, but I think the women would have preferred that somebody else's husband did the fighting.

Reverend Parker blessed the food with a prayer that was nearly long enough to be called a sermon and then after the final amen; declared it proper to begin eating. Despite my promotion to man of the house at home, I was relegated to eating dinner with the rest of the boys in the barn. I really didn't mind since most of the fellows were my age. None of the Copperhead families attended this year's hog killing, so we could speak openly with malice toward the southern way of life. I personally called Jefferson Davis a pot licker, which made one of the boys bring up the occasion of my fight with Burl Stubbs. I might have exaggerated a little about my fighting skill and downplayed Burl's bad luck while recounting the incident, but I seemed to keep everybody on the edge of their seats. "I can't wait until I'm old enough to sign up and fight them Johnny Rebs, myself," I bragged in front of the others. I looked around to make sure Pa wasn't close enough to hear what I was saying. He didn't like anyone who was a blowhard and he would like it even less coming from his own son. When I saw the coast was clear, I let the boys know what I thought about Stonewall Jackson's ancestors.

After the talk died down, a one-eyed man by the name of Uncle Johnny Logan grabbed his fiddle that he called, *Ol' Abigail,* along with a brand new bow that was bought for the occasion and started playing the *Peek-a boo Waltz.* A good fiddle player was held in high esteem on the frontier and Uncle Johnny was the best. The boys moved the tables against the walls of the barn to make room for some dancing and the women brought in jugs filled with warm apple cider. Even the dark cloud of war couldn't stop folks from dancing when *Ol' Abigail* started singing.

At ten years of age I wasn't exactly what you would call an accomplished hoofer. But because Sister Rose loved to dance and was too bashful to get within ten feet of a boy her own age, I was conscripted *(as Pa would say)* into duty. After the waltz, John Maxwell stepped onto the floor and began to call the Virginia Reel.

"Head lady and gentleman forward and back.
Head gentleman and lady forward and back.
Forward and turn with the right hand round.

Forward again with both hands round.

Do-si-do
Do-si-do

Head couple down the center and back.
Right arm to partner and reel".

Grown-ups and children alike followed the calls while those who weren't on the dance floor, kept time with the music by clapping their hands or stomping their feet. After the reel, I decided to take a break and sit a spell when Uncle Johnny started playing a Schottische. Jaybird took my place with Sister Rose and soon had all eyes in the barn looking in his direction. He was kicking his heels so fast, he looked like a chicken with his head chopped off. Instead of being embarrassed, Jaybird became emboldened to dance even faster. Rose was a good sport and tried to keep up with him, but Jaybird was moving his feet so fast she had to fall away. The loss of his partner didn't dampen his spirit any, and he continued to dance his jig all by himself. It wasn't long before a circle had formed around him and he was the only dancer on the floor. Everyone whooped and hollered, which only encouraged him more. Finally, Uncle Johnny ended the song and Jaybird left the floor as the king of the dance.

Even Granny and Pappy joined the fun and danced the square before the night was over. Pa stayed in the background most of the evening and even managed a smile when Jaybird took to the floor for a second time. He never said a word about the subject, but I could tell he was uncomfortable being at the gathering while Ma was alone at home. I suppose it was against his constitution to have any fun while Ma was so unhappy. Looking back, Ma and Pa's happiness was the first casualty of the war for our family.

It was well past midnight when the festivities finally subsided. Despite protests from many of the children, it was time to call it a night. I helped Pa load up the last of the salted pork as everybody said their goodbyes. Pappy hitched the horses and Granny smacked Jaybird's hand for pestering Bub while he tried to sleep in the back of the wagon. Jaybird didn't seem to mind the chastisement considering the amount of fun and mischief he had made that day. It was just water off of a duck's back as far as he was concerned.

Five minutes after we started for home, Bub was fast asleep in Granny's arms and Jaybird was curled up under the front seat—sawing logs as well. With the exception of Sister Rose who was humming a few chords from an old melody, everyone was silent—alone with their thoughts. None of us wanted the night to end. The hog killing along with the feast and night of dancing was a much needed chance to forget about the war and Pa's imminent departure. When we reached the farm and found Ma still awake in her rocking chair, it reminded us of the price our family would have to pay when Pa went to fight for the Union.

—◦◦◦—

Chapter 8

It was a late October morning when Pa told me we were taking the hogs to market at Bristol Landing on the Wabash River. He explained that the Union Army was paying twenty cash dollars per hog. They were to be sent downriver on steamboats to Cairo to feed the troops at Fort Defiance. Pa left our boar and three best sows in the barn so we could build our herd back up and had rounded the rest of the gilts and sows into the horse corral. My heart jumped into my throat when I saw Muddy was in the pen with the others.

"You can't sell Muddy!" I protested.

"We have to, son," Pa replied. "A good hog brings six or seven dollars at best around here. I can't pass up the twenty dollars just so you can have a pet pig. I want to make sure that there is enough to get by on while I'm away. You promised me that you were gonna be a man around here. This is what a farmer does to make a livin'."

"But why can't you sell one of the other sows instead?"

"Those three sows average eight piglets per litter," he answered. "You know for a fact that Muddy ain't never dropped more than four. It wouldn't be in the best interest of the farm to keep her."

"But Pa!" I pleaded. "Remember how she nursed the other sow's pigs when their own mother wouldn't? You said she was the best orphan mother that you ever saw."

"I took all of that into account, Will." His voice now took the tone of a lecture. "But twenty dollars is twenty dollars! There is a war on and we have to sacrifice. It's high time you learned that. I don't want to hear another word on the matter."

I knew he meant what he said so I didn't say anything more. Pa backed the wagon up to the fence while I worked the hogs toward the ramp. None of the pigs would cooperate, so I told Muddy to herd them in. She squealed like it was a game and worked the other pigs from side to side, nipping at their heels until they gave in to her will and made their way up the rickety wooden ramp. Our dog, King, couldn't have done a better job running herd. Once the last one was safely in the wagon, Muddy looked at me in hopes of praise or maybe another game. I walked over and scratched behind her ears. "You too, girl," I could hardly get the words to come out of my mouth. "I need you to get in the wagon with the rest of them."

She looked up at me like it was some kind of mistake. People say hogs are nothing but a dumb animal, but that wasn't how it was with Muddy. She was smarter than any dog or horse on her worst day. She was smart enough to know that when a hog got in the wagon—they never came back to the farm.

"Go—just go." I swatted her on the rump. I knew that Pa was watching me and I didn't want him to see me cry. I knew that's exactly what would happen if I looked into Muddy's eyes. She hesitated for a moment and then scampered up the plank and jumped into the wagon with the other pigs. As much as I tried to look away, I couldn't help but notice that Muddy was looking at me in hopes I would tell her everything was going to be all right. "She's just a stupid pig," I told myself. "You're acting like a baby!" It didn't matter what I told myself. I knew I was lying.

Under most circumstances I would have been excited about the trip to Bristol Landing. Since I was to be considered the man of the family, Pa let me drive the horses most of the way. But every step the horses took toward the river was another step closer to Muddy's demise. I felt like a lowdown turncoat. The fact that Jaybird had come along with us only added insult to injury. Jaybird thought he could do anything I could do, so he fussed about me not letting him drive the team for the first ten miles. I was used to ignoring him, but by the time we reached Heathsville, he had worn Pa down.

"Let your brother take over, Will," Pa sighed.

I raised my eyebrows, but I could see by the look on Pa's face that there was no use arguing. I handed the reins to my little brother without saying a word. *So much for being the man of the family.*

I glanced back at Muddy who stood in the back corner of the wagon away from the nine other pigs. She looked at me with heartbroken eyes, apparently wondering what she had done wrong to end up in the wagon. I had to look the other way before I lost my composure. The only saving grace of the day was that Pa said the hogs were to be loaded onto a steamship headed for Cairo. I couldn't bear the thought of watching her being butchered. There was always hope that the steamship would sink and she could swim to freedom. I knew it was the foolish thinking of a child, but as long as she was alive there was always hope.

Once my brother took over as driver, our pace began to pick up. Jaybird had always been somewhat of a daredevil, but racing a wooden wagon full of hogs was not the best method of displaying his horse racing skills.

Our left wheel hit a rut and the hogs flew up in the air and slammed against the side rails with a thud and the wagon leaned dangerously to the left. Instead of pulling back, Jaybird snapped the reins and yelled "Ha!" The horses took off at a dead run. Pa jumped for the reins, but the wagon hit a log and Pa went flying out the other side. Hogs were squealing with fright and I was holding on for dear life. Jaybird didn't notice Pa's departure and continued to snap the reins like he was riding in the sweepstakes on the Fourth of July. I tried to reach for the reins but he swatted me away and I started to fall out of the wagon too. I was able to grab a handhold on one of the livestock rails and as I was struggling to climb back into the wagon, I was horrified by the crazed look on his face. It was as if the devil himself had taken control of Jaybird's mind, body and soul. We hit another bump and my legs flew over the side once again. My feet bounced off the ground a couple of times, but I managed to pull myself back up to the wagon bench. This time, I decided not to take any chances and slugged Jaybird in the back of his head. I grabbed the reins and tried to coax the horses to slow down, while Jaybird climbed onto my back and started to retaliate. Eventually, I brought the wagon to a stop with my left hand while keeping Jaybird at bay with my right.

I never figured out what got into my brother that never let him walk away from a fight. Never mind that he had commandeered a hog wagon and lost Pa on the roadside in the process. He was mad as a hornet because I had hit him and taken the reins away. He had a fire in his eyes and was determined to get even with me. Nothing else mattered to Jaybird. I smacked him a couple of times on the end of his nose to make him keep his distance, but he kept screaming and clawing at me like a wildcat.

"I'll kill you—you sombitch!" he screamed at the top of his lungs. Tears were flowing in his eyes and spit was shooting from his mouth. "You ain't the boss of me! Let go of me and I'll—"

Jaybird never got to finish his sentence. Pa reached the wagon and jerked him to the ground by the scruff of his collar. The retribution was swift and severe. Pa had Jaybird over his knee and was beating him like a dirty floor rug.

"But he punched me!" Jaybird protested. He could have cared less about the beating. He'd forgotten about his joy ride too. All he could think about was getting even with me. After Pa's swatting arm got tired, he realized this too.

"All right, Jaybird," Pa declared. "You wanna piece of your brother. There he is!"

"I don't wanna fight him, Pa," I protested.

Pa told Jaybird to stay where he was and marched to me at a double time pace. "Listen Will—I don't know what in Tarnation has gotten into Jaybird, but the only one who can beat it out of him is you. He's gotten too big for his britches and needs to be knocked down a peg or two."

"But Pa—"

"Ain't no buts about it. We ain't gonna have a minute's peace until your brother learns his place. We need to get this settled before I leave for the Army. The only rule is you can't use your fists. You have to hit him open handed, so you don't hurt him too bad. Other than that, you can do what you want. He needs to be taught a lesson."

I reluctantly agreed. "Come and get me, you peckerhead!" I called out. I instantly felt the meaty hand of Pa slam against the back of my head.

"Watch your mouth," Pa growled. Apparently *no fists* wasn't the only rule after all.

Jaybird charged me like a bull with hydrophobia. I blocked his roundhouse haymaker and pushed him to the ground. He got up while shouting out cuss words in some unknown language and charged me again. Once again, I put him face down in the dirt. The third time he charged me I backhanded him across the jaw and he fell to the ground. This time I pinned his arms down with my knees and proceeded to slap him across the face repeatedly. I wasn't hitting him that hard because, after all, with our age difference, it wasn't exactly a fair fight. I didn't want him to get hurt too bad.

"Let me up you sombitch and I'll get you this time!"Jaybird cried while he struggled to free his hands.

I looked over at Pa and he just shrugged his shoulders. "Let him up if you want."

Jaybird was all over me as soon as I let go of him. I was sparring with him from a distance, when he threw a sneaky jab that caught me on the cheekbone. I didn't think he had enough mustard on any of his punches to do me any harm, but I saw stars with that one. Once I came to my senses, I was overcome with a rage that I had never known before. Suddenly, my anger at having to take Muddy to the market boiled up in me like an overheated kettle. I knocked Jaybird to the ground with a single blow. Even though I obeyed Pa's command and only used my open hands, I began pummeling him. My mind went blank as I slapped him across the face repeatedly. I vaguely remember hearing him crying for me to stop. I didn't stop. Every bit of anger I had held inside of me came out all at once. I was mad at Pa for killing my pig. I had done everything that was asked of me, but this was asking too much. It was because of him that Muddy had to die. We wouldn't need the money if he didn't go off to war. Everything was his fault.

I didn't care that Jaybird's face was covered in blood. I ignored his tears and kept hitting him over and over again. I heard Pa yelling something, but I ignored him too. Finally, Pa put an end to things by knocking me off of him with the sole of his boot.

"I said that is enough!" Pa's voice echoed through the valley.

When I got back on my feet and took a look at Jaybird, I felt sick and ashamed at the same time. His eyes were swollen and were turning black while blood was gushing out of his nose. He was sobbing as Pa tried to stop the bleeding with his handkerchief. He was no longer the devil-possessed wagon hijacker, but rather a seven year old boy who had just had the tar beaten out of him by his older brother. It was all more than I could bear. I walked into the nearby woods and sat down on a fallen log. I felt like crying but couldn't produce a single tear.

I don't know how long I sat there before I finally heard Pa's voice.

"It's time to go, Will." There was no sign of anger or ill will in his voice.

"I'm sorry, Pa. I don't know what got into me."

"You did what I told you to do, son," he assured me. "I didn't like it any more than you—but Jaybird needed to be taught a lesson. It's better that he gets his hard knocks from his brother rather than someone who intends him harm."

Jaybird was standing at attention next to the wagon when we got back.

"Now you two need to shake hands," Pa declared.

I took Jaybird's reluctantly extended hand. "You whooped me purty good, Will," he admitted. "You're a lot stronger than I figured."

"You got a good lick on me too," I said as I pointed at my swollen right eye. I felt no honor in my lopsided victory. Despite all of his shortcomings—he was still my little brother.

A broad smile appeared on his face as he took a closer look at my shiner. "Yeah, I guess I did," he declared. He puffed out his chest and held his head high. "Just wait until I get bigger and—"

"That will be enough of that, Jaybird!" Pa interrupted. "It's time to go."

And just like that, Jaybird had forgotten about the scuffle and jumped back into the wagon and took his seat as if nothing had ever happened.

—ııu—

Chapter 9

Bristol Landing was bustling with activity when we arrived on the river road. No less than seven steamboats were docked beneath the tree-covered bluff that towered over the Wabash River. Dozens of wagons were lined up for over a quarter of a mile waiting to unload their cargo of corn, wheat, hogs, cattle, sorghum and whiskey. Everything was to be sent to the troops at Camp Defiance in Cairo. There were also several hucksters and peddler wagons filled with pots, pans and elixirs of all sorts ready to sell to the farmers with their newly acquired windfall. Under any other circumstances, I would have been excited as all get out to see all of the commotion. All I could think about was Muddy. I tried to tell myself that she was going to feed the troops and help win the war, but I just couldn't justify what we were doing. She was like a member of the family and was certainly more agreeable than Jaybird most of the time. Pa wouldn't have dreamed of sending our shepherd dog, King, to the slaughter house and Muddy was at least King's equal. It just wasn't fair. I was trying to think up ways to convince Pa to see things my way, but every time I began to argue my point, I got choked up with emotion. I didn't want Pa to see me cry. So I just said nothing.

As we slowly neared the docks, Pa jumped out of the wagon and disappeared into a barn with a sign that said O.W. Lagow & Sons above the door. It was too late. He was selling Muddy for twenty silver dollars. It wasn't quite like Judas collecting his thirty silver pieces but to me it still felt like an act of betrayal.

"Unload four hogs into that pen over there," Pa pointed to a rail pen next to the barn and then walked toward the captain of a steamboat who was standing on the dock.

I pulled the wagon over to the stock ramp and then jumped down to the ground and lowered the tailboard. I was curious why Pa had instructed me to unload only four hogs instead of ten. Maybe they only wanted four hogs for the army. Maybe Muddy wouldn't have to die. But when Pa walked back and said to take the other four hogs back to the steamboat as soon as the first were off-loaded. What little hope I had for saving my pet pig had just been crushed.

I unloaded Muddy with the first group in the pen. I figured it would at least buy her a little extra time by not sending her on the first steamer. While the other three hogs fought over a slop hole, Muddy silently watched me, as if asking what she had done wrong to be treated this way. I found an apple core on the ground and fed her the treat as a gesture of recompense. She accepted the core without hesitation.

After driving the wagon down to the docks, Jaybird and I herded the remaining pigs onto the rickety gang plank to the steamboat named, *The Miss O'Malley*, where a Negro man by the name of Ernie shooed them into a pen with dozens of other hogs that were all squealing to high heaven. At one time, *The Miss O'Malley*, might have been a fine vessel, but in its current condition, pigs were about the only passengers she was fit to carry. And since it was a ship full of hogs, the smell was something I would like to forget.

Pa drove the wagon with Jaybird at his side back to the livestock barn while I remained at the dock. I tried to imagine what life on the river would be like. I noticed that there were several boys not much older than me working on the boats. I was curious how they had managed to get such a fine job at such a young age. After my fight with Jaybird and Pa's decision to sell my pig, I was half-ready to see if I could hire on with one of the ships and leave South Union forever. I was just about to approach a captain, when he noticed some boys who weren't working fast enough. He berated them with words that not even Jaybird would dare to use and then whipped one of the boys with a hickory stick for talking back. *So much for a life as a riverman.* It was hard times for all boys, regardless of their station in life. I decided to reconsider my stance on my own emancipation.

As I was walking up the hill toward the barn, I saw Jaybird herd two of our pigs from the pen toward the barn. I followed him through the wide double doors and then stopped in my tracks. I was horrified when I saw the ropes, chains and pulleys hanging from the rafters. The barn was a slaughterhouse.

Jaybird delivered the pigs to a barrel-chested man wearing a leather apron that was covered in blood. Despite the desperate protests of the animal, the man took a rope and looped it around one of the pig's hind legs and hoisted it into the air. After tying off the rope, he hoisted the second hog into the air beside the first. While I stood there with my mouth wide open, he pulled out a loaded pistol, pressed it against the hog's forehead and pulled the trigger. The squealing pig was immediately silenced.

He cleaned out the pistol and dropped in new powder and ball. Instead of shooting the next hog, he looked directly at me and smiled, exposing what was left of his tobacco rotted teeth. "Your turn, *Sonny Boy;* Come on over here and kill this critter."

I turned around to see if he was talking to someone behind me. He wasn't. "You talkin' to me?" I asked.

"Who else do ya think I'm talkin' to?" He laughed. "You ain't scared are ya?"

"I ain't s-s-scared." I replied. But I was. I couldn't move. I could hunt and kill wild animals for food and had removed many a chicken's head for Sunday dinner. I had watched the men butcher pigs at the hog killing for several years, but this was different. My pig was next in line. This wasn't fair!

I suddenly became aware that Pa and some of the men in the barn were watching to see what I would do. I was expected to kill the sow and then bring in Muddy to meet the same fate. I didn't want to shame Pa in front of the other men, but I felt cornered and wanted to run. It was asking too much. I didn't care about the war or that the Army needed food. At that moment, I no longer wanted to be a farmer or the man of the house. All I wanted to do was take my pig and go home.

Yet the thought of shaming my father kept me in that barn. Each second that passed seemed to be an eternity. My hands were trembling as I tried to make my decision. Either way—I would draw the short straw.

I could feel the tears welling up in my eyes when salvation came from a most unlikely source.

"Let me do it!" Jaybird yelled at the top of his lungs. "I wanna kill it!" I was never so happy to see his swollen black and blue face in my whole life.

"Whoa boy!" shouted the butcher as Jaybird grabbed for the gun. "Don't want ya shootin' me by mistake!"

I backed out of the barn while the other men laughed at Jaybird as he struggled with the oversized pistol. I was hoping that I could disappear without being noticed, but that wasn't the case. Pa had his eyes on me the whole time.

I ran to a mound of river gravel that was piled next to the hog pens and dropped to my hands and knees in a heap. When I heard the crack of a pistol in the barn, I began to sob like a baby. I thought about making a run for it with Muddy, but as I looked up I could see that Pa was already headed in my direction. I was convinced he was going to make me go back inside and shoot my pig. I sat up and buried my face in my hands.

"Are you alright, Son?" Pa asked calmly.

"I can't do it, Pa!" I cried. "I just can't do it. Please don't make me kill her."

"Shhh... Don't fret none. I know what that sow means to you. I wasn't expectin' you to kill the animal."

"I don't want you to be ashamed of me. I've tried as hard as I can to make you proud of me."

"You haven't let me down, Will." He patted my head and draped his heavy arm around my shoulders. "You have a kind heart and I know you will become a fine man some day. You look at the world in your own way. Sometimes the way you see things might not seem fair, but the world is a cold hard place and things need to be done that ain't pleasant. Take that pig of yours for instance. Your pig is the smartest and finest piece of swine flesh that *The Good Lord* ever created. You've worked with her and trained her like she was a trick pony in the carnival. She's lived a fine life for a hog, much better than her sisters in the slop pen. But there is one thing that will never change. A hog's purpose in this world is to provide food for its master. And a hog knows its place. I've never seem a more noble animal than a hog walking to the slaughter. A hog ain't afraid to die and holds its head high as if to say; *"Here I am, Lord. Take me to Hog Heaven."* And that is how it will be with your sow; she will be fulfillin' her destiny. Do you understand what I'm tryin' to say, Son?"

I nodded my head yes, and wiped the last of the tears on my shirt sleeve. I wanted to say something, but the right words wouldn't come to mind.

"You just stay right here and I'll be back to get you when my business inside is done." Pa patted me on the head and then went to the pen to get Muddy and the other sow. Muddy went on her own, but he had to use a stick to herd the other one as they headed toward the barn and their appointment with Jaybird the executioner.

I felt chills run up my spine when I heard the crack of the pistol shot echoing from the barn. I wondered if it was Muddy on the end of the rope. It didn't matter. It was all going to be over in a minute.

But instead of hearing a second gunshot, I heard Pa shouting at me from the barn. "Get over here, Will." There was a tone of anger in his voice.

My knees wobbled as I walked back to the barn. It could only mean one thing. He was going to make me shoot her after all. When I got inside, instead of dangling from a meat hook, Muddy was standing next to Pa. "Will! You loaded the wrong damn sow!" he scolded. "I told you to save this one for breeding stock! Now I have to return twenty dollars to Mr. Lagow just because you didn't listen to me. Now go load this hog back in the wagon!"

"But Pa—"

"Don't sass me! Get to it!" He winked at me and pointed toward the wagon.

I didn't hesitate. "Come on, girl! Let's go!"

I think Muddy understood the situation and scampered straight to the wagon. I removed the tailgate and rolled a stump next to the bed and Muddy used it as a step ladder and climbed into the wagon. She squealed with excitement as I scratched the back of her head while we waited for Pa and Jaybird to appear. I don't know if Muddy realized how close she was to *Hog Heaven*, but I was grateful enough for the both of us.

I finally breathed a sigh of relief after the docks and packing houses of Bristol Hill were behind us. Jaybird jabbered on about killing the pigs for two or three miles, but then the excitement of the day, not to mention the strain from our fisticuffs got the better of him. He ate a hard biscuit and then crawled beneath the wagon seat. He was sound asleep within minutes. Pa and I didn't exchange a dozen words on the rest of the way home. I started to thank him, but he stopped me before I could finish my sentence.

"Some things are best left unsaid among men," he explained.

Pa was never one to make a fuss about things, but I remembered seeing his eyes glisten in the late afternoon sun and realized that he really did love me. I felt ashamed for thinking badly of him.

—᭦ᴟ᭦—

Chapter 10

The holiday season seemed to come quickly in 1861 as Pa prepared to go to war. He was scheduled to join the 49th Illinois Volunteer Infantry Regiment at Camp Butler in Springfield on New Year's Day. He wanted to join one of the regiments made up from local men, however, the 21st and the 38th had already deployed. He then decided to join up with the 49th out of Washington County. Pa learned that his cousin, Berry Farmer, from Tamaroa had enlisted and the regiment was paying a fifty dollar cash bonus for recruits who signed up before Christmas. Pa signed the papers at the court house in Robinson the day after Thanksgiving. He said it would be safer because he and Berry could look out for each other if things got tough. Pappy and Granny agreed with the wisdom of enlisting with kinfolk, but Ma wasn't buying it. She had continually pleaded with Pa not to go, but he held firm. Once his mind was made up there was no changing it. Pa felt duty bound to fight and that was how it was going to be.

Instead of making Pa's last days at home enjoyable, Ma did her best to make him miserable. She had it in her mind that he was surely going to be killed within a year, so she harassed him in advance for making her a widow. "What kind of man abandons his family just so he can play soldier?" She berated him endlessly "Is freeing slaves worth sendin' your family to the poor house?"

Pa tolerated her insolence in silence, but I could tell it weighed heavily on him during those last few days. While Ma considered him a scoundrel, I considered my father to be a hero.

"The Union has to be preserved," he explained to me while we were feeding oats to the horses. "Our country is in as much peril as it was during the Revolution. But instead of crazy King George, this time it's a bunch of slave-owning plantation owners causing the entire ruckus. Most people down south don't own any slaves, but the rich folks there have 'em all worked up about preservin' the southern way of life. I'll guarantee there ain't gonna be any *southern gentlemen* out on the battlefield with their muskets. The *Johnny Reb* army is made up of a bunch of poor misguided secesh boys that have been sold a bill of goods. It's important to me that you know the real reason I have to go fight in this ungodly war."

"I understand, Pa."

"I know you do, Will," he replied. "I just fret that your mother might turn her displeasure in your direction after I am gone."

"Don't worry about me. I can handle Ma."

He smiled and patted me on the top of my head. "Oh, you can?"

"Yessiree, I can!"

"I guess you can indeed. I don't know why I was worried in the first place. You have a good head on your shoulders, but I want you to promise me one thing."

"Anything, Pa. Just name it."

"I want you to learn how to think for yourself."

"I don't understand," I replied.

"This country is a changin' most every day and who knows what way the winds will be blowin' tomorrow. Folks will change their allegiances just as quick. I'm goin' off to fight in this war because I thought things through and decided it was the right thing to do. While I'm gone you are gonna have to make some decisions on your own that a boy of your age shouldn't have to make."

"What about Pappy?" I wasn't sure what he meant. I wasn't used to grown-up conversations.

"Pappy will make the decisions about the farm, but he ain't a spring chicken anymore. You need to help look out for everyone, but I already know that you'll carry the water in that regard. What I'm tellin' you, Will, is that during this war folks will tend to get excitable— especially when they're around other folks. That's how a mob gets started and the next thing you know—you are doin' something against your nature. All I'm askin' is that if you find yourself in that kind of situation, you'll stop and think things through. If something seems wrong to you, don't follow the others. Just walk away. Do you understand what I'm saying?"

"I think so." I scratched my head. "Do you really think folks will get riled up around the neighborhood?"

"Not right away, but things might get lean around here as the war drags on."

"How long do you think it will take to win the war?" I asked.

"Only the *Good Lord* knows for sure."

"Tucker Simons said his uncle told him the *Rebs* can't last more than a few months."

"I pray that to be true, but from what I see in the newspapers, the Confederates seem to be holdin' their own whenever a skirmish breaks out. I'm afraid I might be gone a goodly amount of time. And there is also a chance I might not come back at all."

"Don't say that Pa." I felt like I had been kicked in the stomach. When the boys in the neighborhood talked about war, it was honor and glory that dominated the conversation. The thought of Pa not coming home never entered my mind.

"Men get killed in battle, Son. It would be foolish to think that something couldn't happen to me. That is why I need to know that you will think for yourself and not let others lead you astray."

"I'll do my best, Pa." I tried my hardest to hold back my tears and act like a man. "I promise I will."

"That's all a man can ask for. Now come over here and give your *old man* a hug." I ran into his meaty arms and cried like a baby.

Winter school had been in session for the past six weeks and I was happy for the one week recess for the holidays. Because of the outbreak of hostilities with the rebels, the neighbors who favored secession not only left the South Union Church, but also refused to send their children to the local school house. Enrollment had dwindled from thirty-six to nineteen students and the schoolmaster. Samuel Stout, a young bachelor from Terre Haute had tendered his resignation, effective on New Year's Day. Stout had joined an infantry unit from Indiana and was leaving immediately for the war. Letters had been sent to find a replacement teacher, but in the meantime, the new session would commence under the supervision of Reverend Parker. Sitting through two hours of fire and brimstone every Sunday was one thing, but the prospect of an additional five days a week of Reverend Parker's teachings was another. I began praying in earnest for a new teacher to accept the position.

I had already taken responsibility for most of the chores around the farm by the time the Christmas season arrived. The temperature had dropped below freezing and it had snowed for the previous few days, so I spent the better part of my days cutting wood. Pa spent as much time as he could trying to calm Ma's nerves before his departure, but she ignored the extra attention. She rocked in front of the fireplace for hours on end; staring into the fire without emotion. She ate her meals away from the dinner table and acted like the rest of the family didn't exist. Even her pride and joy Bub, was unable to get a smile out of her. She would hold him for a few minutes, then send him on his way. Sister Rose took charge of caring for my younger brothers, while Granny ruled the kitchen. Pappy kept an eye on things from his seat at the kitchen table while smoking rabbit tobacco from his cob pipe.

With Pa tending to Ma, the task of harvesting the Yule log fell upon my shoulders. Even with the dark cloud of war looming close to home, Christmas was still a magical time around the cabin. As the acting man of the house, I declared my intentions of getting the perfect log for the benefit of Jaybird and Bub's youthful expectations. But, in all honesty, I looked forward to Christmas Day as much as my brothers.

I sharpened the axe to a razor's edge and hiked into the woods until I found a hedge tree that was about two feet in diameter. After an hour of constant swinging, I felled the tree and cut away a three foot section. I immediately realized that it was too heavy for me to carry, so I headed back to the barn to fetch a horse and rope. On my way back, I found a nice little pine tree that would do fine as a Christmas tree and harvested it too. I delivered the pine to the cabin, where Sister Rose made me a piping cup of hot sassafras tea to warm me up before I went back for the log. Pa praised me for my choice of conifers.

I finished the tea and bundled up as the snow began to fall in earnest and headed after the log with our plow horse in tow. The second trip seemed further than the first as I found myself walking into a brisk northerly headwind that was rapidly gaining strength. By the time I reached the hedge tree, the late afternoon sky had faded to dark gray as the blizzard blocked out what was left of the sun. The eight year old roan became restless as snow began to blow sideways and tried to break away from my grip, but I held firm and tied her lead to a tree while I harnessed the log. I jumped when I heard the not so distant howl of a wolf. I suddenly became aware that I was defenseless. I didn't think to carry a rifle and I had left the axe back in the barn.

As soon as the log was secured, I hurriedly untied the horse and started for the cabin. We hadn't taken more than a dozen steps when the wolf howled again. Apparently the roan was more afraid of wolves than me. She reared up, knocked me to the snowy ground and then bolted though the woods on a dead run. Instinctively, I reached for the log, but instead of me grabbing a hold of it; it got a hold of me instead. My left leg got caught up in the rope and I found myself a helpless passenger bouncing through the woods next to the Yule log. At first the joyride was harmless until the mare went left and I went right. I bounced off a leafless sapling and then flew up into the air. I landed with a thump and found myself riding atop the log facing backwards as the horse picked up speed. I tried to kick my leg free, but the rope had twisted tight around my ankle. All I could do was try to stay on the log instead of the other way around.

The horse ran between the trees as the blizzard turned into a complete white out. I had no idea which way we were traveling as my head began to spin like a top. But before I could worry about being lost in the storm, the mare came to an abrupt stop. Once I cleared the cobwebs from my mind, I realized the horse was standing in front of our barn door. Apparently the old girl knew the way home better than I did. I looked around and gratefully realized nobody had witnessed my undignified return. I untangled my foot and gingerly took a couple of steps to make sure everything was still in place. It was. I put the skittish mare into her stall and wiped her down before giving her some hay and a scoop of oats. I didn't know whether to thank her for getting me home safely or punch her between the eyes for almost killing me.

I walked over to the corner of the barn to the small pen where I kept Muddy during the winter and sat down on an old crate. I decided to take a few minutes to catch my breath before rendering judgment on the critter. After talking it over with my pet sow and seeing how I was no worse for the wear; I decided not to hold any malice toward the horse. I had to admit that the ride home was one of the more exciting events of my young life. I also decided not to tell Ma or Pa about what had transpired during my expedition. I wanted to keep them from worrying and also maintain my status of "man of the house."

After catching my breath, I dropped a few acorns and an ear of corn into Muddy's pen and then closed up the barn for the night.

I sat by the fireplace and watched Sister Rose and Bub as they tied red cloth ribbons and thin strips of indigo around the Yule log while Jaybird strung pieces of popcorn on a string for the tree. I wrapped my hands around the steaming cup of hot tea and let the fire from the hearth warm my backside. My stomach growled mightily as Granny was making a corn pone in the Dutch oven and had a venison stew simmering in the kettle over the fire. We were still two days from Christmas Day dinner but as far as I was concerned; the holiday feast had already begun.

A steady stream of neighbors started showing up at our cabin on Christmas Eve and continued to flow throughout the evening. Everyone wanted to pay their respects to Pa before he left for Springfield. Sister Rose kept a pot of coffee on the woodstove and a crock filled with hot cider on the table. Granny offered candied yams and sweetbread to our guests. The men congregated around the fireplace, smoking pipe tobacco and cussing the lack of success in some battle back east. Even with the cloud of war hanging overhead, everyone seemed ready to share a little Christmas cheer.

Reverend Parker presented Pa with a new Bible to carry in his rucksack and Mrs. Parker knitted him a blue wool scarf to match his federal uniform. Uncle Johnny Logan stopped by with his fiddle and after helping himself to three mugs of cider broke into a rendition of Jingle Bells. Pappy joined in with his mouth harp, while the rest of us clapped in rhythm.

Jaybird began to dance a jig that managed to bring a smile to Ma's face. Within minutes, she was clapping her hands and tapping her foot with the music. She even joined in on the chorus. It was good to see her act like herself again. Pa noticed the change and went over and took her by the hand. "A waltz if you would be so kind, Uncle Johnny!"

Uncle Johnny bowed politely and began playing a cross between an old Scottish Waltz and *We Wish You a Merry Christmas*. Pa whisked Ma around the cabin while we all stood back and watched. It was as if the *Spirit of Christmas* had fallen upon her and given her the ability to be happy once again. For the rest of the night, Ma joined the celebration without mentioning Pa's departure or cursing the war.

I would have been happy to watch everybody else, but Rose took me by the hand and forced me to join in the dancing too. I pretended that I was put out, but within minutes I could no longer maintain my frown. What I lacked in skill; I made up with enthusiasm. It was well past midnight before the festivities died down. I stayed up with Rose and helped her wash the dishes, after everyone else had gone to bed.

"I wish tonight could last forever," Rose sighed. "Everyone seems so happy."

"Especially Ma," I replied. "I didn't reckon I would ever see her laugh again?"

"She's seems much stronger now. I just hope she can keep her strength once Pa leaves." As soon as she said it, Rose looked at me apologetically. "I pray to the Lord that she does."

I smiled and nodded. I had my doubts.

Christmas day was a much more solemn occasion as we realized the time for Pa's departure was near. Although when Pa brought in Christmas gifts that were hidden in the barn, things started to brighten. Apparently, he used some of the hog money to buy the gifts. Bub got a top and some building blocks while Jaybird and I each got a new hatchet. We all got a new pair of shoes, along with a sack filled with rock candy, peanuts and an orange. Sister Rose was thrilled when she opened a package filled with a bolt of calico cloth, along with assorted pieces of cotton and wool. Granny got a new shawl and Pappy got a harmonica.

Pa saved Ma's gift for last and presented her with a gold heart shaped locket on a chain. At first she seemed too afraid to touch it but eventually took it and immediately began to weep.

"You shouldn't have spent the money," she sobbed. "We can't afford this."

"Shhh…" He pressed his finger to her lips. "You deserve more, Sarah. I know I'm askin' a lot from you. I wanted you to be able to keep my heart next to your own while I'm gone."

Ma wrapped her arms around Pa and buried her head on his shoulder. "I truly love you, Sam Farmer. I won't be able to draw a breath if something should happen to you."

"I'll come back to you, Darlin'. That's a promise."

Everyone in the cabin was silent as they embraced in front of the fireplace. Sister Rose smiled at me and then led Jaybird and Bub back to the Christmas tree. "Let's leave the grownups alone," she whispered.

I nodded and followed her when Pappy starting playing *My Old Kentucky Home* on his new harmonica. I tried to give my parents some privacy, but I couldn't keep myself from watching them. I prayed Ma could come back from that dark place.

That afternoon we sat down to a dinner of salted ham, chicken and dumplings, sweet potatoes, along with corn pone and sweet butter. We had warm cider and cool buttermilk and fried doughnuts for dessert. Granny even let Jaybird and I drink a mug of coffee mixed with cream after the meal.

After the dishes were washed, we all circled in front of the fire and listened as Granny sat in her rocking chair and read the Christmas story from the Gospel of Saint Luke. It wasn't long before Jaybird and Bub were sound asleep on the floor. Rose started to take them to bed, but Pa told her to leave them be. He said he wanted to watch them sleep while he still could.

All three generations sat around the fire watching the last of the Yule log crackle and pop and then finally disappear in a trail of smoke dancing up the chimney. No one dared to break the silence as we tried to make the moment last as long as possible.

—⚒—

Chapter 11

Ma's Christmas recovery was short lived. She fell back into her rocking chair and a deep state of melancholy within two days of Pa's departure. She had somehow managed to find the strength to ease Pa's constant worry by climbing out of the darkness during the holidays, but she seemed to be much worse now that he was gone. She awakened late in the morning, sometimes staying in her bed past lunchtime and retired shortly after sundown. She had surrendered all of her domestic responsibility to Granny and Sister Rose, unconditionally and without a fight.

Since Rose was timid and never did anything to stir up any trouble. She quietly went about whatever duties Granny assigned to her. I also found myself taking all of my walking orders from Granny as well. Once Granny issued a command, she expected it to be accomplished in a timely manner.

Pappy said little when it came to handing out chores. "A tight lip when needed is the key to marital bliss," he told me when I asked why he let Granny do all of the bossing around. He pointed at the wood pile on the cabin porch. "Take that stack of wood over there. There is probably a hundred ways a feller could stack that wood and none of those ways would be wrong. Now your Granny likes it stacked a certain way. Her method is better than some and worse than others, but in her mind; she knows best. Now I could show her that my way might be better, but I would run the risk of rufflin' her tail feathers. Once that happens, there is a mighty good chance that I'll be eatin' raw taters and a hunk of meat that tastes like the sole of an old boot. This being said, I stack the wood how she likes it and every now and then I get treated to a meal fit for a king and maybe get a slice of apple pie to boot."

I chewed on his words for a moment. "But if Granny is wrong and you don't say nothin'—isn't that the same as telling a lie?" I asked.

"Heaven's, no!" he exclaimed. "I'm just keepin' the peace. There ain't no sin in that! Now, if it is somethin' that is really important, I'll put my foot down then and live with the consequences. But I ain't about to eat no shoe leather on account of no firewood. Just do what Granny says and you'll have no trouble with her. I'll step in if she gets out of line with you, but it's your job to make sure we get an apple pie every now and then. Are we on the same side?"

I nodded yes. "Keep quiet and eat pie."

The cold dark days after the New Year was a busy time for me. I got up and fed and watered the animals and hauled in firewood before dawn while Jaybird carried in water and Sister Rose cooked the breakfast meal. Granny's rheumatism made it hard for her to use her fingers in the morning so she and Pappy would finish off a pot of coffee that looked thick enough to be molasses before starting her day. After breakfast, I threw a bridle and blanket on the roan and then rode her back to the cabin. Rose jumped on behind me while Jaybird rode in front. It took us about a half hour to reach the school with snow on the ground. In better weather, it only took half that time.

Rose had no intention of going back to school after Christmas. She had finished the eighth grade primer and was needed at home. Anything above an eighth grade education was considered a waste on the frontier. Since she was the oldest girl left in school and without any friends her own age, she decided to stay and help with Ma. Only three days into the winter session, Reverend Parker took ill with the ague. Without a suitable teacher to replace the replacement, school was cancelled for the semester.

After a few days of being cooped up with their children, parents realized that a resolution needed to be found for the problem at hand. It was decided that Sister Rose would instruct the children until a new master could be found or Reverend Parker was back on his feet. At first Rose was hesitant to accept the position, but eventually consented. Even though she was shy and backward around adults, Rose was at ease and even outgoing around the children. With the exodus of the Copperhead students, the enrollment at the South Union School was down to thirteen, so Rose didn't expect to have much trouble keeping the classroom under control. The Widow Rush, who lived next door to the school, volunteered to render out any chastisement needed with the business end of her broom. Even though she didn't have any children of her own, she didn't mind beating a child for the greater good of the neighborhood. Rose didn't ask for recompense but the parents all agreed to pay her two dollars cash money or an item for her hope chest if money wasn't available.

Rose was also responsible for keeping the class room warm, which meant I was responsible for splitting and hauling the wood to the stove. A few of the men who hadn't left for war cut and delivered several hardwood logs for the school to use. Unfortunately, none of the wood was split small enough to burn inside. Upon arrival, I grabbed the axe and split enough wood to last until recess at which time I would split enough to get us through the day. A couple of the younger boys offered to help, but since I was the oldest boy left in the school, I considered myself Rose's assistant. With the exception of Jaybird, all of the kids seemed to respect my position of authority.

After school I helped Rose secure and clean up the classroom before riding home through the mud and snow. I put away the tack and wiped down the roan as soon as we reached the farm. Once she was secured in her stall I began the task of feeding the rest of the livestock. Hay and a little bit of grain for the horses and cattle, cracked corn for the chickens and slop for the hogs. I always saved Muddy for last and fed her an ear of corn for a treat. I let her out of her pen so she could accompany me to the wood pile while I split some more wood to replace what was used while I was gone. It seemed like I spent half of my day with an axe in my hands. I didn't mind though. Jaybird was too small and Pappy got tuckered out after three or four swings. He wasn't what you would call feeble, but Granny was worried the strain might be more than his heart could bear. All the heavy work fell to me. It was all part of being the man of the house.

After the wood was cut and stacked, I played fetch with Muddy for a few minutes before it got dark. Our dog, King, came over and watched. I threw a stick for him to chase, but he looked at me in a way that indicated he wasn't interested in learning any new tricks. It didn't matter. He was still a good dog.

I had just finished putting Muddy back in the barn when I noticed a rider approaching on a familiar mule. It was Hub

Wheeler on his way to George Maxwell's house with the mail from Robinson. Maxwell ran the local post office for the Flat Rock area.

"Got a package for Sarah Farmer," he said. "Thought I would drop it off and save ye a trip over to the post office."

"Much obliged, Mr. Wheeler. Wanna come in the cabin and warm up?"

"Thank ye for the invite, but I best be getting on down the road before it gets too dark to see. Give my regards to your elders." He touched the brim of his hat and was on his way.

I studied the package and immediately became excited. It was from Pa. It was dated three weeks earlier. Mail delivery around South Union was sporadic at best. Eventually most correspondence arrived at their intended destination after a few days of misdirection on the wrong stage coach or collecting dust on the shelf of a forwarding post office. Tardy or not, I was excited to hear from him.

Ma's eyes widened and she sprung out of her rocking chair as soon as I walked into the cabin with the brown paper covered parcel. She pushed her uncombed hair out of her eyes and snatched the bundle from my hand as if it were a priceless jewel. It was the first time she had shown any interest in anything since Pa's departure. She opened the envelope that was carefully attached to the package with a twine string and removed several hand written pages. She squinted and held the letter next to the oil lamp to get a better look and within seconds became emotional. "Tarnation!" she cried when she was unable to focus on its content. It was difficult to read a book in the cabin under any circumstances, but deciphering Pa's chicken-scratch handwriting after sundown was next to impossible. Ma gave up and handed the letter to Rose and carried the package back to her rocking chair.

Rose took a seat at the table and placed the lamp in a position where it wouldn't cast a shadow on the letter. She sat up straight with perfect posture and in the same manner that she delivered her lessons at the school house, began to read to us.

3 January 1862
Camp Butler Illinois

Dear Family

I went on duty for the first time today and was assigned to keep the fires going for Company I while the men prepared to move into a barrack vacated by a company that headed off to Cairo. It was cold and damp with snow and ice falling all day, so at least I was able to stay warm. After dark, the officers gave us a dinner of oysters and yams. I ain't never had oysters before, but I learned I had a taste for them and finished a second plate. Cousin Berry thought they tasted like fish bait, so I finished his portion as well. We both agreed that the officers seem to be very smart fellers.

6 January

We seem to march all day long without going anywheres in particular. The grounds are a bloody mess. New recruits arrive everyday and the company should soon be full.

9 January

We had a special dinner tonight in honor of a victorious battle in New Orleans. Captain Brokaw, Major Bishop and Lieut. Harlan ate with the enlisted men. We had salt pork and roasted potatoes. We didn't march today as the melting snow turned the parade grounds into a lobgolly. The boys in the 46th are fussing about not getting paid. Berry says they will surely mutiny if the money doesn't come soon.

15 January
Rumor has it that our troops are leaving Cairo to fight the Rebs in Columbus, Kentucky. Some of the men say we will be moving out soon to join them. I have to admit I am a little frightful about going into battle. Camp is a bit dull. Most of the boys spend their days playing cards and gambling. I stood guard last night and nearly froze to death from the wind and cold. The paymaster finally came by and I received $31.77. I am sending $25 home with this letter to help with expenses. Two days ago, I went to Springfield on a day pass and had two photographs taken in my new blue uniform. They are not very good images.

23 January
A man fell through the railroad bridge over Sangamon River last night onto the ice and was killed. Everyone said he was drunk, but I didn't know him. I was chosen for burial detail. A huckster was drummed out of camp for selling whiskey to some of the men. I went to listen to a preacher who held a meeting in Company K barracks. He had the Spirit of Lord upon him. It made me miss Sunday Meetings with all of you.

29 January
We had to bury three men yesterday who had caught the measles. Camp Butler is not a healthy place. I took an ear ache while marching yesterday and shook all night with an ague.

The noise and racket in camp is trying my patience and it is very cold in the barracks. We are only issued two blankets and there is barely enough straw to cover the floor. I went to sick call and was given two pills by a surgeon. I hope they will give me some relief.

3 February

I just learned that we are moving out for Cairo and then on to Fort Holt in Kentucky. My ear ache is easing and I am grateful to be leaving this place of sickness. I fear that there is a greater chance of dying from a disease than catching a Secesh bullet. I am sending my clothes, as we are not allowed to wear anything other than our uniform. I pray that you are all well and safe. I wish more than anything to be home with you all, but I still believe that I have a sacred duty to fight for this just cause. Let us all believe that the fighting will be over by harvest time. Until my return, know that you are in my thoughts and in my heart.

I remain your faithful husband, son and father,
Samuel Farmer

Everyone was silent as Rose carefully refolded the letter and placed it on the table. I don't know what I was expecting Pa to say in his letter, but the realization of his situation was sobering. I envisioned him as a hero, charging against the Rebs in his navy blue uniform. I saw the stars and stripes proudly waving behind him while drummers kept time with the marching band. I foresaw medals for valor and his return as conquering liberator of the South. I had not seen him infirmed, lying on muddy straw while soldiers died from measles and others played cards. His letter made Camp Butler sound like a prison instead of a training facility.

"I knew this would happen!" Ma cried. "He's gonna catch a death of a fever before he sees a Reb!" She clenched her jaw and slammed the package to the floor. Bub was frightened and immediately began to cry.

"Shame on you, Sarah Farmer!" Granny scolded as she lifted Bub from the floor. "Not in front of the little ones!"

"He's gonna die! I feel it in my soul! If a bullet don't kill him; a sickness surely will."

"Not another word!" Granny fired back. "I'll not have you cursin' my son!"

"I'll curse him for leaving me alone with three boys! I'll curse him to damnation!"

Granny's face turned crimson. She clenched her jaw, walked over to Ma and waylaid her across her face. Ma started screaming like a heathen rooster, so Granny took aim and slapped her again. The second blow did the job.

Ma immediately became silent. Her eyes opened wide and wild and then she began panting like a dog. She looked directly at Granny and acted like she didn't recognize her.

Bub continued to cry and Jaybird looked nervous. Pappy told Sister Rose to take the boys up to the loft while Granny ordered me to fetch a cold wet cloth.

Granny knelt down on the floor and took Ma's hand in her own. "You have to be brave, Sarah. You are scaring the children."

"He's gonna die! I just know it!"

"Poppycock! Samuel is fine. He is not going to die. You have to believe that."

Ma buried her face on her knees and began sobbing.

Granny forced her head upward so she could look her in the eyes. "His life is in God's hands and we have to believe that our prayers are protecting him."

Ma wiped her eyes with a handkerchief. Her sobs subdued to an occasional sniffle.

Granny lowered her voice to a whisper. "Sarah, I know that you are worried. There would be something wrong with you if you weren't. You're not alone. I am scared myself that something might happen to him. But what good does our worryin' do? Not a dad blasted bit. We need to be strong for the children's sake. They look to you for their strength. You need to be their rock; even when you feel like you can't go on. You need to think about the boys instead of yourself. Do you understand what I am saying?"

Ma nodded and rested her head on her knees.

"That's my girl," Granny said and patted her on her back. She let Ma collect herself for a moment and then placed the package on her lap. "Why don't you open this and see what Samuel sent?"

Ma futilely tried to untie the knots and then out of frustration decided to tear into the wrapping paper like a child on Christmas morning.

There were two photographs of Pa in a dress uniform, holding an oversized pistol against his chest. He wore a stern humorless expression on his face. His hair was slicked back, his hand rested on his hip and his eyes seemed to be focused on something far away. The photographs were securely positioned in ornate cardboard frames with Pa's signature in the bottom left hand corner. One photo was inscribed to Ma and the other to Granny. There were three small bags of rock candy for the children, a box of powdered soap for Rose and a pouch of cherry pipe tobacco for Pappy. There was a small envelope with twenty-five dollars of cash money along with Pa's gray flannel shirt and butternut wool pants.

Ma briefly looked at the photographs and the other gifts and then passed them off to Granny without a word. She concentrated on Pa's clothes and gently traced the outline of the button holes of his shirt with her finger. "I made this shirt for him last summer," she whispered. "This was his favorite shirt." She held the shirt to her face and inhaled deeply. "I can still smell him." She doubled over and clung to the garments and began to weep.

"Now, now," Granny said as she put her arm around her. "Why don't we get you to bed, dear. Things will look better in the morning!"

Ma nodded her head and tottered over to the bed and stayed there for the better part of three days. She refused to take her meals at the table and slept all day and night, waking periodically to cry or rant about Pa's demise. After three days Pappy sent me for Doc Lagow in New Hebron.

When we returned home from school that day we found Ma sitting back in her rocking chair with a faraway look on her face. The doctor had given her a dose of Laudanum, which enabled her to get out of bed but that was about it. She nodded and smiled at us, but I don't think she understood what was going on around her. Doc Lagow said to give her a dose of the elixir four times a day until she came out of her melancholy. The word melancholy, accurately described her condition for the past several months. I was convinced she would have to take the medicine for the rest of her life.

—∽∾∽—

Chapter 12

The *Vincennes Sun* reported that the Illinois 49th Infantry regiment saw heavy fighting during the battle of Fort Donelson in Tennessee. Church bells rang in celebration across the countryside in honor of the Union's first significant victory of the war. Ulysses S. Grant became an overnight hero and earned the nickname Unconditional Surrender Grant because he refused to give terms to the rebel commander. The mood in our cabin was a bit more guarded as we had not received word from Pa. The *Sun* reported that 500 Union soldiers were killed in the battle, while 2,000 were wounded and another 200 were captured or missing in action. Ma was convinced Pa was among the dead. We all tried to convince her that she had nothing to fret about, but down deep inside we shared her fear.

I learned quickly that the waiting was the hardest part for the families left behind. Word would eventually trickle in about the local companies, but because Pa enlisted in a regiment that predominately consisted of men from Washington County, news was hard to come by. Reverend Parker told us that we would have received a notice from the Provost Marshall in Olney if anything bad had happened to Pa. "No news is good news," he assured us. "The Devil would like to rule your lives with dread and fear. We all have to stand firm and persevere until the war is over!"

I tried to take comfort from the preacher's words, but I could never quite get the worries to leave the back part of my mind. With the exception of Ma, who figured no news meant that Pa was already dead, we all tried to keep a smile on our face for Jaybird and Bub's sake. Pappy tried to keep the boys entertained and Granny buried herself in her household chores. I heard her shed some tears in prayer when she didn't know I was around. I was careful not to speak of my own fears except when Sister Rose and I were alone. Rose was the only one I trusted with my true thoughts. She was worried too, but reminded me that since we had no real information to go on, everything we were feeling was a figment of our own imaginations. Good or bad, it didn't matter. We had nothing to go on, so it was best to assume he was fine and keep him in our prayers. If something did happen—there would be plenty of time to mourn afterwards. Meanwhile, we had plenty to keep us busy. Rose's words made sense to me, so I tried to go about things just as they were before Pa's departure.

Unfortunately, news of the war was everywhere. It was hard not to get discouraged when all of the reports about the war back east were bad. That's why the victory at Fort Donelson was so important. It gave the Union something to hang their hat on. Until I learned something to the contrary, I decided to believe that Pa was alive and well and that the Illinois 49th was leading the way to a quick end to the war.

In early April we received a short note from Pa that confirmed that he was not injured.

3 April, 1862

Dear Family,

I don't have much time as we are about to cross the Tennessee River to a place called Pittsburg Landing. I got my first taste of action at Fort Donelson. The Rebs fought hard but were no match for us. Fort Donelson was a muddy mess. Glad to be moving south. I was promoted to Sergeant after the battle. I have to leave now. The boat is getting ready to shove off. I pray you are all well.

Faithfully yours,
Samuel Farmer

Granny killed a fat rooster and we celebrated the news with a victory feast. Pappy took the letter to Sunday Meeting and boasted that U.S Grant couldn't have won the battle without Sergeant Sam Farmer at his side. We were all proud as could be. Ma, however, didn't join in on our jubilation. She had worried herself so sick, that the arrival of good news couldn't bring her back from her state of melancholy. Her dependency on laudanum seemed to increase by the day. With every dose of the elixir, she seemed to fade deeper into her own world of darkness. A world in which there was no war, no missing husband, no children and family and no accountability. I desperately wanted Ma to come back to us. I wanted the loving and caring mother who sang songs, cooked apple pies and prayed over us when we were sick. But with every passing day it became more evident that the Sarah Farmer of my childhood wouldn't be coming back. Whether the news of the war was good or bad; it didn't matter. She no longer reacted to anything around her. What little food she ate was spoon fed to her by Rose. Sometimes all she would take would be a few sips of broth. It was when she started ignoring Bub, that I realized that she was gone. Bub was confused and heartbroken. Granny doted over him as much as she could, but he had always been Ma's baby boy and he couldn't understand why he had been forsaken.

I became angry with Ma for abandoning the family when we needed her the most. The anger would eventually be replaced by a heavy dose of guilt. Down deep I knew it wasn't her fault. She didn't choose to be unhappy. She was sick and I was being selfish. After all, I was supposed to be the man of the house. Pa expected me to be strong when things got tough and I didn't want to let him down. Whenever I felt my anger getting the best of me, I would go outside and chop firewood until my arms felt like they were going to fall off. Once I had gotten myself to the point of exhaustion, I didn't have it in me to be mad at her anymore. I found that the easier course was just to stay away from her as much as possible. I wasn't proud of that, but it helped me get through the day. Sometimes that was all that mattered.

It was only a few days after receiving Pa's note that we learned that the 49th was in the thick of things at Pittsburg Landing. The newspapers called the Battle of Shiloh the bloodiest fighting of the war to date. It was said that the fighting at Shiloh made the Battle of Fort Donelson look like a picnic. Once again, Grant's Army of the Tennessee won what was called a "major victory" for the Union, but it came at a heavy cost. It was reported that the Union Army suffered over 13,000 casualties. I didn't know how many troops were in Grant's command, but 13,000 was a number beyond my comprehension. Pappy said that "Grant's boys gave a heck of a lot more than they took." He was certain that Pa was unharmed. Granny—however wasn't so sure. She didn't say anything, but she was visibly shaken. Ma didn't say a word. I don't even know if she understood what was going on anymore.

I was eleven years old and for all intents and purposes, I no longer had a mother. I still loved Ma—or at least what was left of her, but I also began to resent what she was doing to the family. I felt like she had chosen to abandon us. Everybody said it wasn't her fault, but I figured she was so mad about Pa going off to war that she decided to take it out on the rest of us. For the time being, I decided to keep my mouth shut about the matter.

Winter school ended on April 10 when the weather started to warm up. On April 11, it was time to go to work in the fields. The almanac said that it was time to start planting potatoes, so I found myself heading out to the tater patch after a breakfast of bacon and biscuits. Rose and Jaybird came with me, but after thirty minutes of hoeing up the red clay, Jaybird became bored and started throwing dirt clods at blackbirds that had come to dine on the newly exposed night crawlers. I told him to get to work, which resulted in a dirt clod bouncing against my ear. I started to go over and thump my little brother, but Rose intervened. She grabbed Jaybird by the ear and led him back to cabin before I could lay a malicious hand on him. He squealed and squawked all the way. Five minutes into the planting season and my authority had already been challenged. Jaybird, the mutineer!

I found myself chopping away at the ground, alone with my thoughts. Rays of brilliant spring sunshine pierced through a crystal blue sky and warmed the earth between my toes. It felt good to be barefooted after a long dark winter of confining my feet in a pair of undersized boots. I swung the hoe and moved in a rhythm that allowed me to break the most top soil with the least amount of effort. Chop…Chop…Chop and step. Chop… Chop…Chop and step. "Work smart, not hard," Pa always said. I soon realized that muscles needed for tilling the tater patch were different from those used to cut the firewood during winter. My arms and shoulders felt like I had added a millstone to each. After working for what seemed to be an eternity, I looked up to gauge my progress. I had barely made a dent in the field.

Maybe Jaybird wasn't as dumb as I thought he was. By misbehaving, he was punished by being sent back to the cabin while I did all of the work. He took the whole "work smart, not hard" proverb to heart in a much different way. "Why work when you don't have to," seemed to be his motto. I doubt he would have acted up if Pa were still around. The threat of a black leather strap had always served as a deterrent. Now it seemed he was going to test Granny and Pappy's resolve. It was bound to happen, so maybe it was just as well to set the boundaries early this year.

When I saw Jaybird reappear while rubbing his backside, I knew what had happened. Instead of returning to the tater patch, Granny led him to the garden behind the barn at broom point. It was there that he resumed tilling under her watchful eye. Sister Rose joined me with a burlap tater bag and by sundown, there was a half acre of seed potatoes in the ground and I was exhausted. I could brag all I wanted to about being the man of the house, but if the truth be told, I had a hard time keeping up with Rose. She was taller and stronger than me and never complained a bit.

Planting potatoes was one thing, planting corn, sorghum and tobacco was another. Pappy felt the money crops were too important to plant without grown-up supervision. Pappy helped me hitch the horse to the plow and decided where and when we planted. Every now and then he would relieve me for a row or two, but for the most part he found a shady spot under a tree in the fence row while making sure that most of my seeds ended up under the red Wabash Valley clay. "Keep up the good work, Will," he cackled. "Couldn't do a better job, myself."

His toothless smile was a comfort and he knew a lot about farming. He had scratched out a living in the hard scrabble of the Tennessee hills, so the Honey Creek topsoil seemed "rich-folk bottom land" to him. Sister Rose helped Granny back at the cabin on the days when Pappy went with me. Pappy and Rose's approach to working in the fields was like the opposite sides of a coin. Rose and I talked while we worked, but she was all business. She could shame me into working harder, just by the pace she set for herself. It was if she were killing snakes in the Garden of Eden. If I fell behind her, she would stop, raise an eyebrow and give me a stare that made me feel guilty. She didn't have to say anything. The fact that I was getting out-worked by a girl was humbling enough.

Pappy told me to go sit under a shade tree and take a break whenever he took the reins. "Loafin' is good for a boy's constitution," he told me. "Don't be a slave to time. There'll be plenty of time to get everything done. That's why *The Good Lord* gave us tomorrow. As long as there is a today, there will always be a tomorrow." Pappy liked to tell jokes, but when we were alone, he let me see a side that was all business. He admitted he was worried about Pa, but he didn't want anyone else to know. "It's important for us to be strong for the women's sake. They do enough worryin' for the both of us. From what I hear about the fightin' at Shiloh—it sounded like hell on earth. I'd rest a lot easier at night if we got word your Pa was not harmed."

I appreciated the help, but I noticed that Pappy was struggling to keep his balance behind the plow. On two occasions he went to a knee when his foot slipped on the uneven ground. He had to frequently stop and rub his gnarled hands whenever his rheumatism flared up. It got to the point where I couldn't stand to see him agonize in pain anymore. At first he fought me when I made him sit instead of me. Pappy had a lot of pride. I know it hurt his feelings, but down deep I think he knew I was right. He asked me not to say anything to Granny and continued to accompany me to the field. He helped me whenever he could and tried to teach me some things that he said a boy ought to know, but as the temperature grew warmer, my work load grew heavier. I was tired and sore every evening and sleepy and stiff in the morning. I didn't complain. I promised Pa I would take care of the family while he was gone. He had enough on his mind just by staying clear of Johnny Reb bullets, I didn't want to let him down by letting the farm go to rack and ruin.

—⁂—

Chapter 13

It was the middle of June and we still hadn't received any news from Pa or anyone else since the fighting at Shiloh Church. We tried to think only good thoughts, but with the passing of each and every day, the tension and trepidation started to grow. Granny openly feared for the worst, but tried not to say anything when Bub and Jaybird were around. Ma, on the other hand, didn't care who was within earshot. "He's dead and it's his own blasted fault," she cursed from her rocking chair. She would rock some more and repeat the exact same thing a few minutes later. She had become a total stranger since the beginning of the war. I loved Ma, but the woman in the rocking chair was not the same woman who had raised me. I kept quiet and didn't say anything, but I wanted my Ma back. I needed her and so did my brothers. How could she act this way with Pa gone? Fortunately there wasn't much time to fret about it. There was always more work for me to do.

What little news of the war that did manage to find its way to South Union was mostly bad. Shiloh had been considered a major victory for the Union Army, but the cost in human lives didn't leave many of the folks in the mood for much celebrating. Those who were opposed to the war in the beginning were growing bolder in their opposition by the day. Some of the local people started calling themselves "Peace Democrats, Copperheads, and Knights of the Golden Circle." Some called for an immediate peace with the South, while others wanted to organize local bushwhackers and vigilantes and bring the war to the Wabash Valley.

A small but extremely deadly group of rabble used the Confederate cause as an excuse to steal, murder and terrorize the neighborhood in the pursuit of ill-gotten gains. Most of these lived in the back wood bottoms of the Embarrass River near the settlements of Charlottesville, Port Jackson and the Dark Bend. The swamps around the Embarrass had long been a haven for horse thieves and counterfeiters. The area was secluded and provided a measure of separation from the law abiding folks which made up the majority of the county. In normal times, there was safety in numbers. In the past, outlaws had never bothered our neighborhood because the local settlers were heavily armed, and in most cases were actually better marksmen than the scallywags. But since the outset of the war, the majority of able-bodied men had gone south to join the fight. It fell to the men and boys who were too old or too young to join the army to protect the homesteads. There was plenty of gossip coming from the liar's corner at the general store about the danger these outlaws presented; but to date it was all talk. I was almost too tired to care.

As the days grew hotter and longer, my list of chores seemed to grow at an equal pace. It wasn't as if I was alone in my circumstances. Rose worked just as hard in her own way. She helped me whenever she could in the field, but she was desperately needed at the cabin. Granny ran the household and cooked most of the meals, but keeping an eye on Jaybird and Bub along with tending to Ma's demands was a heavier load than she could carry. Rose did whatever it took to make sure everything got done without any hint of a complaint. As much as I wanted to, I didn't complain either. Call it pride if you will, but I wasn't about to be out worked by a girl, even if it was Rose.

Times were tough, but we didn't know anything else. Everyone else around South Union was struggling to get by too. The war had created shortages at the general store, so what little dry goods made it to the shelves were too expensive for anyone to buy. Pappy traded for some salt and saleratus for baking bread since the winter wheat was ready for harvest, but coffee, tobacco or sugar was reserved for the rich families only.

Despite my long days in the field, I tried to spend a little time with Muddy every evening. Part of me felt that I was too old for a pet pig, but another part couldn't wait to see her at the end of the day. Her playful squeal and uncompromising devotion reminded me of the days before there was a war. I didn't have to be the man of the house around her. When we were together, I could feel like a kid again. I could speak foolish and childlike words and she didn't care. It was all fun and games as far as Muddy was concerned. I told her things I would have been ashamed to speak in front any living person. I complained about working too hard and even cried from worrying about Pa dying alone on some battlefield. Muddy faithfully listened for hours on end, pleased to be deemed noble enough to be part of such important conversations. Muddy walked with me to the fields a couple of times, but when we got word that Copperheads were stealing livestock from the farms of absent Union soldiers, Pappy felt it would be safer for her to stay close to the cabin. In the long run, Muddy helped keep Jaybird and

Bub occupied during the day; which in turn, eased Granny and Rose's burden.

I had just finished loading the last bushel of wheat into the barn when I saw the plume of dust rising up from behind a rickety flatbed wagon being pulled by an ancient dapple gray mare. The driver was a weather-beaten man with long snow-white hair and a long white beard to match. Granny and Pappy stepped out on the porch just as the wagon rolled to a stop.

"Howdy neighbors," he spoke in an unnaturally deep bass voice. "Would this be the home of Samuel Farmer?"

"I'd be his Pa and this would be his Ma," Pappy answered cautiously. "Why do ye ask?"

"The name is Thompson. Jeremiah Thompson. I'm a bringin' my youngest boy, Ned, back from the battlefield at Shiloh Church. He has news from your son Samuel."

"Sam is alive?" Granny gasped.

"Yes, Ma'am—he most certainly is. Ned wouldn't be here if it wasn't for your son."

"Praise Jesus!" she cried.

That's when I noticed the frail, thin frame of a man in a blue uniform struggle to sit upright in the back of the wagon. At first glance he looked to be on the far side of forty years of age. His eyes had the weary look of an old man who had seen too many tragedies, but after a closer look they still had the youthful glint of a boy no older than eighteen. He wore a white bandage around his head with a sprinkling of crimson seeping through. He was drenched in sweat and the left sleeve of his jacket was pinned to his shoulder where his arm had once attached to his shoulder. He grimaced in pain, but still managed to produce a small measure of a smile. He nodded toward Granny, "Pleased to make your acquaintance, Ma'am."

"Lord Almighty, he's burning up with fever!" Granny declared. "This boy needs to be in bed!"

"He will be as soon as we get back to our home in Marshall," the old man said. "We've come three hundred miles from the far side of the Tennessee River. He'll last another two days until we can get him into his own bed. But if it wouldn't be too much trouble, we'd be obliged if we could water our horses and camp near your barn. We won't be any bother and we'll be gone by dawn's light."

"Nonsense!" Granny growled. "You'll sleep inside with us. We won't take no for an answer, will we Pappy?"

"I afraid my wife will make life miserable for all of us if we don't do as she says." Pappy smiled as he began to unhitch the horse.

Pappy and Mr. Thompson helped Ned into the cabin while I led the old gray mare to the barn. As bad as I wanted to get into the cabin and hear what he had to say about Pa, I realized the horse was in need of attention. I washed her down as quick as I could and still feel good about the quality of my work, then dried her off and put her into an empty stall with a leaf of hay and a few handfuls of oats. She seemed grateful and didn't pay any attention when Muddy meandered over to inspect the visitor. As soon as she was settled, I dashed back to the cabin.

Ned Thompson was setting upright in bed while Granny was peeling him out of his uniform jacket, despite his sincere protest. "Honest, I don't want to be a bother."

"Be still and let me look at your dressing!" She ordered. Granny carefully unwrapped the blood stained cloth and then let out with a gasp that the scared us all. "When's the last time this bandage has been changed?" Granny asked.

"A corpsman changed it when we crossed the Ohio in Cairo. I guess it's been about ten days."

"Lord help us!" she declared. "That's a might angry shade of red. I am afraid an infection has set in."

"Really, Mrs. Farmer, Ned will be fine when we get him home," protested Jeremiah Thompson. "We've already been too much of a burden."

"Mr. Thompson!" Granny roared. "This boy needs to see a doctor now!"

"But Ma'am—"

"But nothing! This boy is gravely ill!" she snapped, "Get on your horse Pappy. Reverend Parker has got a doctor from Ohio visitin' this week. Fetch him on over and tell him to hurry."

Pappy was gone before either of the Thompsons could say another word.

"This boy can't be moved for at least two weeks," declared Doctor Isaiah Judd from Xenia, Ohio. Doctor Judd was a round man with a round bald head, moon-shaped brown eyes and round gold spectacles that made his eyes look double their normal size. He had a long waxed moustache surrounded by rosy cheeks that would have made Santa Claus jealous. "It's a miracle he's lived this long. I'm concerned that what little arm he has left might be gangrenous."

"Really, Doc," Ned Thompson protested, "it doesn't hurt that bad."

"I want you to look me in the eyes, son. If you do not follow my instructions—you will not be among the living by this time next week. Do you understand what I am saying?"

Ned nodded yes.

"But Doctor Judd—we are so close to home. Wouldn't he be better off in his own bed?" pleaded the elder Thompson.

"I am not a tactful man," Doctor Judd replied. "I have not minced any words, sir. Do you prefer your son dead or alive?"

"What kind of question is that?"

"An honest question," replied the doctor.

Doctor Judd slathered a salve and poultice on Ned's wounds and rewrapped clean bandages on the arm and head. He made him eat some chicken broth that Granny had prepared and gave him a large dose of laudanum for the pain and insisted that he be left alone to sleep.

Ned wanted to tell us about how Pa saved his life, but Doctor Judd insisted it could wait until morning. Ned started to protest again, but quietly nodded off to sleep as soon as the laudanum kicked in.

Rose hung a quilt from the rafters to give Ned some privacy as we all gathered around the kitchen table. Granny started pouring steaming hot cups of coffee. Reverend Parker waited until Rose joined us and then went to the sleeping soldier's bedside and recited a prayer of protection to see him safe through the night.

Doctor Judd said that he would return first thing in the morning and left a bottle of laudanum with instructions to administer two spoonfuls if he should happen to awaken in the middle of the night. "You have a very sick boy, Mr. Thompson. I'm not sure we are completely out of the woods, but I am convinced that Providence most certainly has brought you to this farm on this night, just as Providence has brought me to visit Reverend Parker at the same time. I do not believe that God would orchestrate such a series of events if he did not intend you son to live."

Jeremiah Thompson slowly nodded and choked up as he tried to speak. He took a deep breath and whispered: "Thank you, Doctor. God Bless every one of you."

It was turning dark as Doctor Judd and Reverend Parker left for home. Granny had a pot of beans in the kettle seasoned with a rabbit Pappy had killed during his morning hunt simmering on the stove. The sweet smell of nearly baked corn pone in the Dutch oven in the fireplace filled the cabin. With all of the excitement, I had forgotten how hungry I was. This was remedied as soon as the food was placed on the table.

Jeremiah Thompson hesitantly accepted the chair at the head of the table and quietly finished his meal in a manner that indicated it had been a while since he had eaten. I had so many questions to ask that I felt like I was busting at my seams, but I knew better than to say anything. I would have to wait until the adults spoke and glean whatever I could from their conversation. Despite my duties around the farm, there was still a pecking order and proper manners needed to be observed.

Ma had been sleeping all afternoon and rarely came to the dinner table anymore. Rose tried her best to roust her from bed for the occasion as soon as we learned Pa was still alive, but even that glorious good news couldn't pull her out of her melancholy. She sat up and said "That's nice," and then went back to sleep. I was ashamed to admit it, but at times I preferred her sleeping all day instead of her ranting fits of rage. In less than a year, Ma had gone from a loving and caring mother to a total stranger who was a combination of a helpless child and a crazy relative that was kept in the back room away from company. I knew she was sick and couldn't help it, but I was angry at her for being such a burden to us all during such hard times. I wasn't proud about how I felt, nor would I ever speak those words out loud in front of another soul. But it was truly a source of anger that boiled hotter inside of me with each passing day. It was a bitterness that I did not understand or care to explore. It was what it was. I didn't like the person that I was becoming.

Pappy brought out a tin of rabbit tobacco and offered a pipe to Mr. Thompson.

"No thank you, Mr. Farmer, I don't partake in tobacco, but don't let that stop you."

Pappy smiled. "Well, in that case, I don't mind if I do." He grabbed a stick from the kindling and stirred the coals in the fireplace until it sparked and then lit his cob pipe while puffing like a whippoorwill. He took a deep draught and blew a stream of white smoke into the air.

Mr. Thompson cleared his throat and honked his nose into a linen handkerchief. "There are not enough words to tell you how grateful I am to you all. I wanted to hurry on home, but Ned had promised your son that he would deliver news of his well being, and insisted that I honor his word. If I had not submitted to his stubbornness; I am afraid I would be delivering his corpse to his mother. Your family has truly been the salvation of my son. First, it was Samuel at Shiloh and now the rest of the Farmer family has come to his rescue again."

"Just showin' some Christian charity," Granny told him. "I am sure you would have done the same for us if things was the other way around."

"For my own soul's sake, I hope so Mrs. Farmer." He clasped his hands together, closed his eyes and looked as if he was praying a silent prayer. After a brief moment of silence he opened his eyes. "If there is ever anything I can ever do for you, please let me know. I am eternally in your debt!"

"Well—if it wouldn't be too much trouble—we'd be much obliged if you could tell us what you know about Samuel," Granny asked. "We ain't heard a single word since the Battle at Fort Donelson."

"Forgive me Ma'am," Mr. Thompson apologized. "I've been so consumed about Ned that I've completely forgotten about your feelings. I know Ned has a message from your son, but I will tell you what little I do know."

"Whatever you have to share will be appreciated," Granny assured him.

"It was late April when a rider from the Provost came to our house with a letter that simply stated that Ned was gravely ill in a field hospital at Pittsburgh Landing on the Tennessee River. It didn't describe the injury, nor did it say whether he was expected to live or die. My wife, Elizabeth, and I were beside ourselves. We didn't know what to do. Finally, I decided to get into the wagon and head south. I hired a neighbor boy to help Elizabeth with our dry goods store in Marshall and left the next morning. My people are from Ohio and I had never been south of Clark County in my life, but I couldn't stand the thought of him lying down there all alone.

I pushed my old mare, Matilda, from dusk til dawn. I had no idea where I was going, but once I crossed the Ohio River, I just followed the other wagons heading for the battlefield. It seems I wasn't the only one on a rescue mission. There were scores of men going to Shiloh to bring back the wounded. It seems the Union takes care of its dead, but for the most part, the wounded are left to fend for themselves. I was not prepared for the filth and squalor, or the extent of the inhumanity of the field hospital. There were thousands of bodies laying in their own mess beneath the boiling sun in a cotton field. Besides the battle injuries, there were outbreaks of dysentery, small pox, measles and malaria. What nurses and corpsmen I saw seemed undertrained and unmotivated to render aid. There were piles of amputated body parts left for the vultures and no food and water for the wounded."

Mr. Thompson asked for a mug of water before continuing. "I had to bribe a guard to take me to Ned. He brought me to a broken pile of bones moaning and near death. That is also the moment I met Samuel Farmer. He was spoon feeding Ned a bowl of fish broth beneath the shade of a lean-to made from a pair of feed bags. I thought for sure my son was going to die at any minute, but Samuel said that Ned had actually improved over the past few hours. I wanted to pack him up and leave for home that instant, but Samuel said he was too sick to travel. He was right of course. I wasn't thinking clearly at the time. He suggested that we move Ned into the wagon and move him beneath the shade trees upriver from the camp. There would be access to clean water and it would help with Ned's nerves."

"How did Sam look, Mr. Thompson?" Granny asked cautiously.

"I am sorry Mrs. Farmer. I have been so consumed with my own worries that I have neglected to ease your own. You son looked as well as can be expected. The 49th Regiment was on the front line and was overrun by the Johnny Rebs within minutes. Apparently General Grant didn't send out any scouts and there were thirty thousand Rebs only a half hour from where the boys slept. Ned was shot in the arm and your cousin, I think his name was Berry, was killed instantly."

"Oh, sweet Jesus," Granny gasped. "Was Samuel hurt?"

"Miraculously, no," answered Thompson. "While the others retreated, Sam refused to leave Ned for the bayonet and stayed with him until it was safe to pull him from the battlefield. He carried him over two miles to safety, then went back to join the battle. I am afraid I don't know many of the details of the battle beyond that. Apparently, after the fighting was over, Sam came to the field hospital to check on some of the boys in the regiment and needless to say he wasn't happy with what he found. More soldiers were dying from disease and sickness than the enemy's bullets. A surgeon said there wasn't any medicine and whatever food was in stock, was needed for the troops who were doing the fighting. I suppose once a soldier is injured, he has outlived his usefulness to the army. It was as if they couldn't die quick enough. This didn't set well with Sam, so he started to forage the countryside for food and herbs for poultices. At the time of my arrival, he had helped over twenty men. A doctor from Michigan said that if it hadn't been for Sam's camphor leaf wrap, Ned would have died from gangrene."

Pappy exhaled a plume of blue smoke and noticeably puffed out his chest with pride. "I would have expected nothing less from Sam."

I have to admit I was mighty proud too. I knew Pa was a hero and now the rest of the world would know too.

Mr. Thompson cleared his throat before continuing. "Unfortunately, it wasn't long before the surrounding area had been picked clean, so Sam had to become more resourceful about gathering supplies. He started to venture further and further to find provisions and eventually he found himself behind enemy lines. When he arrived at the field hospital with a case of medicine marked Confederate States of America; several officers took notice. I think they felt his skills were being wasted as an infantry soldier. He received orders one night and was gone before dawn. He did manage to stop by and deliver a message to Ned for all of you before leaving. Ned promised he would not let Samuel down and that is why we are on your doorstep at this very moment. As far as what the message is— Ned has not confided in me. He will have to be the one to finish this story."

"Lord Almighty!" Granny exclaimed. "What in blazes is going on?"

Pappy furrowed his brow in thought and then cleaned the ashes out of his pipe. "I reckon they is makin' a spy out Samuel!"

"They wouldn't!" she cried.

"I'm afraid they would, Darlin'" he replied. "It don't matter if you is a fightin' Redcoats, Injuns or Johnny Rebs. An army wants to know what the other feller is doin' before he does it. Sam has got a good head on his shoulders. I could see why they would want him."

"But they hang spies don't they?"

"I ain't saying Sam is a spy. Maybe he's just a scout. But whatever it is—it sounds like he's in the thick of it."

Granny got up and cleared the table without saying another word.

That night as I went to sleep, I said two prayers. One was for Ned Thompson to live through the night and the other one was not to let the Johnny Rebs hang my Pa as a spy.

Chapter 14

Ned confirmed what Pappy suspected. The Union Army was using Pa as a spy behind enemy lines. "It was all because he was too good at taking care of the men at the hospital," said Ned. "I don't know where he found what he found, but it was the difference between life and death for a lot of us. But it was the two cases of morphine that got the attention of a Colonel who was in charge of recruiting spies. It had been several days since there had been any medication at the hospital. There wasn't even a bottle of rotgut hooch to kill the pain during amputations. Sam decided to do something about it. He hiked several miles into Mississippi, behind Confederate lines, and commandeered a Johnny Reb uniform that a lieutenant had hung on a tree to dry. He changed into that uniform and marched right into their supply tent and walked out with two cases of morphine, a case of chloroform and a box of Cuban cigars that were supposed to go to General Sterling Price, himself. He wore that Johnny Reb uniform until he got to our lines and then changed back into the blue. He marched past the guards like he had made a trip to the general store. Once word got around about what Sam Farmer had done, he became a hero around the hospital. It was also what got him conscripted into the spy corp. From what Sam told me, he didn't have much say in the matter. He was to report to that colonel in the morning and didn't have a clue as to where he was goin' once he got there."

Ned had been excited while telling us about Pa's exploits, but then he looked troubled. "Sam told me to let everyone of you know that he is well and loves you more as each day passes. He also wanted me to tell you that because of the sort of job he was about to take, he wouldn't be able to send or receive any letters. He said you would have to trust that the *Good Lord* would take care of him and bring him home safely once his duty was completed."

Granny was upset that Pa would take such a risk, but I had to admit I was more proud than scared. Ma acted like she didn't hear or care what Ned had to say. She simply stared at something that nobody else in the room saw and then went back to bed.

Ned Thompson's recovery was going slower than Doctor Judd had expected. But after five days, he declared that he considered him to be out of immediate danger. Doctor Judd arrived every morning after breakfast and cleaned Ned's wounds with alcohol and gave him a dose of laudanum for the pain. He also taught Sister Rose to change the bandages and on the sixth day allowed her to clean the wounds by herself. Rose was a natural nurse and didn't stop with cleaning the wounds. She was constantly changing the blankets and turning his pillows. She had cut his hair twice and had cut away his beard exposing the baby face of a teenager. Despite his protests, Rose shaved him every day whether he needed it or not. Granny said that Rose was smitten with Ned. At the time I didn't know what the word 'smitten' meant, but she sure spent an awful lot of time at his bedside. Mr.

Thompson helped with my chores, but Granny threw a tizzy. She didn't feel it was proper for a guest to work. So to keep things peaceful, Pappy and Mr. Thompson spent much of their day sitting on stools in back of the barn, keeping an eye on Jaybird and Bub. I don't know how much supervising was getting done, but neither boy drowned or got kicked in the head by a horse, so I suppose they passed muster. Both boys liked Mr. Thompson who was a great story teller and could keep them quiet for hours on end. That alone was worth his weight in chores.

Even though Ned was showing improvement, Dr Judd said it would still be a couple of weeks before he could go home. Mr. Thompson said he felt he had already been too much of a burden and offered a trade of sorts. "I'm indebted to you for the care of my son, but as a God-fearing Christian, I couldn't put you out any longer for my board and keep. Since it seems that you will be caring for Ned a while longer, why don't you allow me to take the two younger boys for a visit with me to Marshall? I've been away from my wife for too long now and since we don't have any children at home, it would liven up our home."

"I expect it would, at that," laughed Granny. "But that would be askin' a lot. I don't know if you noticed, but Jaybird is a might high spirited."

"Nonsense!" replied Thompson. "I've raised three boys. I am familiar with the species."

"Please, Granny!" Jaybird begged. "Can I go with Uncle Jeremiah?"

"Uncle Jeremiah? You're laying the molasses on a little thick ain't you boy?" she bristled.

"Don't be hard on the boy, he reminds me so much of Ned at that age."

"I don't know—" she tapped her index finger against her temple. "What do you think Pappy?"

"I'd say we are gettin' the better part of the bargain, but if Uncle Jeremiah wants the boys, I don't see any harm in it."

"I guess it would be all right," Granny reluctantly agreed, "but I don't want you to be spoilin' the boys. Bub won't give you any fuss, but you better keep a tight hold on Jaybird's reins."

Mr. Thompson grinned widely. "We won't have any problems. Will we boys?"

"No problems at all, Uncle Jeremiah," Jaybird promised with the sincerity of a snake oil huckster.

Jeremiah Thompson headed north at daybreak with my two brothers for Marshall. I had never been to Marshall and all I knew about it was that it was on the National Road and it took two days to get there by wagon. Since Doctor Judd said Ned needed at least another month to recover, he and his wife would return with the boys in four weeks and then return home with their son. We were to send a letter by the stage coach if there were any change in Ned's condition, but if no letter was received, everything was to be considered just fine. Jaybird and Bub waved frantically from the wagon as it disappeared around the bend. It was their first time away from home without a family member and both believed they were on a great adventure. Within fifteen minutes, our cabin seemed eerily quiet. Too quiet.

The dog days of summer had set in and I had pretty much caught up with my chores around the farm. Everything in the fields seemed to be under control, so all I had to do that week was take care of the livestock. The corn was waist high and the wheat was in the barn. That's when Pappy came to me with a task that seemed to be too good to be true. The wheat in the barn needed to be taken to the mill in Palestine and Doctor

Judd needed some medicine and supplies from the apothecary. Since my work was caught up and the boys weren't around, he and Granny decided to send Rose and I by ourselves.

At first Rose protested, insisting that Ned couldn't live without her constant attention, but Doctor Judd promised that her patient's level of care would not suffer in her absence. She finally agreed. She had some money saved from teaching school and said she wouldn't mind getting some material for a new dress. Rose had been more concerned about her appearance since the arrival of Ned Thompson. She had always been too bashful to talk to boys, but Ned was in need of care and was barely conscious during their getting acquainted period. Ned wasn't a bit shy when talking to our family as a group, but he was uneasy around Rose when she tended to his wounds. He seemed to be ashamed about his missing arm. He turned away and at times struggled to hold back the tears.

"There is nothing to be ashamed of," she assured him in her dove-like voice. "You are alive and that is all that matters." She was gentle and tender as she faithfully cleaned his wounds and before long, you could hear them carrying on conversations for hours on end. At times I felt ignored and tried to see what they were talking about, but Granny said I should give them their privacy. When I asked why, she and Pappy smiled at each other and said: "You'll understand someday."

I hated answers like that. I was *man-enough* to do all of the work around the farm, but not grown-up enough to know why I couldn't talk to Rose and Ned. It didn't matter how much work I did around the farm; everyone still looked at me as a child. That was one reason why I welcomed the trip to Palestine. The other reason was that word had it—there would be a circus in town.

Rose and I left for Palestine after a breakfast of flap jacks and eggs. Rose packed a basket full of corn dodgers and salted pork while I finished up feeding the livestock. There were twenty six bushels of wheat for the mill and a list of medicine to buy for Doctor Judd and another list of dry goods for Granny.

Rose carried the cash money, but it was my job to drive the wagon. It would take a day to get to Palestine and then probably another day of waiting for the wheat to be milled into flour and then another day for the trip home. Pappy said that he would expect us back in three days, but if anything came up and we couldn't get away on the morning of the third day, we were not to leave until the following morning. He didn't want us to leave in the afternoon, which would force us to camp in the country on the way home. "Only camp in town!" he told us. "I've been hearin' rumors that the Copperheads are ridin' around the countryside at night, lookin' to stir up some trouble. It's too dangerous to sleep out by yourselves. You'll be safe as long as you stay in town at night!"

"I ain't afraid of no Copperheads!" I bragged.

Pappy smacked me on the top of my skull with his empty corn cob pipe. "You best lose that way of thinking right now!" Pappy scolded me. "It's a good way to get yourself killed!"

"Sorry Pappy." I was ashamed. I had never heard Pappy so much as raise his voice before, let alone put a knot on my head.

"It's okay, Will. It's just that I don't want anything to happen to you two. These are dangerous times and there are a lot of people out there looking for trouble. And because of that, Rose will be the one who decides when it is safe to leave for home. Is that clear?"

"Yes sir."

Pappy smacked the old mare on its backside and we were on our way.

We had traveled half of the fifteen miles to Palestine when we reached the small hamlet of Morea. I knew from our trip to Bristol Landing, that Morea had a public watering trough and a good shade tree to sit under while we ate our lunch. After watering the mare I walked her over to a green patch of fescue and left her to graze. As I was walking back to the shade tree, I happened to look through a big glass window into a doctor's office and stopped dead in my tracks. I felt my heart beat a tattoo all the way to my throat. Behind the dust and grime of that window was a human skeleton looking back at me. I had never seen a skeleton before, but I knew exactly what it was. I had seen picture books about Halloween and Reverend Parker had a book that had a picture of the Devil dancing on the bones of Israel. It was a skeleton; no doubt about it. Part of me wanted to run, but another part of me realized that it wasn't everyday that a feller got the chance to study a pile of bones that used to be alive. The sign above the door said the office belonged to Doctor J.A. Ingles, Esquire. I checked the door handle to see if anyone was inside, but it was locked.

I jumped three feet in the air when I felt a heavy hand grab a hold of my shoulder. "Kinda scary lookin' ain't he?" said an old man with long white hair and a longer white beard. "He just stands there all day and all night with that silly smile plastered on his face from now until eternity. He never utters a single word. He just stands there and smiles at the folks as they pass by. Although I don't spect he's got anything better to do with his time."

"D-d-does he b-belong to you, Mister?"

"Naw," he replied. "He belongs to Doc Ingles, but I did help boil and skin him."

"You skinned him!" I wanted to run, but my feet were frozen to the ground. "Was he still alive?"

"Heaven's sake, no!" The old man laughed. "What kind of heathen do ya take me for?"

I was afraid to answer, so I didn't.

"His name was Billy Ray," the old timer continued. "They hung him for stealing horses down on the Embarrass a few years ago. Doc always wanted a skeleton to look at when settin' broken bones and such, but they was so expensive from the medical schools back east, that he decided to go a different route. When Doc heard that nobody claimed Billy Ray's body, he had me hitch up my flat wagon and we went south to the county line and cut the body down, before anybody else claimed him. It was a might fretful sight, I have to admit. He was bloated something awful and the buzzards had already started to work on him. I held my breath as best I could and loaded him in the back of the wagon. He smelled somethin' awful on the trip back home, but I managed somehow. The stink was so bad— folks know'd we was coming a half mile before we got there. It was a dirty job, but I wasn't about to turn down the Yankee silver dollar he was payin' me. When we finally made it back to the office here; it was time to pick the bones clean. Doc had me fetch a wooden barrel and set it in the woods behind this office. We soaked ole Billy Ray in some kind of acid for a week and he just kinda melted off of his bones. Then we took what was left of him and boiled him in a cast iron kettle of salt water over an open fire for a full day. After that we laid his bones out in the sun to bleach for a few days. Once Doc was satisfied with the color, we wired him back together and he's been in that window ever since. So there he is—smilin' like he ain't got a care in the world. I've got a key to the office if you'd like to go in for a closer look?" He beamed a devilish grin that eerily resembled the smile of Billy Ray.

"No thanks, Mister," I groaned. And as soon as I felt him ease the grip on my shoulder, I darted for the shade tree, where Sister Rose was waiting impatiently for me.

"Where in the devil have you been, Will Farmer? I was startin' to worry that you had gotten yourself in some kind of trouble."

"No trouble," I panted.

She took a closer look at me and frowned. "I do declare, Will. Your face is so white, I'd swear you must have seen a ghost."

I started to answer, but thought better of it.

"Well anyway—you better eat up. We need to make sure we get to Palestine before sunset." She handed me a corn dodger and a piece of pork.

I tried to eat, but every time I started to take a bite, all I saw was Billy Ray's bony face smiling and laughing at me. I couldn't have eaten anything if I tried. I wrapped the food in a towel and put it back in Rose's basket. "Let's get movin'," I said. "I'll eat when we get to Palestine."

I ran back and fetched the mare and wagon. We were back on the road to Palestine within five minutes. As we left, I tried my best to keep from looking back into the window of Doctor J.A. Ingles, Esquire, but I couldn't help myself. Billy Ray was standing tall with his smile fixed on his face forever. *Come back and see me again, Will. I'll be here waiting for you.* Even though I swore to myself that I would never pass through Morea again as long as I lived, I had an uneasy feeling that I would be seeing Billy Ray's smiling face in my dreams.

We were barely out of Morea when Rose started to talk about Ned. "I wonder how Ned is feelin'...I hope Doctor Judd cleans his wounds before breakfast...It's time for Ned's Laudanum. I hope Granny remembers to…"

"Ned. Ned. Ned. Is that all you can talk about?" I whined.

"He's just so helpless," Rose said. "I'm just worried he'll get worse while I'm gone."

"Doctor Judd won't let anything happen to him," I assured her.

"I hope you are right."

"Tarnation, Rose, you sound like you're in love with him."

Rose turned red as a beet and slugged me square on my shoulder with her bony fist. "Sometimes Will Farmer, you are entirely too big for your britches."

"You are in love with him!" I shouted playfully.

Rose started to say something then buried her face in her hands. Moments later she started to sob and then hiccupped uncontrollably.

"Please don't cry, Rose," I pleaded. "I was only jokin'."

"I don't know what's wrong with me," she cried. "It hurts me to be away from him. My insides are all churned up. I feel like I'm gonna bust."

"Maybe you ate a bad piece of meat for lunch," I suggested.

"It ain't nothin' I ate, Will," she answered. "Can't you see? My heart is breaking."

She started bawling again. I didn't know what to say. How was I supposed to know she had a broken heart? She had looked just fine to me before the crying fit fell upon our conversation. The more she cried, the more I decided that keeping my mouth shut would be my best course of action. I drove the rest of the way to Palestine without uttering another word.

Looking back, I realize that Palestine wasn't much of a town as far as towns go, but to my eleven year old eyes, it could have been Philadelphia or Cincinnati. I had never been to a settlement with more than a hundred residents. Palestine had over a thousand. There were dozens of stores offering everything from eastern-style fancy dresses and shoes to Cuban cigars and rock candy. I counted three blacksmiths, two coopers, two hotels, two taverns and at least a half dozen general merchandise dry goods stores. There were five restaurants and just as many churches, two barbershops, three livery barns and a store that sold only hats.

Before we left for our trip I had overheard Reverend Parker explain to Doctor Judd that Palestine was a Presbyterian town in a way that made it seem like a Presbyterian was almost as bad as being a heathen. I, myself, had no idea what a Presbyterian was in the first place, so I didn't give it much thought until we passed a large and ornate Presbyterian church. It was the biggest building I had ever seen in my life. It was beautiful. There was a sign in front that said "Pray for our troops." I wondered why Reverend Parker didn't like a group of people who built such an extraordinary building and prayed for Union soldiers to boot. From where I was sitting, they seemed to be on our side, so they couldn't be all bad. I would have to speak with the Revered about the matter when we got back home.

I couldn't wait to explore everything. Hopefully, there would be plenty of time for adventure while the wheat was being milled. We drove north past the business section of town until we reached the grist mill owned by William Wilson. I stopped the wagon at a small out building with a sign that said it was the office.

A small man with gold-rimmed glasses said that everyone had gone home for the day and there wasn't anyone around to unload our wheat. He said if we came back in the morning, there would be someone there to take care of us. When Rose asked if there was a safe place where we could camp for the night, he said that there was a campground on the east end of town near the ruins of the old fort.

I sighed in disappointment. As much as I wanted to roam downtown, I knew I wouldn't get a chance to survey the wonders of Palestine that night. Twenty six bushels of wheat was not a small bounty in those days. I knew we couldn't let our cargo out of sight until it was safely in the hands of the mill workers.

We followed the rutted dirt road away from the setting sun until we saw several wagons parked beneath the shade of a grove of hardwood trees. After deciding that this was the campground the man at the mill had told us about, I snapped the reins and pointed the horses southward. As we got closer to the trees, I couldn't help but notice that many of the wagons were unusually large and painted in bright colors. At first I thought it might be Gypsies. Every now and then a Gypsy would pass by our farm with a wagon full of trinkets or snake oil to sell. Their wagons were similar to the ones in the grove, but not exactly the same. Pa had taught me that Gypsies couldn't be trusted, so I approached the campground with trepidation.

As we moved closer, I could see that there was writing and pictures painted on the side of the wagons. After straining to decipher the letters, I almost jumped out of my seat with excitement when I realized what was in store. The words on the wagons were all identical: THE ROBINSON & LAKE CIRCUS.

—w—

Chapter 15

I was put out with Rose when she insisted that we camp on the back side of the grove which was as far as we could get from the circus wagons. "Why do we have to set up so far away?" I complained.

"We've come here on business and that's exactly what we are going to do." Rose spoke in a tone usually reserved for school marms and old maids. "We are going to take our wheat to the mill, buy our supplies and then head straight for home. Everyone is counting on us, Will. We have to think and act like grownups. Remember your promise to your father. You are supposed to be the man of the family. Besides, I've heard horrible stories about circus people. Give them half a chance and they'll rob you blind. Worse than that—I hear they'll slit your throat for the clothes on your back."

Suddenly, I felt a well of resentment rise up in me. Yes, I promised Pa that I would be the man of the house and I had done everything in my power to keep my word. I worked every day from sunrise to well past sunset. I had plowed and planted, weeded and hoed every acre of the farm. Twice a day, I had fed and watered every head of livestock and done every chore I was asked to do without complaining or causing any strife. I did the work of a man and yet everyone still treated me like a child. Granny and Pappy talked in hushed voices when they made important decisions. They made me leave the cabin with my younger brothers when Doctor Judd and Reverend Parker spoke about Ned's injuries or Ma's declining disposition. It was just fine for me to act like a grownup as long as there was work that needed to be done, but when it came to everything else— they still looked at me like I was a dumb kid. Worse than that, I felt like I was no better off than a slave.

"Who told you stories about the circus people?" I snapped.

Rose hesitated. "Different people. Why do you ask?"

"It was Granny—wasn't it?"

"Well—yes" she admitted. "Why do you ask?"

"Because she told me the same story about getting my throat slit for the clothes on my back. Only instead of circus folk, it was Gypsies. Pretty soon it'll be the Hard Shells or Presbyterians. You're just mad because you had to leave your boyfriend at home."

"What is wrong with you, Will Farmer?"

"Tarnation Rose! There ain't nothin' wrong with me," I answered.

"Why are you being so hateful? There is a war going on after all, or have you forgot about that. Who knows what kind of danger your father is in. What about Ned? He's lost an arm and has been through hell on earth! This ain't a time for celebratin'!"

I could tell by the tone of Rose's voice that my words had hurt her. She was right. I was being selfish. Even though every word she spoke was true as the Gospel and even though I figured that I would end up doing the responsible thing—there was a part of me that couldn't give up hope of getting a look at the circus folks. "I'm sorry Rose. I'm just tired of not havin' any fun."

She nodded her head reluctantly while trying to hold back the tears. "I know you are, Will. I know how hard you work, but folks are countin' on us. Don't you think I'm tired of taking care of everybody? Jaybird and Bub are a handful and your Ma—she might as well be a young'un too."

"And now you have Ned to take care of to boot," I added.

"Yes, but Ned is different." A hint of a smile appeared on her face and her eyes widened a little. "It's not like work when I tend to Ned. He needs me and I can tell he is grateful."

I began to feel a bit jealous. "We all need you, Rose. I'd don't know what we would do without you."

"I know you do," she laughed as she messed my hair with her fingers, "but it's not the same."

"I don't understand," I asked.

"I don't know as if I understand myself," she admitted.

"Do you love him?" I asked.

She sighed and then took a deep breath. "I don't rightly know. It hurts every part of me to be away from him. He is all I can think about. Every time I close my eyes, I see his face. When we crossed that creek just outside of town, I thought to myself that it would be a wonderful place for a picnic with Ned. Even now, I wish Ned were with us."

"Do you mean instead of me?" I growled.

"Heavens no! I wish he was here with us."

"Oh sister—you have got it bad!"

Rose sighed again. "I reckon I do."

I pursed my lips and surveyed the situation. "I reckon I wish Ned was with us too."

"Why is that?" she asked.

"If he was here to keep you company, maybe you might loosen up the reins on me a little."

"And let you sneak over to the circus camp?"

"There ain't no harm in taking a peep," I complained.

"Did you ever hear the sayin' that curiosity killed the cat?" she asked as she hopped out of the wagon.

"What's a cat got to do with the circus?" I replied.

"Never mind, Will. It's just that I thought I saw you sproutin' a new set of whiskers and the beginning of a long furry tail."

I looked at Rose and shook my head. The whole world seemed to be goin' crazy.

After gathering enough wood to get a fire started, I grabbed a wooden bucket and hiked down a winding trail to a shaded creek bed. I drew enough water to fill our small cooking kettle and then poured the rest into a wash basin. I watched Rose add two scoops of beans and a strip of jowl into the kettle and then carefully place it atop some coals next to the fire. She was alone with her thoughts. I chuckled to myself. I wondered if she would see Ned's face when she looked into the pot of beans. He appeared to be everywhere else.

I realized that it was going to be a while before supper would be ready. "I'm goin' back down to the creek and get some water for the horse."

She nodded and started singing a song while stirring the beans.

"I think I'm going to take a swim and wash up in the creek while I'm down there, do you want to come with me?" I asked.

"Someone needs to stay with the wagon," she answered. "Just be careful while you're down there. Supper will be ready in about an hour."

As soon as I reached the creek I headed downstream for five minutes and happened onto a shaded pool that looked to be shoulder deep. The water was crystal clear and cool as a deep well. I was out of my clothes and into the water within seconds. I had come up for air and was about to dive under again when I saw her beautiful brown eyes staring at me.

"You're quite the little swimmer, Sweetie." She was standing in the water, no more than ten feet away. Her hair was raven colored, pulled tight against the back of her head with a yellow ribbon. Her pearl white smile glistened in contrast to her wet crimson-colored skin. As she bobbed up and down with only her head and the top of her shoulders exposed above the water, I suddenly became aware that just like me, she had decided to go skinny dipping.

"How did you— I mean—I didn't see you—I mean—"

"Calm down, hon. I ain't gonna bite," she assured me. "I was just down here coolin' off. There's plenty of room for the two us."

I had never been so embarrassed in my life. "I didn't see you. I am truly sorry, lady. If you'll kindly turn your head, I'll get out and leave you alone."

"No need for that," she laughed. "Besides, you are already wet. My name is Cliffy. What's yours?"

"Will. Will Farmer."

"Pleased to meet you, Will Farmer. Are you from Palestine?"

I couldn't believe how calm she was. My insides were churning like melted butter. "But I don't have any clothes on, I shouldn't be here."

"Relax, Will Farmer, you ain't got nothin I ain't seen before. I've got younger brothers and I've given baths to every last one of them. You didn't answer my question. Are you from Palestine?"

"I live on a farm about fifteen miles west of here. We brought our wheat to the mill."

"You said we; did you come with your Ma and Pa?" She seemed nice and all of a sudden I forget that we were swimming naked.

"My Pa is off at the war and my Ma is sick in bed. Sister Rose and I came by ourselves."

"Where is your sister now?" she asked.

"She's back at the campground cookin' up supper. Rose is my aunt—not my sister. We call her Sister Rose on account that she is only three years older than me."

"And how old are you, Will Farmer?"

"Eleven, but I'll be twelve next February."

"Why you're practically a man." She laughed again and splashed at me, then disappeared under the water. I waited for what seemed like an eternity and then started to fret when she didn't resurface. I considered going for help when she popped up thirty feet behind me.

"You scared me half to death!" I shouted at her. "I thought you drowned!"

She laughed again. "Oh sweetie, don't worry about me, I can stay under water for five minutes if I need to. It's what I do for a living."

"You stay underwater for a living? What kind of job is that?"

"It's just part of what I do. I'm with the circus. I walk a tight wire, dance on a rope, jump into a barrel of water from a high tower. After that they lock me into the barrel. I hold my breath for six minutes before they let me out. To tell the truth, I only stay in the barrel for a little over four minutes.

They use an hour glass that runs fast. The ring master gets the crowd worked up, so it seems like I'm in the barrel for ten minutes. Then they act like they can't get the lid off. They create a panic with the audience and then finally break the lid with an ax. The crowd holds their breath thinkin' I'm dead, but when I jump out with a smile on my face, they all stand and cheer."

"You're a circus girl?" I asked. My head was spinning. Fate had put me in a situation that was far beyond the wildest of my schoolyard lies. Granny and Rose's warnings about circus folk being cutthroats had been greatly exaggerated to say the least She was the most beautiful girl I had ever seen and she was a circus girl on top of that. I had to admit, the fact that she wasn't wearing any clothes was unnerving. I decided to pretend not to notice her nakedness the best I could. I was in uncharted waters to say the least.

"I've been with the circus for the past three years. At least I think it was three years ago last April when Pa sold me to Mr. Robinson.

"You're Pa sold you? Are you a slave?"

"I'm what they call a bond girl, but I might as well be a slave. They'd come after me if I tried to leave."

"Isn't that against the law?" I asked. I remembered enough of Reverend Parker's sermons to know that it was against the law to buy or sell anybody in the state of Illinois.

"It might be against the law, but Sam Murphy would kill me before he'd let me go."

"Who's Sam Murphy?" I asked

"He's the circus boss. He runs the show when we're on the road. It's not as bad as it sounds. I don't go hungry and I'm away from my old man. He's was mean as a snake and liked to use his belt when he got drunk and that was mostly every night while I was growin' up."

"And Sam Murphy treats you better?"

"He treats me different. I wouldn't exactly say it was better."

"It don't sound right to me," I told her. "The reason Pa went to war was because he said we needed to get rid of slavery forever. It doesn't seem to me that there is a lick of difference between being a slave and a bond girl. A person is free or they ain't. I don't rightly see that there is any middle ground on the subject."

"Don't you go frettin' about Cliffy."

"Cliffy is a funny name," I told her.

"Cliffy is my nickname. If you think it's funny—just wait until you hear my whole name! It's Cliffphilia Willow Maya McGee. I was named after my Grandma. She was a Pottawatomie squaw from Wisconsin. My Grandpa bought her while she was on her way to the reservation. He gave up a red colored mule, a saddle and two blankets."

"You're lying," I laughed.

"No—I ain't joshin' you." she said. "I think there might have been a jug of whiskey involved too, but I ain't for sure. It was during the trail of tears and the tribe was on the way to Oklahoma. Grandpa Shamus was fresh off the potato boat and wanted a wife. He couldn't pronounce her Indian name, so he gave her a new one. When he first saw her, she was standing under a cliff in a field of wheat under a willow tree. That is how he came up with Cliffphilia Willow. After he bought her he always said "she's mine forever." He added the name Maya so that she would never forget that she was his property."

"It sounds like your family has a history of sellin' your women-folk. It's just not right," I told her. "If I had any money, I'd buy you and set you free."

"Why Will—that's the sweetest thing anybody ever said to me. If you was a year or two older, I reckon I might have to run off with you."

Suddenly I felt embarrassed and tongue tied at the same time. I didn't know what to say so I splashed water at her and dove off in the opposite direction. We laughed and swam for a while longer and then we heard a voice shouting upstream. I couldn't make out what the man was saying, but he sounded big and he sounded mean. Cliffy's smile suddenly disappeared.

"It's Sam Murphy," she whispered. "Hurry—get your clothes and hide in those bushes on the far side of the creek."

"What's wrong?" I whispered back.

"Nothin' I can't handle. Just do as I say, Will."

I made her look the other way as I put on my britches and waded upstream. I crawled behind a fallen log and covered my eyes like I promised as she got dressed. She was pulling on her boots when Sam Murphy appeared. He was the biggest and meanest looking man I had ever seen in my life. Six and a half feet tall and wide as a horse barn. He had a bushy head of reddish brown hair tucked under an undersized derby. His beard covered a good portion of his massive chest. He looked like a bear as he roared. "There you are you little scamp. I've been lookin' all over camp and creation for ya."

"I just came down to wash up," she snapped back. "Surely I don't need your permission to take a bath, Sam?"

"You do if I says you do!" His eyes bulged with a jealous crimson. He snorted and stomped along the creek bank until he towered over Cliffy. "If I didn't know any better—I might think that you slinked down here to meet up with a fella." He cleared his throat and spit a wad of tobacco juice on the ground. "And we both know that you wouldn't dream of doin' such a thing Cliffy darlin'—don't we?"

"I would never—" Cliffy stopped in mid sentence.

"You're damn right you won't—you little tramp." Murphy grabbed her by the wrist and with the back of his free hand, landed a crushing blow against her jaw. "Now where is he? I know you weren't down here alone. I heard voices—I did!"

"Let go of me, Sam," she cried. "You're hurting me!"

"Answer me or there will be plenty more to come!" he growled. "You'll tell me where he's a hidin' if you know what's good for you."

She cried out as he slapped her repeatedly. "Where's your boyfriend now, Darlin'? T'ain't much of a man who would hide in the bushes and let you take a beatin' on his account."

"I haven't been with a man—I swear!" she pleaded. "Please stop."

"Liar!" He backed away, took aim and delivered a final horrific blow to the side of her head. Cliffy fell to the ground in a motionless heap.

My heart was racing as I peeked from beneath the log. I didn't know what to do. I wanted to help, but my body refused to move. The circus boss was as big as a sixteen hand mule. What could I do? I had just about decided to do nothing when Murphy took two steps back and then kicked Cliffy directly in the ribs. Her body convulsed, but she didn't make a sound. "I knows you're out there—you coward! Come out where I can sees ya, or I swear I'll kick this girl until she meets Saint Peter himself!"

I couldn't stand it anymore. I climbed over the log and started walking toward them. "Here I am. Now leave her alone!" I found myself walking into a situation that reminded me of my altercation with Big Burl Stubbs. I had been lucky that day when Pa had come to my rescue. Unfortunately, there wouldn't be anybody to come to my rescue this time. He had a puzzled look on his face as I marched directly towards him. I knew it would be hopeless without a weapon, so I reached into the creek and picked up a rock that fit nicely in my hand. I held the rock up where he could see what I had in store for him and then delivered my ultimatum. "Get away from her or I'll brain you with this rock!"

Murphy remained as still as a statue and then suddenly broke out in a roar of laughter. "Well, I'll be blasted. She's been steppin' out with a leprechaun."

"I said get away from her and I ain't no leprechaun!"

He held his hands up and took two steps backward. "Easy does it, sonny boy—now why don't you drop that rock. Ol' Sam ain't goin' to hurt nobody." He opened his tobacco stained mouth and displayed a smile that a sainted mother would have a hard time loving.

I looked over at Cliffy and saw that she was beginning to stir. I dropped the rock and sprinted to her side to see if I could help. "Are you alright?" I asked as I took her hand.

"My head," she sighed.

"She's fine," Murphy growled. "I've given her much worse than that. Besides that's what she gets for sneakin' around behind my back."

"We was just swimming, Mister. Cliffy hasn't done anything wrong! You didn't have to hurt her!"

"Don't be tellin' me how to run my affairs, Sonny Boy, or I'll gives you what I gave her!" He walked back over and then he lifted me off of the ground by my collar.

I kicked and strained to get away, but the harder I struggled the more I felt my shirt strangle me. Things were starting to grow dark when Murphy let loose and I fell to the ground. My head bounced off a rock with a thud and I immediately saw stars. I was aware of a commotion going on around me, but it seemed far away. A part of me knew that as long as I stayed on the ground I would be helpless and vulnerable. Another part of me told me it was the safest place to be. I heard two angry voices doing battle and then they faded away to a single gentle cooing sound. Finally, the sensation of cool water on my face brought me back. I opened my eyes and found myself in Cliffy's arms.

"Will, are you alright honey?" She was wiping my face with a damp cloth while surveying the back of my head for damage.

"I think so. What happened?" I asked.

"Sam Murphy is what happened, but he's gone now."

I sat up and looked around to make sure. "That fella is as big as a bear."

"And just as mean," she added.

"Why was he so mad at you?" I asked.

"He's just afraid I'll run off with the first man who asks me. It ain't like he loves me or anything like that. I'm just something that he owns like a prize dog or horse."

"Why don't you run away?" I asked. "You could come home with Rose and me."

Cliffy smiled and patted my face. "That's sweet of you, but Sam would search the four corners of the earth until he tracked me down. He's always saying that he would kill me before he'd let go of me. I believe him too. I saw him beat a man to death with his bare hands, just for stealin' a pint of whiskey. Ain't no way to get away from him. But I am proud of you for standin' up to him like you did. You're mighty brave."

"All I did was get a knot on my head."

"I'm sorry about that, but to be honest with you—you're lucky that is all you got. He wouldn't lose a wink of sleep if he killed you. I think you surprised him. Sam Murphy ain't used to people fightin' back. I'll never forget the look on his face when you called him out. You are—and always will be, my hero."

"Some hero…" I complained.

"Don't cut yourself short, Will Farmer," she laughed. "Someday you're gonna make some lucky girl happy. Now you better get out of here before Sam changes his mind and comes back for a second helping of your hide."

"But what's gonna happen to you?" I didn't feel comfortable about her going back to Murphy.

"Don't worry about me. I'll abide. I always do." She held me tightly in her arms and then softly kissed my forehead. "Now go while the gettin' is good."

I reluctantly stood up and started for the wagon. After twenty paces I turned around to take one last look. With the last rays of sunlight falling against her cheeks I could see the tracks of her tears as she silently sobbed. I started to walk back toward her, but she motioned for me to leave and abruptly turned away.

I felt a pain in my chest that hurt worse than a mule kick. I stood like a statue for what seemed to be an eternity and then, because I couldn't think of anything proper to say—I turned and ran for the campground. I felt like anything but a hero.

—⁓—

Chapter 16

After a campfire breakfast of black coffee, biscuits and beans, I hitched the mare and we headed back toward the gristmill. It had been a restless night. At first, I decided not to tell Rose about my encounter with Cliffy, but after a few hours of having my insides tied into knots, I figured I would bust if didn't talk about her. Rose was understanding, but when I told her about Sam Murphy's attack, she couldn't help but hit me with an "I told you so," in reference to her warning about circus folk.

"We should take her home with us," I suggested.

"Are you crazy?" she asked. "She told you he would hunt her down and kill her if she left. You'd be likely to get us all killed."

"But I can't sit around and do nothing."

"That's exactly what you're gonna do, "Rose snapped. "The troubles of that girl are none of your concern. You just met her. I'm sure she was nice to you and you want to help, but what could you possibly do for her? She's a grown up woman and you're just a boy."

Her words hit me between the eyes like a brickbat. As much as I wanted to argue with her—I couldn't. She was right. I was just a stupid kid. A green, fresh from the farm, know nothing kid from South Union. I couldn't describe what I was feeling, other than it hurt. It hurt me in a way that I hadn't known before. I rolled away from Rose and started to cry.

I was ashamed of myself, but I couldn't help it. The tears continued to flow.

A few moments later, I could feel Rose's hand rubbing my back. "Oh brother—you've got it bad." Her voice was gentle and full of concern.

"Got what?" I sobbed.

"Why, you're lovesick—that's what."

I bristled when I heard her begin to laugh. "It's not funny!" I snapped.

"I know it's not, Will. I'm not laughin' at you. As a matter of fact, I know what you're feeling."

"How could you know?"

"I know because I've been bitten by the same bug myself."

"Bug bite? What are you talking about?" I asked.

"I know how you feel because I'm in love with Ned. Sometimes I feel like I can't eat or drink on account of I love him so much. That's why I've been so surly on this trip. I can't stand to be away from him. Sometimes love makes you act like you've completely lost your head."

"I thought lovin' somebody is supposed to make you feel good. Right now I feel like I just ate a bad piece of meat."

"That's what I'm talking about, Will. Love can turn you every which way but loose. You'll get over Cliffy," she assured me." "It's all part of growin' up."

"Do you think you'll get over Ned?" I asked.

"I don't intend to." There was not a shred of doubt in her voice. "I'm going to marry him."

"Marry him?" I was stunned by her proclamation. "You're only fifteen."

"Your mother was only sixteen when she married your father. Besides, nothing is gonna happen for a while. It wouldn't make sense to do anything before the war is over."

"Does Ned know anything about this?" I asked.

She paused. "Not exactly—but I know down deep he feels the same way about me."

I thought about what she said as we rode along the dusty trail back toward Palestine. I had to admit she was right about one thing. She had turned into a love-struck lunatic over Ned. I would have never dreamed that Rose could act this way. She was always so backward and shy. Now she was acting like one of the Wesley Sisters. They were famous for falling in love with any boy who happened to look in their direction.

It was different with Cliffy. I would leave town as soon as the flour was ready and would never see her again. It just didn't seem fair and there was nothing anybody could say that would make me feel any better. She would be gone forever. Ned would be waiting for Rose when we got home. It wasn't the same. I was afraid that I was going to cry again, so I forced myself to become angry. I wasn't mad at anybody in particular—just at the world in general. As long as I kept a scowl on my face, the tears managed to stay away. I refused to act like a blubbering lovesick sissy.

I decided I would just have to try to forget about her and act like the man I was supposed to be. I didn't want anybody to think I was some lace wearing pansy crying over some circus girl. Not me. I wasn't going to let any love bitin' bug get the best of me. I was going to go back into town and take care of business and then go back to the farm. There was a war going on and there wasn't time for any such foolishness. Rose could swoon all over Ned if she wanted. I had work to do.

I repeated these things all the way to the mill. But the more I tried to push away any thoughts of Cliffy, the clearer her smile became in my mind. I knew Rose was right. Cliffy was a woman and I was just a boy. A foolish boy, who ought to know better.

The same man with the gold-rimmed glasses was waiting for us as I eased the wagon next to the loading dock at the mill. "Glad to see you two young people again on such a fine morning. Back your wagon to the dock and I'll find someone to unload the wheat. We should have your flour ready by tomorrow afternoon."

"Tomorrow afternoon?" Rose was agitated. "Why can't we get it this afternoon?"

"Why normally, that wouldn't be a problem, Miss, but we are not milling any grain today on account of the Independence Day festivities. We just came in for a couple hours to finish up an order. I'm afraid it's the best I can do. If you'd rather trade elsewhere—"

"Tomorrow afternoon will be fine," Rose replied.

After the wagon was offloaded, I found a shady place to leave the mare, while we walked to the town square. Even though it was still early, dozens of people were already gathering to get a good spot in front of the makeshift stage, which was nothing more than two flatbed wagons draped in red, white and blue bunting. I stopped to read a poster detailing the order of speakers, singers, dancers and dignitaries. A final performance of the world renowned Robinson and Lake Circus would begin at seven o'clock, followed by fireworks a half hour after sunset. If you were going to be stranded in town for an extra day—this would be the day to do it.

Rose was visibly disappointed about spending an extra day away from Ned, but she said there was nothing that could be done about it. She wanted to go shopping for linens and other frilly items, which appealed to me as much as a trip to a tooth pulling dentist. I suggested that we go our separate ways and meet up later at the town square. Rose was against the idea and only agreed when I promised not to go anywhere near the circus camp. As much as I wanted to see Cliffy again, I was afraid to go any place where I might run into Sam Murphy. A boy who tangles with a bear and survives is lucky. A boy who knowingly walks into a bear's den a second time deserves what he gets. I decided to ignore that funny feeling inside my stomach and honor my promise to Rose. Besides, I had a little over two dollars burning a hole in my pocket and there seemed to be dozens of suitable places to spend it.

I walked up and down the wooden sidewalks before walking into Auntie Gogin's Mercantile and purchased a paper sack full of peppermints for a dime. On my way back to the square, I bought a cup of lemonade from a widow woman for a nickel.

Palestine was a beehive of activity. I had never seen so many people in one place. Everyone was coming and going with no particular destination in mind. I watched and listened and finally took a seat on a stump near a group of men who were talking about the latest war news.

"As far as I'm concerned—George McClellan ain't nothing but a yellow-bellied coward!" shouted a burly round man with a mug of beer in his hand. "If Abe Lincoln had a lick of sense, he'd take McClellan and stand him up in front of a firing squad. As long as McClellan is in charge of the Army of the Potomac—we are doomed!"

"He sure ain't no match for Jeb Stuart or Stonewall Jackson," added another man.

"Problem is—there ain't no boys from Illinois fighting back east. If *Honest Abe* would send Ulysses "Unconditional Surrender" Grant and a regiment of *suckers* from Illinois to Virginia, this blasted war would be over in a month," declared a third man.

"Only if he can stay sober long enough to get there," laughed Beer Mug. "Although he did show them Rebs a thing or two at Donelson and Shiloh—I have to admit."

"My Pa was at Shiloh," I interceded. "He's with the Illinois 49th."

The three men turned and began sizing me up. Children were expected to be seen and not heard, but I figured if I was old enough to bring the grain to the mill, I was old enough to shoot the breeze with the ne'er-do-wells on the fourth of July.

"That's nice, Sonny," snorted Beer Mug, "now why don't you move along and leave the grownups alone."

When the other two men started laughing, I began looking for a rock to crawl under. I had joined the conversation with the best of intentions. I wanted to talk about the war. I had just as much right as anybody to be heard. The war had turned my world upside down, but nobody cared. I felt my face turn red with embarrassment but then my shame turned to anger. I didn't do anything wrong. I bit my lip and was just about to say something I would most assuredly regret later, when a rail thin bald man wearing a dapper black Sunday-suit stepped between me and the three laughing men.

"You're father is a hero and a patriot, son" he said as he wrapped his arm around my shoulders and ushered me away from the hooligans. "You must be proud of him."

"I'm real proud sir."

"You don't have to call me sir. Oliver Woodruff Gogin is the name. Most folks around here call me Uncle Woody. And who might you be?"

"My name is Will Farmer."

"Pleased to meet you, Will Farmer. And where do you come from?"

"I'm from South Union. My sister and I brought wheat to the mill. We were going to head for home today, but the flour won't be ready until tomorrow."

"Sorry about your delay, but you couldn't have picked a better day for a layover. It looks to be a dandy of a celebration, although I would advise you to stay away from roughnecks like those men over there. They'd like nothing more than to have a little mischief at your expense."

"They were talking about the war and I tried to join in. I didn't know I did anything wrong."

"You didn't, Will," he answered. "But some men need to belittle others to feel better about themselves. My wife Eliza and I have some extra room on our picnic blanket and plenty of extra food; why don't you join us?"

"I should probably find Rose and see about—"

"And would this beautiful young lass be Rose?" he asked.

I turned and saw Rose walking toward us with a puzzled look on her face. He stepped around me and greeted her with an impish smile and a bucket full of charm as he ushered her to a blanket beneath the shade of an ancient oak tree. Within minutes I was eating a fried chicken leg and Rose was showing off her indigo and lace to Mrs. Gogin.

Uncle Woody explained that all of his children were grown and had moved away. He said he missed having young ones around during celebrations. When they found out that Rose and I were camping and about my run-in with the circus boss, they insisted that we spend the night at their house in Palestine. Rose didn't see anything wrong with the idea, so we agreed.

As Captain of the Palestine Home Guard, Uncle Woody began the festivities with a speech about helping families whose men had gone away to fight and then ended with a patriotic poem. The crowd cheered and then a brass band began playing 'Yankee Doodle' and 'John Brown's Body'. Politicians and Abolitionists and Peace Democrats ranted and raved all afternoon while people ate, drank, argued and fought over every topic under the sun. One man would speak of the glory of war and another would curse the destruction of the same. It seemed like everyone had an opinion and wanted to beat his neighbor over the head with it, whether he wanted to listen or not.

The war was the subject of every conversation in Palestine that day. But to most, it was just something to argue about. I wondered how many of these people were actually suffering hardships because of the war. The beer drinkers who tried to give me a hard way to go didn't look like they had missed any meals. Why did they get to stay home and complain about cowardly generals? I was curious why some of the loudest voices of dissent were men of fighting age. Why did they get to sleep in their own beds, while my father spent every night in peril? It wasn't fair. To them the war was a far away conflict fought by others. They were in no danger. They didn't lose any sleep worrying about family members. Because of the war, I spent almost every waking hour working in the fields, while they sat around in taverns and complained. I wasn't alone. Rose worked as hard as I did. Pappy and Granny did as well. Worst of all, Ma was going crazy since the war started. Why should my family suffer so much while others felt no pain at all? Why should they celebrate while Ned Thompson fights for his one-armed life, or while Cousin Berry's body lies in the ground at Shiloh? These were the same men that didn't want to hear what I had to say because I was just a boy. The more I listened to the dissenters, the more I felt the fire grow deep inside. Uncle Woody must have noticed a change in my disposition.

"You look like you're fixing to wrestle a wildcat. What's on your mind, young Will?"

"Something just doesn't seem right about celebratin' while my father is off fighting and others are sufferin' mightily."

Uncle Woody removed his glasses and scratched his balding scalp. "I reckon it can seem a little odd at that," he admitted. "But many of the very same people out there are suffering, just like you. See that woman over there selling blueberry pies?" He pointed to a round woman in a loud blue dress, laughing and guffawing with two potential patrons as they haggled about the price of a pie.

I nodded yes.

"That's the Widow Griggs. She lost her husband four years ago when he got kicked in the head by a horse in Hutsonville. She had to sell her farm and move into town. Her two boys had helped her with some of the bills, but they joined up with the twenty first infantry as soon as the war broke out. They were supposed to send money home to help, but to date, none has reached their mother. So she takes in laundry and mends clothes to get by. If she doesn't have a right to complain—who does? But does she? No. What good would it do? She smiles and does the best that she can. She uses her own money to bake those pies and gives all of the proceeds to the poor."

"Why doesn't she keep the money for herself?" I asked.

"Even though she works like a dog to make ends meet; she manages to get by somehow. And she knows there are several around who can't put food on the table. That's why she celebrates. She celebrates waking up every morning. She celebrates a cool breeze in the evening or a warm fire in the winter. The quality of the life we live depends on how we look at things. See that young lady over there beneath that maple tree?"

"The one with the white hat?" I asked.

"That's the one. She's eight months pregnant and her husband is somewhere in Tennessee with his cavalry unit. She hasn't even told him that she's with child because she doesn't want to worry him. She's here to celebrate because it's the only way she can show support for the troops. By being strong for others, it forces her to be strong for herself. Can you understand what I'm saying?"

"I think so."

"Since your father left for the war, you have had to shoulder many burdens that a boy your age shouldn't have to carry. It is really not fair, but in all honesty, life is not fair. Because your father went to fight for what he thought was right, the war has directly changed your life. You work long hours for little thanks and no wages. You're carrying a man's load instead of spending your days at the swimmin' hole or stealin' watermelons. This rebellion has upset the apple cart for every person you see in this courtyard. Some considerably more than others. This war will continue to change our lives until it mercifully comes to an end. Most of these changes will be beyond our control. They will be forced upon us against our will and they will come with horrible consequences. The only thing that we control is the manner in which we conduct ourselves. The way I see things, there is only one way we can go. We simply do the best we can with whatever means we have at our disposal. This means we work to keep the farm running, or help a needy neighbor, or in this case we celebrate the birth of our nation and the men who fight to end the unholy practice of slavery. Yes, we are hurting because our loved ones are far away from home. And the thought that they may never return is a thought too painful to bear. But if we are not diligent here at home, we will become another casualty of the war, just as if we died on the battlefield. Either we remain strong and fight, or we give up and die. It's as simple as that Will."

I closed my eyes and tried to sort out what he had said. "I think my Ma has given up," I admitted. "Sometimes I feel sorry for her and other times I just get so blasted mad at her for quitting. After that I get mad at myself for getting mad at her. It makes me feel all torn up inside."

"What you are feeling is called guilt," he told me, "and guilt can weigh heavily on you if you hold on to it."

"How do you let it go?" I asked. "It seems like I'm constantly tryin' to work things out in my head, but no matter how hard I try, I never come up with an answer that I feel good about."

"I'm afraid there is really no good answer to that question, Will," he admitted. "All you can do is try to live your life with honor and try to do the right thing. You thank *The Good Lord* for today and you hope for the best for tomorrow."

"So it's not wrong to have fun even in times like these?" I was trying to let his words soak in, but I felt just like I did when

Reverend Parker delivered one of his hour long sermons. I heard what he was saying, but I didn't exactly know what to do with his words.

"Not only is it not wrong—it's absolutely the right thing to do! There is a time for work and a time for play. The 4ᵗʰ of July is a time for celebration. It would be downright unpatriotic not to have a good time today."

"Do you really think so?"

"I know so," he declared. "And I think I know exactly what is called for in this situation."

"What is that?" I replied.

"Front row seats for tonight's performance of the circus."

"But what about Sam Murphy?" I could still feel the knot on the back of my head from my first run-in with the circus boss.

"You'll be safe as long as you're with me. Besides, I know your dying to see your lady friend perform. What do you say? Let's go have a good time tonight."

There was a boyish twinkle in his eye and he gave me a mischievous grin. And just like that, I felt like a yoke had been lifted from my shoulders. How could I say no?

—❧—

Chapter 17

Dozens of gas lanterns illuminated the big top tent as three elephants from the dark continent of Africa paraded trunk to tail inside the center ring. A dark-skinned trainer with an ornate feathered military helmet barked out commands in a foreign language while cracking the tip of his bullwhip at the animal's feet. The elephants jumped through giant burning rings, balanced precariously on step stools, danced on hind legs to a waltz played by a fifteen piece brass band. A lion and leopard appeared after the elephants disappeared, followed by clowns with monkeys and then three men in sequined suits standing on white stallions from Austria.

The Robinson and Lake Circus claimed to be the greatest show between the Atlantic and Pacific Oceans. From what I saw that night; they weren't lying. The animals and performers were unlike anything I had ever seen or imagined at South Union. It was if they had come from another world. When I looked over and saw the expression on Sister Rose's face, I realized she was as amazed as I was. Uncle Woody and Mrs. Eliza seemed to be enjoying the show as well. From the moment I first met Uncle Woody, I realized that he was different from any man I had ever met. He was fun loving. That was a given, but then a lot of grownups loved to have fun. Pappy fell into that sort. But Uncle Woody seemed to look at the world through the eyes of a young boy. He said the world was full of wonders, but most folks were too busy to notice. Life was too short and he didn't want to miss a thing. He laughed, clapped and slapped his hat against his leg without a care for what anyone thought of him. He seemed to know every person in town and didn't have a mean thing to say about anybody. I had only met him a few hours earlier and it felt like I had known him for my entire life.

As soon as the horses left the arena, the lamps were dimmed and the ring master appeared with an oversized megaphone and a hush fell over the crowd. "Ladies and Gentlemen! Cast your eyes upward and be prepared to be amazed. Coming to us from the nether regions of Katmandu; we present the death defying beauty, the flower of the Orient, Maya the Magnificent."

And there she was; Cliffphilia Willow Maya McGee. She was positively and absolutely, the most beautiful vision I had ever seen. She wore a skin-tight red sequined leotard with yellow tights with matching ribbons in her raven hair. She waved to the crowd from her perch some thirty feet above and with catlike agility, dove into the air and caught a single rope that dangled from the tent rigging. She began twirling to the music and then leapt over to a second rope which suddenly appeared from another direction. She looped the rope around her ankle while a man grabbed the rope from the ground and began spinning her like a whirling dervish. At first, she spun in a tight spiral, but when the top of the rope was lowered she began to dangle wildly until she was only a few feet above the top row of onlookers. Two more men joined the man on the bottom and rotated the rope in unison to a speed where it seemed impossible for her to hold on. Her arms waved wildly while the crowd "ooed" and "awed" in unison. I knew it was part of the show, but I couldn't help but believe that she was going to be injured or killed. It was at this point her foot slipped from the loop and she tumbled through the air. But just before she fell into the far side bleachers, she reached out and grabbed the second rope and playfully twirled to the ground in the middle of the ring. She raised her arms into the air and the crowd went wild with applause.

Uncle Woody joined in and playfully nudged me in the ribs. "Your girlfriend is quite the performer," he teased. "She is quite a bit younger than I had expected."

I felt myself turning red, but I had to agree. Cliffy was something else indeed. She played to the crowd while the three men rolled out a large oaken barrel filled with water into the center of the ring. I waved wildly with approval when she looked in my direction. Her eyes widened as soon as she saw me and, without warning, she somersaulted in my direction and hopped to a sudden stop directly in front of me. She took me in her arms and before I could react, kissed me directly on my lips. The crowd went wild. I was confounded and didn't know what to do. I couldn't move. And then without warning, Cliffy flipped back into the center of the ring as if nothing had happened. Uncle Woody was smiling, but Rose had a less than approving look on her face.

While the crowd was still cheering, she grabbed the rope and, without effort, shimmied back up to the platform. She bowed to the crowd and then waved an umbrella into the air. The roar of the crowd quickly went silent when it became evident what she was about to do.

"Ladies and Gentleman," the ringleader barked once again into the megaphone. "Maya the Magnificent will attempt a feat so dangerous…so unthinkable…so outrageous that it is out-lawed in most civilized countries in Europe, not to mention seven states above the Mason and Dixon Line. Please, be totally silent and be prepared to be amazed."

Cliffy grabbed a rope and made several passes over the bar-rel to build up the tension of the crowd and then floated back to the platform and once again took the umbrella into hand. The lights were dimmed except for a single lamp above the barrel in the center of the ring. A drum roll began as Cliffy closed her eyes for a moment and extended her arms in front of her. She adjusted her stance, took a deep breath and with-out hesitation leaped into the flickering light. She tucked her knees to her chest and completed a full flip and then opened the umbrella just before she disappeared into the barrel with a splash. The crowd remained silent until she popped back up with the umbrella on her shoulder and a smile on her face. The crowd once again roared in unison.

Almost immediately, the three men lifted Cliffy out of the barrel and began to bind her with shackles and chains while filling the barrel up to the brim. As soon as the water began to overflow, the men placed locks on the chains and then they lifted her back into the barrel and sealed the lid above her with a mallet and nails.

The ringleader immediately appeared with an oversized sand timer and began to explain that no human could hold their breath for more than six minutes, which happened to be the amount of time measured by the timer. He said that Maya the Magnificent had given instructions not to open the barrel until the last grain of sand had emptied from the timer. The crowd waited with trepi-dation as the seconds slowly passed by. The ringleader worked the crowd into a frenzy and even though Cliffy had explained to me how the stunt would work, I was convinced her life was in danger. Sister Rose dug her fingernails into my arm with dread. But just as she had warned, the assistants couldn't get the barrel opened after the timer had emptied. They seemed to panic until the ring leader grabbed a nearby ax and, with a dramatic blow, shattered the lid into splinters. The crowd went completely silent and then Cliffy popped up free from the chains and shackles. Once again, the crowd roared with approval. The men helped her out of the barrel and she bowed repeatedly to the crowd's standing ovation. She wrapped herself in a velvet cloak and then ran out of the tent as another girl on a black horse rode into the ring to take her place.

Once the crowd was focused on the rider as she performed back flips on the horse, I slipped away from my seat and went out onto the midway. As I searched for Cliffy, I caught a glimpse of her as she stepped into one of the ornate circus wagons. I surveyed the area to make sure I wasn't being watched and then took an indirect route that kept me in the shadows until I reached her door. I gently tapped on the door. "Cliffy! It's me. Will Farmer," I whispered. I waited for a moment, but there was no answer. I tapped on the door a little harder. "Cliffy! It's Will—" The door suddenly swung open. She grabbed my wrist and I found myself tumbling head over heels into the pitch dark wagon.

"You shouldn't be here, Will." She seemed frightened. "Sam would tan my hide if he saw you. He don't allow any visitors in the wagons without his approval. No exceptions."

"I made sure nobody saw me," I assured her. "Murphy is still in the tent."

She cracked the door open and peeked outside. Once she was convinced we were alone, she pulled the door shut and secured the lock. She fumbled for a match in the dark and then lit a kerosene lantern that was hanging from the wagon's rafters. "We'll be safe for a while," she whispered. "There are eight more acts to go and Sophie Mae goes on last. He's more worried about her than he is me, so we should have at least a half hour before I have to be out for the closing parade."

"Does he own her too?" I asked.

"He thinks he does. With Sam Murphy—that's all that matters. How did you like the show?" She motioned for me to turn around as she slipped out of her wet clothes.

"You were wonderful," I told her. "You looked like an angel."

"How about the kiss?" she laughed.

My mind went blank. My tongue went numb and my heart began to beat at a rabbit's pace. "You were wonderful," I repeated myself. To date, it had been the biggest thrill of my life, but I didn't have a clue how to tell her. I wanted to say something, but the words just wouldn't come.

"You're wonderful too, Sweetie, but why are you here?"

Her question brought me back to the business at hand. "I met a man today who can help you. His name is Uncle Woody Gogin."

"You can turn around now," she said. "Help me? What are you talking about?"

"Uncle Woody said that it's against the law to hold you as a bond girl. He said it ain't no different than slavery and Illinois is a free state. If you want your freedom, let me know and he will be here first thing in the morning with the sheriff. They will protect you from Murphy, but Uncle Woody said you had to be sure, cause once the sheriff got involved—there would be no turning back."

A blank look came over Cliffy's face and she dropped heavily onto a wooden stool. "Oh Will—what have you done?"

"I'm getting you away from Sam Murphy. I thought that's what you wanted."

"There's nothin' more in this whole wide world I want more, but it ain't that simple. He'll kill us all."

"Uncle Woody said the sheriff can protect you. Murphy won't be able to lay a hand on you," I assured her.

"Sam Murphy won't let a backwoods sheriff stand in the way of killing me. The man is pure evil; spawn of the devil, himself. He will wait until all of the protection is gone and then slit my throat when nobody is looking."

"In a few weeks, the circus will be a hundred miles away," I replied. "He won't be able to hurt you then."

"As long as that man draws breath—he'll never give up until he kills me and those who helped me." Cliffy began to sob. "Before me—there was a girl named Molly O' Harahan. Murphy owned the contract on her just like he does on me. After a show in Cleveland, Molly ran off with a politician, who had some of his henchmen rough Murphy up and then married the girl. Murphy didn't say a word, but three months later, Molly and the politician were found dead in an alley. They suspected Sam, but they couldn't pin it on him because the circus was in New York and there were thirty people who swore he never left his wagon. A few days later Murphy showed me a blood covered lock of Molly's bright red hair. He warned me that the same fate waited for me if I ever double crossed him."

"I'll protect you, Cliffy," I told her. "I ain't afraid of Sam Murphy."

"That's sweet of you, Will, but you should be afraid of him. He is a monster. Besides, there is a war on. People end up dead all the time. Nobody is going to spend any effort protecting a circus girl and nobody is going to lose any sleep if I end up dead. I couldn't live with myself if anything happened to you. You need to leave this wagon and forget this conversation ever took place."

"But Cliffy—what will happen to you?"

"There'll come a day when I'll make my move," she said. "He'll make a mistake and then I'll be free. But I have to make sure he won't be able to come after me. I can't let anyone get hurt on my account."

"But—" She put her hand over my mouth.

"Don't say another word, Will Farmer. This is the way it has to be. If you were a couple years older—I'd marry you in a minute. Who knows—in a few years maybe we'll run into each other and you can make an honest girl of me. Cliffy Farmer. I think I like the sound of it."

I started to protest, but she tightened her clasp on my mouth. "Not another word." she warned and then let loose of me. She dimmed the lantern and then opened the door wide enough to make sure the coast was clear. She drew me into her arms and once again kissed me on my mouth. I closed my eyes and thought I was going to faint. I wanted the moment to last forever, but she abruptly pulled away. "I love you, Will Farmer," she whispered.

She grabbed me by the collar, pushed me out of the wagon and then bolted the door before I could say a word. *I love you too, Cliffy.*

—⟋⟍—

Chapter 18

After a restless night, the Gogins treated us to a breakfast of flapjacks, salt pork and eggs. Mrs. Gogin's pancakes were lighter and thinner than I had ever tasted, but as good as they were, I couldn't force myself to finish my plate. I had a sour taste in my mouth ever since I left Cliffy's wagon. I had made my way back to the big top to watch the end of the show and get one last glimpse of her. She waved goodbye and blew a kiss in my direction and then disappeared. I wondered if that would be the last time I ever saw her. It was painful to even think about it.

After the circus concluded, we made our way back to the village square and watched the fireworks show as the band played patriotic songs. It was a loud and spectacular display, but I rarely looked upward. I didn't want anyone to see the tears in my eyes.

I tried to convince Uncle Woody to get the sheriff anyway, but he insisted that Cliffy knew her situation better than we did. By trying to help her against her will, we might end up doing her harm or even worse—get her killed. I knew he was right, but doing nothing just didn't sit right with me. But what could I do?

After breakfast Sister Rose helped Mrs. Gogin wash the dishes and then took a tour of the garden while Uncle Woody helped me hitch the mare to the wagon. Rose seemed to enjoy our time with the Gogins, however she was anxious to get to the mill and head back home to Ned. After leaving Cliffy, I had a better understanding of how she felt.

Mrs. Eliza packed a lunch basket for our return trip and made us promise to stop by whenever we got back to Palestine. We agreed without hesitation.

We stopped by the apothecary and picked up Doctor Judd's supplies and serums for Ned and I used the last of my money for another bag of jawbreakers and peppermint sticks. It was probably a good thing that South Union was so far away from Palestine. With all of the candy counters, I would never be able to keep any money and my teeth would surely rot away.

When we reached the mill, the familiar clerk greeted us and said they had just finished with our order. Rose went into the office to take care of the paperwork, while I helped a dock worker load the flour into the wagon. We were almost finished when I heard a cannon blast originating from somewhere near the village hall. At first I thought it might be part of the holiday celebration, but then I noticed a flurry of activity that didn't seem right. Men were riding by on horseback at breakneck speed, while wagon wheels sent dust plumes skyward. Everyone was moving at a frantic pace. Something was happening and it didn't look like it was good news. I was impatiently waiting for Rose to return, when Uncle Woody came running toward our wagon.

"Thank goodness your still here," he panted. "The Copperheads attacked farms in Honey Creek Township last night. Apparently they were targeting family members of Union Soldiers."

Suddenly, everything that happened during the last two days seemed petty and unimportant. "Rose! We need to go!" I yelled as she walked out of the office door. "The Copperheads are raiding back in Honey Creek!"

She began trembling and immediately broke into tears.

Uncle Woody helped her into the wagon and then jumped in beside her. "I'm going with you," he said firmly. "It's too dangerous for you two children to go alone."

Normally, I would have protested about being called a child, but in this case he was right. He said two dozen members of the *Palestine Home Guard* were already riding south.

We could see black plumes of dark smoke rising into the sky from miles away. It was hard to judge distance from the wagon, but there seemed to be a smoking tower coming from the vicinity of our farm. I worked the old mare as hard as I could, but the flat wagon was not built for speed. To make matters worse, the horse was getting lathered up and at Uncle Woody's insistence, we stopped for water and rest. I felt utterly helpless, but there was nothing that could be done, except to wait.

The closer to home we got, the more distraught Rose had become. She sat on the ground with her back against a walnut tree. She wrapped her arms around her knees as if pulling herself into a cocoon. "Please Lord—let Ned be safe." She repeated the prayer over and over.

"Keep the faith girl," Uncle Woody encouraged, "there are hundreds of farms in your part of the county. Hopefully, there is nothing to worry about."

She feigned a smile, but was beyond consolation. I think Uncle Woody feared for the worst also, as he never took his hands away from his shotgun. I didn't know what to think.

After a while we were back on our way. The closer we got to home, the more people seemed to be armed. Pistols, shotguns, rifles and clubs. Everyone had some sort of weapon in their hands. But it wasn't until we reached the area around the Flat Rock Post Office that we began to see the devastation. Houses and barns were burned. Livestock was slaughtered, and cornfields were trampled. By the time we reached the edge of our farm, it was clear that our worst fears had come to fruition. From a distance, we could see that our barn, chicken coop and smokehouse had been charred to cinders. The cabin had also been set afire, but the back half had miraculously been spared and was still standing. We didn't see any activity when we first reached the cabin, but then I thought I heard voices around back. I jumped out of the wagon and sprinted around the root cellar then stopped dead in my tracks. I had to take a second look to make certain that my eyes weren't lying. I was paralyzed with horror. At that moment, my life was changed forever. The last of what innocence remained of my childhood was kicked out of me. I couldn't breathe. My eyes filled with tears and I fell to the ground. And then I heard Rose wailing beside me which only confirmed that I wasn't dreaming. Revered Parker was pounding a handmade cross fashioned from two oak twigs into the ground over a freshly dug grave.

Uncle Woody helped me up and wrapped his arm around my shoulders as we walked toward the cross. I tried to ask the question, but the words just wouldn't come out of my mouth.

Reverend Parker must have sensed this and answered my question without making me ask. "It's your mother, Will," he whispered. "The Copperhead cowards killed your Ma."

I went numb and Rose became inconsolable. "We need to get you out of sight just in case they're still around." Reverend Parker took Rose by the arm and led her down the trail that went to the creek. Uncle Woody and I silently followed.

Rose immediately quieted down when she saw Ned and Pappy sprawled out, side by side, on makeshift pallets next to the springhouse. Granny wailed a cry of relief and agony at the same time. "Praise Jesus! You children are safe!" She let the water bucket fall to the ground and ran to embrace Rose and then waved at me to join them. "When you didn't show up yesterday—I was afraid you were bushwhacked too."

When Granny looked at Uncle Woody with trepidation, I explained how he didn't want us riding home alone.

"Much obliged, Mr. Gogin," she thanked him.

"They are special young people, Ma'am. I just wanted to make sure they arrived home safely. And now I am at your disposal."

She hesitated and then nodded with a reluctant smile of acceptance.

"Pappy and Ned; are they—?" Rose sheepishly asked.

"Doc Judd gave them something to sleep, I thought for a while we was gonna lose them both—" Granny burst into tears. She was exhausted. We helped her to a stool beneath a peach tree and Rose went to fetch a ladle filled with water. Granny pulled me close and I rested my head on her shoulder. She patted my back and hummed a familiar hymn.

I closed my eyes and tried to hold back the tears. I didn't want anyone to see me cry. But it was useless.

"What happened?" Uncle Woody asked Reverend Parker.

"About fifty Copperheads launched raids against every farm in the area that had a soldier away fighting for the Union. I guess they figured they could do the most damage terrorizing old folks, women and children. But they weren't satisfied with just burning the homes, destroying the crops and killing livestock. Their intent was to massacre the families of any man who dared to join the Union army. They would have succeeded if it weren't for Reverend Allison. He's the preacher over at the Good Hope Hardshell Church, about a half mile east of the Flat Rock Post Office. Allison noticed several unfamiliar horses at the meeting house yesterday afternoon and went to investigate. Things didn't look right, so instead of barging into the church, he crawled under the foundation of the building until he was directly beneath the pulpit. He said they were men from south of the Embarrass and that they wanted to strike a blow on behalf of Jeff Davis on the Fourth of July. Reverend Allison waited until the meeting disbanded and then jumped on his horse and rode the countryside like Paul Revere—warning everybody he could. Allison said that they were going to attack after dark, so most folks hid out in the cornfields or back in the woods. Riders were sent to New Hebron, Robinson and Palestine to find men to help, but there just wasn't enough time. Doctor Judd and I rushed down here to warn everybody, but unfortunately, this was one of the first farms that they attacked. They carried torches and wore white hoods to cover their faces. Ned and Mr. Farmer tried to hold them off as long as they could, but they were outnumbered twentyfold. After setting fire to the barn and fields, they managed to get a torch to take hold in the cabin. Everyone managed to escape out the back door, but the excitement was too much for their Grandfather's heart. He collapsed as soon as they cleared the house. Ned and the elder Mrs. Farmer managed to drag him to the springhouse, but with all of the commotion, Sarah, young Will's mother must have wandered back into harm's way. She—well let's just say she never had a chance." Reverend Parker looked at me and stopped.

"Go ahead Reverend," Uncle Woody said, "The boy has a right to know."

Reverend Parker pursed his lips and reluctantly nodded. "Yes, I suppose he does." He turned and spoke to me directly. "As you know, Will, your mother had been fighting the melancholy ever since Samuel left to fight in the war. The separation was just more than she could bear. I know it's been hard for you to watch her deteriorate over the past few months, but it wasn't her fault. She had a sickness in her mind that was beyond her control. It would be the same if she had come down with consumption or a cancer."

"What are you trying to tell me?" I asked.

"Because of her sickness, her mind was not able to understand what was happening last night. From what I can tell, your mother went out to defend her house with her bare hands and the blasted demons showed her no mercy. They—" he couldn't go on without getting choked up.

"What did they do to her?" I demanded. I wanted to know

Reverend Parker took a deep breath before continuing. "It's best you don't know, Will. That's why I already laid her remains to rest. What is buried on that hill is not your mother. It is best that you remember her as she was before her sickness. Rejoice that she is now in a better place."

"I want to know what they did to her!"

"No, you don't." Reverend Parker's voice was firm. "You may think you do, but you don't. I've made a vow before The

Lord Almighty never to tell a living soul what they did to your mother. So please, don't ask me again. Your mother was a good God-fearing woman; and that is how you need to think of her. She was a victim of the war just like a soldier who gets killed on the battlefield. She died defending her home and family. You can honor her best by remaining strong and help your family get through this time of grief."

"But—" I didn't know what to say. I walked over and began pounding my fists against the rough bark of a birch tree.

Uncle Woody put his hands on my shoulders and led me to a stump where he forced me to sit down. I buried my head in my hands and began to sob. It wasn't long before I found myself, prostrate on the ground, crying in a fit of pain and anger. I was overwrought with guilt and regret. I had resented and at times even hated Ma for the way she acted over the past few months. I was mad at her for getting sick. Reverend Parker was right. It wasn't her fault and yet I had blamed her as if it was. She had needed me and I had rejected her. While she had been defending the farm—I was off chasing a circus girl. I was a horrible boy. A horrible son. My mind went back to the special things she had done for me over the years and I remembered how she made me feel loved. When I was little, she always told me I was the apple of her eye. Even though she was gone, I could still feel her love. And as soon as I felt the love—I realized the loss. She was gone forever. She deserved better. She deserved a better son and a better life. She deserved to be safe and she didn't deserve to be killed by a mob of Johnny Reb cowards hiding behind hoods and masks.

And it was at that moment that a hatred was conceived in me. A dark, soul consuming rage that came from a part of me that I didn't know was there. Ma was gone and there wasn't a thing that I could do about that. She was gone and the cowards who had killed her were out there planning their next raid. They were not soldiers. They were not honorable men. They were animals who preyed on defenseless women, children and old folks. They needed to be stopped and they needed to be punished. I didn't know what I was going to do or how I would go about doing it, but I made a vow to myself as I bawled on the South Union clay. The men who killed my mother needed to be punished and I would not rest until her death had been avenged. I had been living in a world that was somewhere in between childhood and adulthood. I wasn't a kid and people kept reminding that I wasn't a grownup either. Until that moment, I didn't know where I belonged. Those days were over. From that day forward—I would never be the same.

—ɯ—

Chapter 19

News about the war seemed to get worse that fall. The Union Army was making a little headway in the west, but the cost in human life was in the thousands. The war in the east was another matter entirely. General George McClellan's Army of the Potomac had failed miserably that summer during the Peninsula Campaign and fared even worse in Northern Virginia that autumn. Despite having a much larger army, McClellan was outgeneraled and outfoxed by Robert E. Lee at every opportunity. Most war supporters, along with the local men who had volunteered to fight for the Union, had believed that the war would last no more than ninety days. Eighteen months later, everyone realized they had been wrong and any hope for a quick end of the war seemed hopeless When Confederate guerillas began to raid towns on the north side of the Ohio River a black cloud of uncertainty fell over the Wabash Valley as well. Those who were pro-union feared for the worst, while the Copperheads in Honey Creek Township became emboldened by the success of their attacks. They felt that by harassing the families of Union soldiers, support for the war would wane and the South would be able to succeed. Their tactics had the opposite effect on me.

A hatred burned inside of me for anything to do with *The South* or the southern way of life. Looking back—it was the hatred that gave me the strength to get through those days after Ma was killed. Pappy remained on the verge of death for several days after the Copperhead attack. Doctor Judd said that his heart had nearly given out and that only a strong will and cussed orneryness had kept him alive. Even though he was making steady progress, he was only able to take a few steps at a time before tuckering out. He still maintained his smile and tried to joke around whenever he could. However, the mood of the farm was anything but cheerful.

Ned had been able to get out of bed during the attack and even shot off a few rounds from his revolver at the raiders. He somehow had found the strength to carry Pappy off to safety with his good arm and even went looking for Ma before passing out from exhaustion. Doctor Judd said he might have died with fever if we hadn't arrived with the medicine from Palestine. After ten days of recovery and around the clock attention from Rose, he managed to get out of bed for good. Unlike Pappy, Ned seemed to grow stronger everyday and began to help with some of the easier chores around the farm. Ned sent a letter to his family to let them know about the attack and that he was recovering. He told them about Ma and asked if they could keep Jaybird and Bub for a while longer until things settled down. Ned said he felt obligated to help because Pa had saved his life and he wanted to pay him back by helping our family. Pappy said it was a noble thing to do, but also said that he figured our Sister Rose was the real reason.

Several men from around the neighborhood helped to repair the cabin so we could at least get out of the weather, but we would have to fend for ourselves as far as rebuilding the barn and fences. People tried to help the best that they could, but most were in the same situation as us and needed to protect their own homes. All of our livestock had been stolen or had run away and two thirds of our field crops had been trampled or burned. Everything that I had worked so hard for all spring and summer had been destroyed over night. Even our garden had been burned.

At least we had the flour from the mill. If we would have arrived home a few hours earlier, the bounty of our winter wheat crop would have been lost too. Uncle Woody Gogin stayed for a couple of days and helped clean up before the last of the *Home Guard* left for Palestine. Granny gave him most of the cash money we had saved in order to replace what we had lost. He returned with far more than we had paid for. Two dozen chickens and a fine rooster, along with a milk cow and a herd of six pigs with one sow ready to drop a litter. He brought baking powder, corn meal, whiskey, tobacco, sugar, coffee along with fresh linens and beddings. Apparently his wife Eliza had solicited donations from their neighbors. We all thanked him and offered to pay him back for the extras, but he wouldn't hear of it. He stayed overnight and left early in the morning. He said he was arranging for the Home Guard to patrol our neighborhood until the Provost Marshall in Olney could arrange for Union Regulars to be sent to protect us.

I was grateful for the extra supplies, but not even Uncle Woody's boyish charm could lift me from the dark place I had put myself. I was mad at the world; especially the southern half.

The only bright spot came from an unexpected, but reliable source. It was two days after the attack and I was ready to drop from exhaustion after ten hours of hauling charred timbers to the dump pile down by the creek. My hands were dappled red from splinters and slivers of glass. The muscles in my arms and legs felt like I had been beaten with a club. Worst of all, I had to walk past Ma with every trip. The morning after the attack, Reverend Parker read scripture at Ma's graveside, while Rose, Granny and I held hands. We stood there for ten minutes at the most and then went back to work. I felt like I never had a chance to say goodbye to Ma. She had been sickly for some time, but I never gave any consideration to her dying. I suppose I had tried to keep her out of my thoughts entirely when her mind started to leave. I had resented her for being a burden on the family and for the most part had ignored her for the past few months. Somehow, I knew she would never get better, but I didn't want to admit it. I had treated her badly. I had held back my affection to punish her for being sick. Now I would do anything to have Ma back. I didn't care if she was sickly. She was my mother and had loved me with all of her heart. I tried to pretend that she would be sitting in her rocking chair as I made my way back to the cabin. But every time I passed her grave, the mound of dirt and crooked wooden cross was there to remind me she was gone forever. It seemed like everything I loved had been taken away from me.

I sat on a log next to the creek and buried my head against my knees. My chest hurt so bad I struggled to breathe. I wanted to cry, but had used up all of my tears. It was the lowest point of my life. It seemed like the more I prayed the worse my life seemed to get. I could feel the fury building inside of me when I was startled by a grunt and a prod in the middle of my back. I fell off of the log and spun around quickly; ready to pounce on the intruder. My alarm immediately became jubilation. It was my pet pig, Muddy.

She had several open cuts and was covered in soot and mud. Much of the wiry black hair on her was completely singed away. The tips of both ears were missing, but under the circumstances—I thought she was beautiful.

I had just assumed that she had been slaughtered or stolen with the rest of the livestock. The Copperheads had done such a thorough job of pillaging our farm, it seemed beyond hope that she could have survived. She was bloodied and battered, but she was alive.

It was probably wrong to put so much value on an animal, but under these circumstances, Muddy's resurrection back into my life gave me the will to go on. The Copperheads hadn't taken everything after all. She might have been just a dumb pig in the opinion of most, but she was much more than that to me. She was a reminder of happier days—long before I ever heard of places like Bull Run or Shiloh; simple days of fishing and swimming and childish games. Muddy was as much a part of my childhood as were my own brothers. I heard people say that animals didn't have a soul, but that wasn't the case with my pig. Muddy was an old soul with human-like understanding. She seemed to realize how much I was hurting and rested her head on my shoulder. I wrapped my arms around her dirty, foul smelling neck and planted a kiss on her jowl. Before I knew it, I was laughing so hard that I started to cry.

Granny and Sister Rose's reaction was much the same; laughter and tears. All work stopped while we celebrated. The sudden appearance of my pig couldn't replace the loss of my mother, but Muddy's miraculous return seemed to give us a small measure of hope. We thought she was lost and given her up for dead and yet she was alive. We all agreed that it was a sign for us to keep praying for Pa's safe return and a quick end to the war. We prayed for Pappy's recovery and for Ned to regain his strength. Hope was all that we had, along with the cruel reminder that life must go on whether we wanted it to or not.

—◊—

Chapter 20

November of 1862 was cold and gray. It seemed to rain or sleet most every day and was foggy and damp on the days when it didn't. We were only able to harvest about a quarter of our crop due to the constant night time raids by the Copperheads. After the surprise of the initial attack in July, the residents of South Union were never far away from a firearm of some sort, therefore the guerillas were reluctant to attack homesteads. Instead, they found burning crops and barns and slaughtering livestock to be a healthier if not a more cowardly method of attack. The Copperheads waited until right before the crops were ready to harvest and then attacked with vengeance under the cover of darkness.

I had grown accustomed to pain and loss in my life that year, but losing our crop on the eve of harvest was beyond evil, even by Copperhead standards. I hated anything to do with the South or the rebellion, but I had cultivated a special sort of hatred for the Copperheads. They were northerners that killed helpless women and children. They wore white hoods to hide their identity. They were too cowardly to fight out in the open, but because nobody knew who they were, they were able to live among us in secret. People didn't know who to trust other than the closest of friends and neighbors.

It was during the early days of that November that some of the men in South Union decided to strike back. Even though I hadn't quite achieved the status of manhood yet, I was able to join the militia as a lookout. There was some resistance in the beginning, but two neighbor farmers, Addison Parker and Charlie Jones, stood up on my behalf. They said I had earned the right to claim a pound of flesh on account of everything I'd been through. Eventually, they agreed to let me keep watch for Copperhead meetings near *The Flat Rock*. The Flat Rock was an enormous limestone boulder with a flat top near a spring. When George Maxwell became local postmaster, his house became known as the first Flat Rock Post Office because of its proximity to the rock. Even though the rock wasn't in Flat Rock proper, its location was well known. Since it was off the beaten path and surrounded by dense forest, it was the ideal place for secret meetings. There were rumors circulating through the neighborhood that the Copperheads were using it for that purpose and a meeting place for smuggling contraband to the south.

A blind of leaves, cattails and evergreen boughs was built in the thicket with a clear view of the Flat Rock from a distance of seventy-five feet. The blind was supposed to become my home for the next few weeks.

Granny and Rose were adamantly opposed to the idea of me getting involved in such a dangerous endeavor, but finally gave up when they realized they weren't going to stop me. I had performed my duty and harvested every gourd, bean, ear of corn from the ground along with every apple, nut or persimmon from every tree I could find. The animals that needed to be slaughtered for meat had been butchered. The cabin and barn had been rebuilt and every fence had been mended and repaired. I had kept my promise to my father and had acted like a man. Because I had carried my fair share of the load, I felt I had earned the right to seek a measure of revenge from the yellow-bellied Copperhead cat scratchers. They had taken far too much from my family without receiving any retribution. Granny said that it wasn't our place to judge. She said that it was up to Abe Lincoln and The Lord Almighty to render vengeance, but I wasn't buying what she was peddling.

I wasn't alone in that way of thinking. "An eye for an eye and a tooth for a tooth" was the creed of many from the neighborhood. The manner of punishment however, was an entirely different matter, as there were two different schools of thought. Some of the men wanted to send them to prison at Camp Douglas in Chicago. Others wanted to avoid official channels by killing them on the spot and then dumping their bodies in a hog lot. My feelings were somewhere in the middle. I felt that the Copperheads deserved to meet their maker, but secretly, I didn't know if I was brave enough to pull the trigger. I had enough hatred in me to kill, but the thought of taking a life went against everything Ma and Pa had taught me to believe.

Fortunately, the ambush planned by the locals was to take place two and a half miles west of the spring at Flat Rock and I wouldn't be put to the test. A fine field of late yellow corn within view of the heavily traveled Robinson Road was left unharvested in hopes of drawing a burning party to attack under the cover of darkness. If and when the attack occurred, the Copperheads would walk into an ambush of heavily armed farmers, ready and willing to send them to their graves.

My job was to report any activity at the Flat Rock Spring. I was to stay hidden in the blind for an unspecified period of time and keep watch for anything suspicious. There were reports that The Copperheads and Knights of the Golden Circle were using the spring as a meeting place and as a staging area to launch their attacks. A red-headed mountain of a man by the name of Josiah Highsmith was elected as leader of the local resistance. He preferred to take any raiders to justice who might be captured, but admitted circumstances may dictate other remedies. Highsmith was responsible for my assignment at the spring and promised Granny that he would keep me away from gunfire if humanly possible. I was anxious to help in any manner possible, so I agreed to be a lookout without hesitation.

I crawled into my hidey-hole on an early Monday morning and by mid-afternoon; I was ready to go stir crazy with boredom. The only activity was the occasional squirrel fight over an acorn or the warning squawk of a blue jay. I soon realized that maybe my role with the local militia wasn't as important as I had hoped. After sundown, I began to wonder if I had become the butt of a joke. It felt eerily similar to the time some neighborhood boys had taken me snipe hunting and then abandoned me in the woods in the middle of the night.

I had to continually tell myself that Josiah Highsmith was a principled man and would not make a fool of me. He had said that my job was important and necessary and had warned that I might not see any action at all. However, he did tell me that he believed that the Copperheads would eventually show up when we least expected it. Because of that, I would have to stay put in the blind for a minimum of two weeks to avoid discovery.

The first night seemed to last forever. I soon learned that my tattered wool blanket and threadbare linsey jacket were not enough protection against the biting chill of the

November air. I wrapped myself into a ball and rocked back and forth like an old man with the palsy. Since eating seemed to help, I finished two days worth of corn dodgers before dawn. I tried to ignore the aches in my muscles as the temperature dropped, but it took all of my strength to keep from whimpering like a baby. Thoughts of running back to our farm for more blankets and a heavier coat began to consume me, but the fear of letting the others down kept me hunkered down. Someone was supposed to come by with supplies and check on me at midmorning. I decided I could wait and ask for more blankets at that time. Sometime shortly before dawn, I managed to finally fall asleep.

I almost jumped out of my skin when I heard someone whisper my name. "Are you in there, Will?" It was a girl's voice. I rubbed the sleep out of my eyes and looked out my peep hole. All I could see were two scrawny legs in home-made potato sack moccasins. "Let me in, Will!" she demanded. I moved the grass-covered hatch out of the way and Lizzy Maxwell pounced into the blind with the quickness of a wildcat. "I didn't think the lookout was supposed to sleep on duty," she laughed.

"What are you doing here?" I asked. "I thought that—"

"Thought that they would send somebody else?" she interrupted.

"Well—now that you mention it—I was expectin' Josiah Highsmith."

"Sorry to be a disappointment, but it'll be me who will be checkin' up on you. Josiah Highsmith is stayin' close to the cornfield. Most of the men think that's where the Copperheads will hit next. Besides, nobody's gonna pay attention to a girl pickin up nuts and acorns in the woods." She opened up a burlap bag and handed me some corn dodgers, a piece of salt pork and a half loaf of bread wrapped in a tattered piece of cloth. "It ain't much. But it'll have to hold you over until I come back tomorrow morning."

"I don't know if I'll last til morning. I nearly froze to death last night. I can't even feel my fingers."

"Well you are a bit on the blue side," she admitted as she wrapped her hands around mine to warm them. "See if this helps."

It did, but I began to grow uncomfortable as we huddled together in such a small area. Lizzy was a year older than me and I had always considered her a tomboy. She had several older brothers and played tag with the boys instead of *Ring around the Rosie* with the girls. I had been around her in school and in church for years and never gave her a second thought. However, as she tenderly rubbed the feeling back into my fingers, I became aware that she was indeed—all girl. She wasn't beautiful like Cliffy, but she wasn't homely either. "Th-th-thanks," I stammered. Her warm hands made me realize just how cold I actually was. After a few minutes, I closed my eyes and began to relax. I sighed and before I knew it, I had fallen asleep.

I didn't know how much time had passed when she jostled me awake. "Wake up, Will. I got to get goin' or they is gonna think something happened to me."

"How long was I asleep?" I was groggy and my head felt like an anvil had landed on it.

"Not that long," she answered. "Besides, you looked like you needed it. Oh—I almost forgot. Do you have anything to report?"

"Not a thing," I replied. "Not a darn thing."

"Try to stay warm and I'll see you in the morning." She peeked outside to make sure we were alone and then disappeared into the daylight. I looked through the opening and watched her as she scampered away with the grace of a young doe. I looked forward to her return.

The second day was just as boring as the first. I'd been so anxious to get into the war and fight the Copperheads that I said I was willing to do anything for the cause. Hiding out in a groundhog hole wasn't exactly what I had in mind. The minutes seemed to pass like hours as the temperature dropped and the chill of the ground sapped my strength. I was miserable. I tried to think about happier times to keep my mind from fretting about the chill in my bones. My life had changed so much since the first shots were fired at Fort Sumner that it seemed like I had become somebody else. Granny and Pappy arrived and Pa left. Ma went crazy and died and Ned moved in while Jaybird and Bub went to live with Ned's folks in Marshall. Pappy's heart nearly gave out during the raid and he was still too feeble to do much around the cabin. Jaybird and Bub came back, but Ned decided to stay. Not that he had any choice in the matter. Sister Rose was attached to him like a fat tick on a hound dog. Ned asked Granny for permission to marry Rose. Granny said she had no objections as long as they waited until the summer when she turned sixteen. Rose was again hired to teach another term of winter school and was in the process of preparing her lessons. Overnight Rose had become an adult. She was always what folks called an *"old soul"* and was wise beyond her years, but the change in her had unnerved me a bit. We were still close, but now Ned was the most important person in her life instead of me. I suppose I was a little jealous, even though Ned seemed to be a great fellow. It was hard to explain, but I guess I just felt sorry for myself. I realized I had responsibilities at the farm and did my best to fulfill my obligations, but I felt like I just didn't fit in anywhere. I was growing more frustrated and mad as the days passed. I had hoped that fighting back against the Copperheads would help, but freezing to death in silence on the frosty November ground wasn't what I had in mind. I daydreamed about Cliffy, but that brought no relief either. The thought of that circus ape, Sam Murphy, and his dirty hands all over her, was more than I could bear. Deep in my heart, I knew that I was too young for her, but that didn't matter. I was convinced that I would love her until the day I died.

The sun was starting to set and the temperature would be dropping even lower. I wanted to go home. I wanted to jump between the covers in my own bed and sleep for days. I couldn't stand the thought of another night alone. The only thing I dreaded more than the cold was the thought of being ridiculed by the men of the local militia. As much as I wanted to—I couldn't leave my post. I would have to hold out until Lizzy Maxwell came with a blanket in the morning.

After sunset, I decided to take a chance and slip out of my hiding place and stretch my legs. I had been told not to leave the den under any circumstances, but the thought of making a privy inside the blind made my stomach spin. Besides—after a day and a half of solitude, I had come to the conclusion that it was unlikely I would ever have any visitors at all.

After taking care of my necessary business, I hiked down to a creek and found a long-needled pine tree and cut away an armful of the lower branches. After shaping them into a bundle, I hauled them back to my blind and forced them through the small opening. The task was made more difficult as my joints struggled to thaw out from the chill. I began running in place and after a couple of minutes my muscles began to loosen at the exact time I started to run out of breath. "What a miserable predicament," I muttered. I determined that two more trips would be necessary to gather the raw material needed to fashion a proper conifer mattress. Not that I had ever made an evergreen mattress before—I hadn't. I hoped that the feathery bulk of the pine garland would provide some insulation. The cold damp ground was sapping the life out of me. I didn't know if it would work or not, but at least it was something to keep my mind busy instead of constantly fretting about my circumstances.

After stuffing the last of the pine into my hideout, I decided to survey the area. I followed a deer path to the top of the hill and quieted my breathing and listened for any signs of company coming. Nothing. Absolutely nothing. Chills ran down my spine. It was so quiet, I suddenly felt as if I were the only person left in the world. I was alone and vulnerable. I was stirred from my daydreaming when I heard a nearby wolf howl into the night. I ran back to my hiding place and dove through the door on the dead run. *Some brave soldier,* I thought. Maybe Granny was right. Maybe I was too young to be out here on my own. I wanted to prove everybody wrong, but I was beginning to question my resolve.

I fashioned the pine boughs into a nest, rolled myself into a ball and wrapped my measly blanket around me. For now—I would stay.

My mattress seemed to help for a while, but then the temperature began to drop and I found myself worse off than before. I could feel my fingers and toes beginning to grow numb and the minutes began to pass like hours. I felt like crying, but I didn't have the energy. I had no choice, but to suffer through. I found myself quietly moaning as the chill reached down into my bones. I was in agony. I thought about packing up and heading for home, but I was afraid I wouldn't make it. I decided that my best chance was to hunker down and wait for morning. Mercifully, somewhere around midnight—I drifted off to sleep.

"Wake up, Will! Please wake up!"

I could hear the familiar voice pleading with me and felt the hand slapping my face, but couldn't force myself to open my eyes. I didn't want to wake up. I felt like I could sleep forever.

"Can ya hear me, Will Farmer?" Lizzy Maxwell cried. "You have to wake up, now!"

When she hit me hard enough to kill a tomcat, I was jarred back into the world of the living. "Ouch! What are you doing?" My teeth started chattering and I began shaking uncontrollably.

"You're chilled to the bone!" she cried.

She pulled her body close and wrapped her arms around me while simultaneously covering us in a heavy patchwork quilt. "I knew I should have come in the middle of the night. It got so cold—our pond froze solid overnight! Ma said you'd be fine and I believed her."

"I'm okay," I muttered. "You don't have to—"

"Be still," she ordered.

I was too weak to argue.

As I watched her rub my hands between hers, I realized I couldn't feel a thing. "I can't feel my fingers, Lizzy."

She sighed. "We need to get your blood flowing." I could feel her fidgeting beneath the blanket and before I realized what was happening, she grabbed my hands and held them tightly against the bare skin of her stomach.

I started to pull away, but she wouldn't let me. "What are you doing?"

"T'ain't no time to be shy," she whispered as she tightly wrapped her arms around me. "Gangrene will set in if we don't hurry."

Gangrene was a frightening word. I didn't know exactly what it was, but I knew if you got it, there was a good chance you were going to lose an arm or a leg. Even so—I was taken aback by Lizzy's brassy behavior. But despite my boyish embarrassment, within minutes I began to regain some feeling in my fingertips. Unfortunately, what I did feel was comparable to a thousand angry bumblebee stings.

I buried my head against the warmth of her bosom and tried my best not to cry out. Any other time, I would have been horrified for a girl to see me so helpless and acting in such a sissified manner, but she seemed to know what she was doing. I tried not to think about the compromising situation in which I found myself and let her tend to my chill.

We remained silent and still for quite some time. I began to listen intently to the sound of her heartbeat as we clung together in that tiny grass hut. Soon my inhibition disappeared, and I found myself longing for her touch.

It wasn't the same way that I often thought about Cliffy. Lizzy made me feel safe in the same manner that Ma used to when I was younger. I had spent the past year and half trying to prove that I was a man, but at that moment, I wanted to be a boy. Sister Rose had filled in the best that she could, but once Ned showed up, things hadn't been the same. I was willing to stay in that moment in time and pretend that my world hadn't gone to the devil over the past two years. Lizzy seemed to notice and held me even tighter. Because of her kindness, I could no longer contain myself and began to sob.

Once I warmed up and was able to compose myself, Lizzy and I began to talk. The reality of the war had affected her life as much as it had mine. Much of the work around her family's farm had fallen to her when three of her older brothers enlisted in the Union army. She had performed whatever task that was asked of her, whether it be working in the barn or toiling in the field. After the harvest, she pleaded with her family to let her get involved with the local war effort. It was unthinkable to allow a thirteen year old girl to take up arms with the militia, but with perseverance, she managed to talk Josiah Highsmith into allowing her to act as a messenger. He said that a girl would be able to move about the neighborhood without suspicion, even if the Copperheads were watching. "T'ain't nothing happened yet," she complained. "I most surely have walked a hundred miles, just to let folks know that nobody's seen nothin'. It's too darned cold for them Johnny Rebs to make mischief."

I agreed with her on that point. I still couldn't feel my toes, but her company had eased my nerves to a tolerable state. "Did the militia spend the whole night in the field?"

"Shucks, no! Those blue-bellies got out of the cold and ske-daddled home around midnight."

"And left me all alone to freeze?" I asked.

"I guess they figured you was tough enough to take it," Lizzy said as she placed my right hand between hers and rubbed hard enough to start an Indian fire. "I was plenty worried about you, Will."

"At least somebody was," I complained. "I wonder why they didn't relieve me." I felt abandoned. I had suffered through the night for nothing.

"I suppose they plum forgot. Most men ain't all that smart, you know. Sometimes I swear they don't have enough sense to quit milkin' a steer. Now, be still before you get frostbite!"

My hands began to warm again as she continued to rub them. "Where did you learn about doctoring?" I asked.

"I've been ridin with Doc Judd when he makes his rounds thru the neighborhood." She said that Reverend Parker thought it would be better for the doctor from Ohio to travel with a local girl; not only to comfort the folks of South Union, but also for Judd's safety. There were reports of the Copperheads kidnapping doctors to tend to their wounded. Judd said it wasn't necessary, but conceded at the preacher's insistence. "Doc Judd's been teachin' me to be a nurse. As soon as I turn fifteen and if the war ain't over, I'm fixin' to join the army as a regiment nurse. Doc says I take to nursin' kinda natural; like a fish to water."

"They don't let girls go off to war!" I sniped.

"They're takin' all the nurses they can get and there ain't nobody gonna stop me. I can't put it into words, but I feel that God has put me on Earth to help others. Besides all my brothers have gone off to fight the Secesh. I need to do my duty too."

I couldn't argue with her. A doctor couldn't have given any better care than Lizzy did that morning. "I 'spect I'll enlist next year as a drummer boy. It's not the same as soldier'n, but it's better than sittin' back here—not knowin' what happened to…" I stopped myself before finishing the sentence.

Lizzy sensed my pain and wrapped her arms around me again. After a few moments, she broke the strained silence. "Have you heard anything from your pa at all?"

"Not a word," I whispered. "Everybody says Pa is dead, but I know he's not and so does Granny. She says a mother can tell when her children pass on and says she can still feel his spirit. I know what she means. When Ma died, it was like part of me died with her. It's not like that when I think about Pa. It's like I can feel him trying to get home. So, as far as I'm concerned—he is alive and nobody is going to tell me anything different."

"Does anybody have any idea where he might be?"

I paused before answering. I knew I wasn't supposed to say anything, but I was busting on the inside. I wanted to talk about Pa. After the events of that morning, I decided I could take Lizzy Maxwell into my confidence. I sighed and then closed my eyes. "Ned said that Pa went behind enemy lines after Shiloh and said that we might not hear from him for a spell."

"What do you mean when you say 'he went behind enemy lines'?"

"I think he's pretending to be a Johnny Reb. I think Pa is a spy."

"A spy? Lord Almighty!"

"Shhh!" I scolded her. "You can't tell a single soul! If one of the Copperheads found out, they could send word and it could cost him his life."

"I hear they hang spies on sight. How could they send a man with a family, or…"

"Or how could a man with a family agree to go?" I finished her sentence. "I've asked myself the same thing a hundred times. How could he go and leave us to fend for ourselves?" I could feel the anger rising up in me. I got mad every time I thought about it and then after a while I would begin to feel guilty for being selfish.

"I'm sure he had his reasons, Will," she consoled. "Your father is an honorable man,"

"I reckon he agreed to the suicide mission in the name of honor. Damn the consequences!"

"Shame on you!" She scolded me and slapped my hand. "You need to repent for thinkin' such a thing. A soldier has to follow orders, whether he likes them or not."

"But how could he leave his family? He knew Ma was in a bad way and he went anyway. I've worked like a dog since the day he left and it still isn't enough! How could he do that to me?" I couldn't believe that I was saying these things to Lizzy. My father was my hero. There wasn't a dishonorable bone in his body. It was like words were coming out from somewhere deep inside of me. I was confused and immediately ashamed of myself.

"Do you think that you are the only person suffering on account of this war? My ma has blisters on her knees from prayin' night and day for my brothers. Archie, Joe and Bill are somewhere down in Tennessee. We haven't heard a word from any of them in weeks. Everybody thought the war wouldn't last ninety days. Now it looks like it'll go on forever. Ma says she dreams about three caskets bein' lowered into the ground."

"Who is in the caskets?" I asked.

"She doesn't know, but fears it is her children. Sacrifices for the sin of slavery, she says. It's God's punishment on this country."

"That's what Pa said before he left. He said that the war was God's retribution. Funny thing though—before the war started, he never spoke a word about slavery. I don't know what changed him."

"*Uncle Tom's Cabin*," she replied. "It was probably Mrs. Stowe's novel. Pa bought a dozen copies to pass around the neighborhood. I know it to be a fact that he gave one to your father shortly after the Rebs fired on Fort Sumter."

"Pa was always reading something, but he never said anything about it. What does the book say?" I asked.

"Can't really say for sure," she replied. "I ain't read it for myself. Sister Sarah used to read it aloud when we went to bed at night." Lizzy's older sister, Sarah Maxwell, died in the summer of 1860 when an outbreak of Yellow Fever came through the neighborhood. "But what I do remember is that it was a sad story about Southerners mistreatin' their slaves. A negra woman escaped to Canada with her boy and an old slave by the name of Tom got sold downriver and made friends with a white girl. That's when Sarah got sick, so I don't rightly know how it ended. Pa said that it showed that a person just couldn't call themselves a Christian if they kept slaves. I keep tellin myself that I need to finish the book to see how it ends. I just can't understand…"

"Shhh," I whispered and cupped my hand over her mouth. "Somebody's coming."

Lizzy nodded. I slowly pulled my hand away and rolled my body toward the opening of the blind. I fiddled with the grass and sticks to make sure the door was well camouflaged and then eased myself toward the peep hole. She pulled herself tight against me and buried her face against the back of my neck. I could feel her heart beat a tattoo and her breathing quickened as the heavy footsteps grew near. At first, all I could see was an oversized pair of buckskin moccasins, but when he stepped into the opening by the spring and I saw the eye patch, I felt my heart step in time with Lizzy's. It was One Eye Skaggs!

Folks said that Kenneth Ray Skaggs was born mean as a snake to begin with, but his daddy, Lyman Skaggs, wasn't satisfied with that. He hit him upside of his head with a hickory stick for even the most insignificant of infractions and whipped him with a buggy whip if he cried after the discipline. When Skaggs reached the age of fourteen, he told his father that he wasn't going to take any more of his beatings. Lyman took exception to the insolence and grabbed a piece of barn wood with the intention of teaching his son a lesson he would never forget. The elder Skaggs slammed the board squarely in the middle of Kenneth's face. The rotted beam shattered into a thousand shards and the boy fell hard to the ground. One of the splinters speared directly through his closed eyelid causing a permanent blindness in his right side. As a tribute to his father's cruel discipline, young Kenneth refused to cry. He picked himself up, walked into the barn and with the business end of a pitchfork, sent Lyman into eternity.

Because of the abuse to which the boy had been subjected, the local authorities ruled that he had acted in self-defense. With his father gone, One Eye Skaggs began what was, up until that point, a twenty year reign of terror in the lower Embarrass Valley. He started with horse stealing and worked his way up to kidnapping, armed robbery and if the rumors were true—even murder. The outbreak of the war had given him a chance to continue his criminal endeavors under the banner of fighting for the southern cause. He had been credited with burning over a dozen farms in the area and stealing hundreds of horses to be sent south to the rebels. He claimed that he was commissioned as a Captain in the Confederate Army by Jefferson Davis, himself. I don't know if anyone believed his claim, but nobody was going to deny the terror his band of guerillas had brought to Southeastern Illinois.

Josiah Highsmith had sent me to be a lookout at Flat Rock because he figured there wouldn't be much of a chance for me to see any action at such a remote location. He had allowed a thirteen year old girl to be the messenger for the same reason. Despite Highsmith's best efforts to keep us out of harm's way, Lizzy and I found ourselves alone with the cutthroat leader of the Copperheads.

—◊◊—

Chapter 21

One Eye Skaggs silently squatted and warmed his hands over a small fire as the afternoon began to fade away. Two men with southern accents had appeared on horseback a few minutes after the burly outlaw. They spent most of the afternoon smoking dreadful smelling cigars while admiring Skaggs's new LeMat revolver "I heard about these *Grapeshot Revolvers*," said the taller of the two newcomers. "I was under the assumption that they was made for Confederate Officers. How did you happen to come by yours?"

Skaggs spewed a wad of tobacco into the fire and then wiped the remains from his bushy beard with the sleeve of his shirt. "I took it from a dead peacock major down in Tennessee." He grinned broadly, exposing the gap in the middle of his teeth. "He thought he could deal from the bottom of the deck and I wouldn't notice." His sadistic laugh sounded as if it were coming from a demon.

Lizzy punched me in the back after hearing his boast. "Did you hear that?" she whispered. "If he doesn't think twice about killing his own kind—what do ya think he'll do to us?"

"Shhh!" I pushed my finger against her lips. "We'll be fine as long as you keep quiet!" she nodded and then pressed herself tightly against my back once again. We had been trapped in our hideout for hours while the three men waited only a few footsteps away. The blind had worked as intended, but was too far away for me to hear about half of their conversations. As far as I could tell, they hadn't said anything that revealed what they were up to.

A few minutes later, a fourth man appeared from the south, leading his roan gelding down the deer path. "It's about damn time you showed up," One Eye roared, "Another fifteen minutes and we was gonna leave without you."

"Good thing you didn't," replied the newcomer. "My boy heard somebody braggin' that they was gonna ambush some Copperheads in a cornfield west of Honey Creek. That got me to thinkin'. Why would anybody leave a patch of good field corn standin' when we've been burnin' farms, right and left? That corn should have been harvested three weeks ago."

"So you think these nigger lovers have set a trap for us?" asked One Eye.

"I know so for a fact," he answered. "I crawled up a hill on the backside of the farm and saw a dozen men on horseback hidin' in the cattails above the creek bed and another dozen hidin' in the fence row to the west. Everyone of em has a musket or squirrel rifle of some sort. Looks like they're trying to draw us in and then catch us in some sort of crossfire."

I could feel Lizzy's fingernails dig into my back. I turned around and nodded that I heard what was said. The newcomer's voice sounded familiar, but I couldn't quite place it. I inched myself closer to the peephole and tried to get a better look at him. I recognized him immediately. It was Virgil Stubbs! The Stubbs Family hadn't been back to church since that Sunday when Virgil and his overgrown son, Burl, tried to pound me in the ground. There were rumors that Stubbs had been involved with some Copperhead raiding parties down by Port Jackson. Apparently those rumors were true. Things couldn't get any worse.

"No good double-crossin' abolitionists!" growled One Eye. "Try to put a bullet in me— will they?"

"So Captain—are we gonna give 'em a little of their own medicine and take 'em from behind?" asked one of the men.

"No, you idiot!" One Eye replied. "The fact that they've gone to the trouble of settin' a trap in that cornfield, means that they probably got some surprises in store for us. But this does give us an advantage in another way."

"What do you mean?" asked the man with the LeMat.

"Since all of the able-bodied men are in that cornfield, it means that we can do as we please somewhere else." He smiled and clapped his hands. "Hey Stubbs," he yelled at the newcomer, "anything worth burnin' to the north of here?"

"Nothin' but a few small farms and the South Union Church."

"Is it a Yankee church?" One Eye asked.

"Yes indeed, Captain. It most certainly is a Yankee meetin' house."

One Eye smiled as he opened the cover to his silver pocket watch. "Alright boys—gather up your men and have them back here by two hours after sundown. Looks like there's gonna be a little fire and brimstone preached at the meetin' house tonight."

"Where are they?" asked Reverend Parker as he spied out the window of the log cabin church.

"They should be here by now," I told him, but I was starting to worry myself. One Eye Skaggs and the three other men left the Flat Rock Spring shortly after sundown. Lizzy and I left a few minutes later. Since Lizzy's farm was close to the field where the neighborhood men were gathered, I sent her to warn them. I made the two mile trip to the Reverend Parker's house on the dead run in a matter of minutes. The preacher had just sat down to supper with Dr. Judd and the Widow Rush when I banged on their door. By the way they were looking; I realized that I must have been quite a sight. I was winded, half frozen and had spent the last two days in an oversized groundhog den. After repeating my story for a second time, Reverend Parker grabbed his shotgun from the mounts above the fireplace and handed it to Doctor Judd. He grabbed an oversized revolver and a bag of lead for himself. He asked if I had a weapon with me. When I said no, he ordered me to go home, before the trouble started.

"With all due respect, Reverend, I'm not going anywhere, "I declared. "I'm not a kid anymore. I've spent the last two days freezing my—well, what I mean is—I was out in the cold all night while the other men went home to their own beds and I'm the one who heard what was said and…"

"Confound it!" interrupted Reverend Parker. "I'm not challenging your right to be here, Will, but what good are you if you aren't armed?"

"I can hide out in the bushes and act as a look out, or I can climb up on the roof with a club or some rocks…"

"That is enough! I don't have time to argue." Reverend Parker turned to the old woman at the table. "Mrs. Rush, do you still have any of your husband's old rifles?"

The silver-haired widow rolled her eyes and scratched the wart on her chin. "I have a flintlock long rifle. I think there is still some powder in the horn and some lead balls in the dresser."

"Good. Take young Mister Farmer with you and see that he is provisioned. I want you to lock your doors and find a safe place and stay there until I come get you." She nodded, clutched my hand with her bony fingers and started for the door.

Reverend Parker cast his eyes back in my direction. "Don't tarry, Will. I want you inside the church with us as soon as you have the musket."

It had been over an hour since I arrived at the church with the late Ezra Rush's oversized musket and we still hadn't heard a sound outside. I primed and loaded the squirrel shooter with buckshot and powder. Since the rifle was longer than I was tall, I knew it would be hard to take a clean shot. By using shot instead of a ball, I figured I had a better chance to actually hit something.

"Are you sure they said they were coming tonight?" asked Doctor Judd.

"They were going to meet two hours after sundown and then head this way," I answered. I doubted that I would be questioned so much if was older. "I'm sure of it, Doctor."

"Why aren't they here yet?" complained Reverend Parker. "What if the Maxwell girl didn't get through?" He paused and then his eyes opened wide. "What if they don't believe her? We're sitting ducks in here."

"I'm sure she made it," I assured him. "Lizzy knows the woods around Flat Rock Spring as well as anybody. As far as believing her, Josiah Highsmith knows Lizzy wouldn't lie."

"What if the Copperheads get here first?" Doctor Judd asked frantically. "The men are on horseback. They've had plenty of time to cover the distance. Something must have gone wrong."

I shrugged my shoulders. I didn't have an answer for him.

"Maybe we should negotiate with them," Judd suggested. "After all, this is a house of worship. Surely these Copperheads have some measure of Christian decency."

"I don't think we can count on it with this bunch," warned Reverend Parker. "One Eye Skaggs may have acquired the title of Captain, but he isn't anything but a scoundrel and horse thief."

"Lord help us!" Beads of perspiration appeared on the crown of the bald doctor's head. He cleaned his spectacles and then wiped his brow with a red and white checkered handkerchief. "What about the other man? What did you say his name was? Vernon…"

"Virgil Stubbs," Reverend Parker corrected him.

"You said this Virgil Stubbs used to be a member of your congregation. Surely he could be reasoned with," Judd pleaded.

"Ha!" I almost choked while trying to swallow my laugh.

"This is no laughing matter, Will," scolded the doctor. "Somebody could get hurt or even killed."

"The boy wasn't trying to be fresh," Reverend Parker jumped in to defend me before I could apologize. "To make a long story short, let us say that the Stubbs family didn't leave our church on the best of terms. You might even go so far as to say that Virgil Stubbs holds a grudge against both Will and I."

A single shot from the darkness shattered the glass window on the far side of the church and then ricocheted between the windows. "Get away from the windows!" cried Reverend Parker as he began to overturn furniture.

Judd and I joined him and within seconds, we had built a small barricaded fort in the middle of the sanctuary. There was an ear splitting *Rebel Yell* from the south followed by another volley of gunfire. Two or three shots plinked against the log exterior of the church, but most of the gunfire seemed to be pointed in another direction.

"They're shooting at each other!" explained Reverend Parker.

"I told you Lizzy would get through!" I bragged. "They must have been waiting outside to bushwhack them." I decided to keep my head down when a second bullet crashed through the window.

The battle raged for several minutes and seemed to be moving away from the church. Reverend Parker and Dr Judd cautiously made their way to the window to get a better look. I was worried about another stray bullet and decided to stay put, but after a couple of minutes, I worked up enough nerve to get a look-see for myself. Instead of joining them at the window, I headed toward the door. Just as I grabbed the latch handle and stated to peek outside, the door boomed open sending me to the puncheon floor on my backside. It took me a second to gather my wits and then realized I was in trouble. One Eye Skaggs was standing in the doorway with a hickory torch in one hand and his Johnny Reb pistol in the other. From the look on his face, he was surprised to see me too. Apparently he wasn't expecting to see a boy. He quickly got over it and pointed the pistol at my forehead and pulled the trigger. *Click!* The gun was jammed.

"Damn it!" Skaggs bellowed and started to work on his gun.

I wasn't going to wait around for him to fix it, so I sat up straight pointed the squirrel shooter in One Eye's direction and pulled the trigger. There was a quick flash followed by a boom that sounded more like a small cannon than a rifle. The kick-back sent me tumbling back several feet and once again I was looking at the rafters. Not being familiar with the old weapon, I had guessed about the amount of black powder to use with the shot. Not wanting to error on the side of using too little, I decided to go in the opposite direction. The discharge immediately filled the church with plumes of blue smoke and the eye-watering tang of sulphur.

As the smoke began to clear, I saw One Eyes Skaggs rolling on the ground just beyond the threshold. His hat was on the ground ten feet behind him, His face was covered with tiny pools of red. The hair on the left side of his head was drenched in blood. He explored that area and let loose with a scream that made him sound like a wounded bear. "You shot my ear off! I'm gonna kill you, you little bastard!"

As he struggled to get to his feet, I figured I had better act while I still had the advantage. I didn't have time to reload, so I decided to use the old rifle as a club. I took him by surprise and landed a blow against the side of his neck, sending him back to the ground. Unfortunately, he blocked the second blow with his hand and refused to let go. We played tug of war for a few seconds, but when Skaggs saw Reverend Parker and Dr. Judd coming with their guns, he let loose and limped away into the night.

"Shoot him!" I yelled. "He's getting away." But neither the preacher, nor the doctor was prepared to shoot a man in the back; even if it was One Eye Skaggs.

"I'm a-gonna kill you boy!"Skaggs shouted from somewhere in the darkness. "I'll spit in your grave; if'n it's the last thing I do!"

Lizzy did indeed get the message to Josiah Highsmith in a timely manner. Highsmith decided to ambush the Copperheads before they got to the church instead of defending it from the inside. Since the home guard thwarted Skaggs's mob while suffering only a couple of minor injuries in the process, it seemed to be the correct decision. Highsmith said, in retrospect, he should have made sure the church was empty before the commencement of hostilities. As it turned out, Reverend Parker, Dr. Judd and I acted as bait to the trap. Skaggs apparently had sent a scout to watch the church before the gang arrived. When the scout reported that the church's only defense was two old men and a young boy with hunting rifles, Skaggs got careless. Instead of surveying the surrounding area, he assumed they could take the church without any meaningful resistance. The Copperheads all stood in the front yard of the church, exposing themselves to Highsmith's militia. Highsmith's men opened up on the rebels as soon as they fired the first shot at the church. Two Copperheads from Lawrence County were killed outright and four of their wounded men were captured while the rest of their gang high-tailed it south without them.

Among those that got away was One Eye Skaggs, minus his left ear. However, Skaggs's misfiring LeMat combination ball and grapeshot revolver did not go with him. During all of the confusion of our confrontation, Skaggs had dropped his prize weapon. Despite the protests of Reverend Parker, I claimed the prize sidearm as my first trophy of battle.

I took a lot of good natured ribbing from the men in the neighborhood, but I felt like I had earned their respect. Once you've actually been under fire, or see the elephant for the first time as the soldiers say, people look at you differently. From that day forward I went from Will Farmer to the Yankee boy who turned One Eye Skaggs into One Ear Skaggs.

—◊◊◊—

Chapter 22

An early December blizzard covered the ground with two feet of snow and managed to quiet all hostilities in the neighborhood. Granny said it was on account of that God decided to give us a reprieve from bloodshed at Christmas time. I don't know if what she said was true, but the wind and snow had the desired effect. It took most of each sun-shortened day for me to care for the livestock and split enough wood to keep the cabin warm. It was hard work, but I didn't mind. The drifting snow that made even the simplest chore difficult, also offered us a measure of protection. Since the roads were impassable, for the first time in months, we could breathe a sigh of relief in knowing that we were safe from Copperhead retribution. Apparently the Rebs needed the rest as much as we did.

About a week before Christmas, on Granny's orders, I harvested a seven foot tall pine tree from a thicket down by the creek and hauled it back to the cabin shortly before sunset. Rose and Ned along with Jaybird and Bub garnished the tree with pine cones and popcorn while Granny warmed apple cider in a kettle over some coals in the fireplace. Pappy did his best to knock out a Christmas Hymn on his harmonica. None of us cared when he hit a flat note. It was good to see him smile again. Our store-bought ornaments were destroyed in the fire last summer, so to me the tree seemed a little sad. Rose did her best to make things festive by crafting *hand-made* replacements, but as hard as I tried, I just couldn't get into the Christmas spirit. I couldn't help but think about Ma and Pa being gone. I just didn't feel I had the right to be happy. Ma was gone and I grieved for her; especially for the way she was before she took ill. But she was dead and buried. I could visit her grave whenever I wanted. But it was different with Pa. Folks were beginning to say that he was surely dead. "You'd have heard something by now if he was still alive," or "Lord knows what ditch in Dixie he's laying in." Even the most optimistic of our friends figured he was captured and being held in a rebel camp. Prison was better than dead, but there was news trickling northward about the hellish conditions at a place called Andersonville in Georgia. There were stories of unspeakable cruelty and torture, along with disease and famine. It all sounded to be a fate worse than death itself. Either situation was unthinkable for me. How could I join in the games and act as if nothing was wrong? I realized that a sour disposition didn't help the situation any, but I owed it to Pa to remain miserable.

Despite my lack of participation Sister Rose was determined to make a merry Christmas at the cabin. She sang carols and played games with the younger boys until they couldn't keep their eyelids open. She had been secretly making gifts for the past several weeks, so there were plenty of presents for everyone under the tree. Since the arrival of Ned Thompson, Rose had changed from a shy backward girl to a lively young woman who kept the household running. Granny still ruled the roost, but it was obvious that the day would soon come when Sister Rose would be in charge. I didn't think Granny would mind all that much. She still had the constitution of a mother bear, but the stress and strain of the past two years had taken its toll on her. Her face had aged ten years since the beginning of the war and she seemed to run out of pepper before the end of the day.

Rose picked up the slack by taking on more of the day to day chores around the cabin. At first Granny resisted. She didn't want to give up her seat on the throne, but as time went by, she began to welcome Rose's help.

Pappy kept a cheerful outlook on everything, despite the fact he had just started to recover from the heart attack he had during the summer. Doctor Judd said that his recovery would be slow and he might never come all the way back to where he was before. Pappy still managed to keep a smile on his face anyway. He was just beginning to speak clearly again, which allowed him to tell his stories to Jaybird and Bub. He told them about the olden days in *Ol' Kain-tuck* for hours at a time. Whether he was fightin' Injuns or killin' panthers; they hung on his every word. They were spellbound and Rose and Granny appreciated the help.

Ned was rapidly regaining his strength each day. He had to learn how to do things with only one arm, but even with his handicap, he could work circles around most men. He had gone to Marshall to visit his folks in November, but now was back for good. For the time being, he was sleeping with me in the loft. He spent most days cutting lumber in the barn for a room addition he intended to build once the weather broke this spring. He planned on having the room finished for their wedding day on the fourth of July. Ned's folks offered to help them buy some land for a house of their own, but he and Rose wanted to stay with us to help with my brothers. Granny assured them that she could handle everything and that young people should go out on their own, but seemed relieved when they declined her offer.

Ned also served to keep me humble. One day after church, I was showing off One Eye Skaggs's LeMat and started bragging how I'd seen the Elephant. Once a soldier had seen battle for the first time, it was said that he had seen the elephant. It was a rite of passage into the brotherhood of soldiers. I was in the middle of my story when Ned walked up and interrupted me. "Will, you make war sound like some sort of game. I'm here to tell you that it ain't no game at all. I ain't taking away the fact that you have been under fire and that you acted brave with Skaggs and all, but you haven't seen the elephant yet and I pray to God that you never do. You were in a skirmish alright, but you haven't seen the destruction of a battle." Everyone's eyes turned to Ned. He placed his hand on the stub where his left arm used to be. His eyes rolled and then focused on the rafters of the church. For the first time since I'd met him, Ned began to describe what he'd witnessed at Fort Henry, Fort Donelson and finally at Shiloh where he had lost his arm. "The noise is so loud when the cannons start, that you can't hear yourself think. Smoke is everywhere and your eyes burn from the sulphur and you can't run away. If you do, a Reb sniper will put a Minie Ball between your eyes before you take your first step. Your own sergeant will do the same if you turn and run the other way. Guts, blood and body parts are strewn across the ground, blown to pieces by cannon balls. Grown men crying for their mamas and praying for God to let them die. I swear to Heaven above that Ol' Scratch, himself must have personally invented the cannon." Ned paused and took a deep breath before continuing with the story. His eyes began to glisten and he turned away to blow his nose with a threadbare handkerchief. "Then the order comes to attack. And good soldiers always follows orders. You stand in front of the enemy, side by side in a straight line and march out into the open field. You get so close you can actually smell the stink of their butternut and gray uniforms. You take aim at a man standing in the opposite line, while watching him aim at you. That's when the shooting starts. Death comes instantly to those around you. If you're lucky enough to survive the first volley, then you have to try to reload while under fire. After the second shot, the smoke is so thick; you can't see a damn thing. At that point, the fighting is hand to hand. Rebs come at you with bayonets, knives and swords. After that, you fight with the butt of your rifle, a rock or anything else that you can get your hands on. If you're still alive at the end of the day, then you can say that you've seen the elephant."

Ned wasn't being mean spirited, although he did knock me down a peg with his recollection. It was the only time I ever heard him talk about his battlefield experience. He said it was just too painful to think about. Unfortunately, his missing left arm served as a reminder each and every day of his life. From that point on, out of respect for what Ned and Pa had endured in battle, I decided to choose my words carefully when it came to my encounter with One Eye Skaggs.

Everyone seemed to be fitting into their place—with the exception of me. Rose and Granny took care of my brothers. Ned was taking over many of the chores on the farm. I was too young to join up with the army and after the events of the last couple of years; I felt I was too old to play childish games. I figured I should be doing something to help find Pa, but everybody said there was nothing to do. Hard as I tried, I just couldn't find any joy in my life.

Uncle Woody Gogin had written several letters of inquiry to the Provost Marshall in Olney, on behalf of our family, regarding Pa's whereabouts. But every reply said the same thing; Samuel Farmer was listed as missing in action. There wasn't any information as to where he had gone or what he was doing.

Ned said that just because there wasn't any word from the war department, it didn't mean Pa wasn't alive. "Once a spy goes behind enemy lines, he's cut off from everybody until he comes back home. When the army says they don't know nothin'—it's not a lie; it just means they don't know where he is. Maybe he's just waitin' for the right time to cross back over to our side of the lines. We have to be patient and not give up hope."

I did feel he was alive, but it was frustrating as all get out not to be able to do anything about it. Regardless of my melancholy, I decided to do my best not to ruin Christmas for the others.

The longer the war went on, the harder it became to justify keeping Muddy. Although, no one ever said anything, I knew things were getting lean around the neighborhood and a hog was put onto the Earth to be used as food. We had enough food in the root cellar to make it until spring, but it was going to be close. Others in the neighborhood weren't so fortunate. People shared whatever they had to make sure nobody went hungry. Muddy represented several meals for several people. Deep in my heart, I knew I could never justify keeping a pet pig while people were suffering. I prayed it never came to that, but I was all too aware that Muddy had a dark cloud hovering over her pigpen. For most of the winter, I let Muddy loose to forage in the woods for food. She never wandered too far away and managed to keep her weight on without using the feed and grain earmarked for the other animals. In that way, she wasn't a burden. However, a heavy blanket of snow covered the ground and made foraging next to impossible. I had to do something to make sure she didn't starve. While standing on the creek bed. I broke the ice over a knee-deep pool with an axe. I then seined the creek bottom with a net made out of old seed bags. After a dozen passes, I usually managed to catch a bucket of minnows along with a few small trash fish. I mashed the fish into a pulp and then added a few harvested cornstalks, until the silage was covered in the fishy slop. It smelled like the devil, but Muddy seemed to favor the concoction. It was enough to sustain her until the snow melted.

It was a couple of days before Christmas and while on my daily trip to seine for fish, I decided to take a short cut by walking on the frozen creek instead of following the trail. I had almost reached my fishing spot, when I heard a loud crack and a pop. Before I could react, the ice gave way beneath my feet and I was completely submerged underwater. The immediate shock of the ice cold water was replaced by the horror of being pulled downstream by the force of an undertow.

I tried everything to escape, but was helpless. It felt like I had been shot out of a cannon. I was going downstream at the speed of a running horse. I was spinning around and couldn't tell which end was up. I didn't know how deep the water was because I couldn't touch the ice above or the creek bottom below. I was completely helpless to do anything. It had all happened so quickly, that I didn't have time to take much of a breath before going into the water. I was running out of air. I was certain I was going to drown. I fought the urge to exhale as long as I could, but then my body betrayed me. Just as freezing cold water began to pour into my lungs,

I was released from the undertow and I found myself wedged between a frozen sand bar and a sheet of ice. I got to my knees and pushed upward with my back. I didn't have much strength left. I was ready to give up when I felt the ice give a little. Desperately, I hunkered down as low as I could get and pushed up with everything I had left.

The ice snapped and then broke apart, allowing me to shoot up into the daylight. Water exploded out of my mouth and nostrils and I gulped air into my burning lungs. I reached for a low hanging branch and pulled myself to the safety of shore. The undertow had taken me to my fishing spot where the ice wasn't as thick. If I would have landed anywhere else; I'd have been trapped until spring thaw. I was lucky to be alive.

I collapsed in a snow drift beside the creek and proceeded to vomit uncontrollably. Water spewed from me like a well-oiled pump. I must have swallowed gallons. When I finally stopped with the spasms, I was exhausted. My chest ached and my innards burned. After a few minutes, my mind started to calm down and I began to feel the biting cold stinging every inch of my body. I began to shiver. I knew I needed to get out of my wet clothes, but for some reason, I hesitated. *Just rest a few minutes and then head back to the cabin.* The longer I waited; the warmer I felt. The voice inside of me was screaming to get up and get going, but I wasn't listening. "*A little longer...* " I mumbled to myself.

Gradually the pain started to drift away and I began to feel sleepy. I stopped shivering and a peaceful calm came over me. *Must get up and run home. Must get up and...*

Granny poured a boiling pot of water into the tub, while Rose frantically rubbed my hand between hers.

"Keep your eyes open, Will," Ned ordered. "You've gotta stay awake." I felt a tinge of pain when he slapped my face. "Look at me, Will! You cannot go to sleep!"

My mind seemed to be lost in a fog as I tried to understand what was happening to me. I felt numb. I could see Rose patting my hand, but I couldn't feel a thing. "Can you feel this?" she asked. I shook my head, no, which induced her to rub even harder.

I had no recollection of how I had come to be in the bathtub in our cabin. The last thing I remembered was coming out of the icy creek. After a few minutes, my fingers and toes began to sting and even though I was being boiled in a big metal pot; I began to feel a chill in my bones.

"I can't take anymore," I turned my head as Granny forced the last spoonful of the chicken broth mixed with castor oil into my mouth.

"Just one more and then you can get some sleep," she promised. I agreed and three spoonfuls later she gave me my reprieve.

Rose arranged my pillows as I jumped beneath a pile of quilts and blankets. Ned and Jaybird had moved my bed next to the fireplace where an extra large log had just been added.

"You gave us quite a scare, Will," said Rose. "I don't suppose you'll be completely satisfied until you get yourself killed."

"I'm sorry, Rose. I didn't mean to fall through the ice."

"Just like you didn't mean to get in a shootout with that Skaggs fella." Her voice became agitated. "What were you doin' on the ice anyway?"

"I was going to catch some fish for Muddy. I thought it would be quicker to walk down the creek."

"You know better than to walk on ice over moving water. This family has gone through enough, without you actin' like a blasted fool. It's hard enough around here without you dancin' with the devil every chance you get. I know you're hurting on the inside, but you're not the only one. You're being selfish. All you can think about is how bad you feel. Well, how do you think we'd feel if you drowned out there, Will Farmer? Instead of building a cozy fire for you to sleep by, I'd be diggin' your grave in the frozen ground next to your mother. Don't you ever…"

Rose broke into tears before she could finish her sentence. A hush fell over the cabin. Ned walked over and tried to comfort her, but she motioned him away. She used her apron to dry her tears. After a painfully long silence, Rose kissed the back of my hand and then held it tight against her. "I'm sorry for losin' my temper, Brother Will, but I love you too much to see you leave me so soon. This family cannot survive without you. Promise me you'll be careful for my sake—if not your own."

I could feel the tears well up in my eyes. "I'm sorry, Rose. I won't…"

"Shhh!" She pressed a finger to my lips. "I don't want you're apology. I want your promise."

"I promise," I whispered.

She pulled the top blanket up to my chin and softly kissed my forehead. "Now, get some sleep."

Rose turned toward Jaybird and Bub. "Who feels like some popcorn and apple cider?"

Both brothers immediately volunteered. I rolled over and stared at the fire while Rose shooed everyone over to the kitchen table. I realized that I had cheated death that day and from now on I was on borrowed time. Rose was right. I had been feeling sorry for myself. I had been using Ma's death and Pa's absence as an excuse to be miserable. I'd been feeling left out when actually, it was me who was pushing them away. It was at that moment I realized I was where I was supposed to be; here with my family who needed me. I fought sleep as long as I could to no avail. I dozed off while listening to my family sing: *Silent Night.*

—◊◊—

Chapter 23

Lizzy was all business as she swabbed my forehead and neck with a damp towel. "You're still burning up!" she said. "Time for another dose of the tonic!"

"Not again!" I protested. "I'd rather eat a dead skunk! That stuff tastes awful."

"I'm sure it does, but you still have to take it. Now open up." Lizzy shoved the wooden spoon into my mouth as soon as I parted my lips. "Doctor Judd said we'd have to put you in another ice bath if your fever didn't break."

I gagged and tried not to vomit the elixir of dogwood bark, laudanum and whiskey as it trickled down my throat. Apparently my tumble into the creek had given me pneumonia, or lung fever as the locals called the affliction. On the first night, I felt like I was freezing to death. I lost the feeling in my fingers and toes and my bones were iced to the core. Ten blankets and a roaring fireplace didn't help at all.

The next morning the fever moved into my lungs and the opposite was true. My clothes were drenched and I felt like I was being boiled in a kettle of oil. Every joint began to ache and I found myself struggling to draw a breath. Rose sent Ned for the doctor.

Doctor Judd arrived an hour later along with Lizzy. Now that the Copperhead threat had subsided, Lizzy had gone back to studying with the doctor in hopes of becoming a nurse with an infantry unit. Judd gave me a quick look over then ordered Rose to fill the bathtub with a mixture of snow and cold well water. Once the water was roughly the same temperature as the icy creek, they dropped me into the tub; long johns and all. I shot straight up as soon as I hit the water. I tried to climb out, but a half dozen arms pushed me down until I was submerged to my chin. I didn't see how holding me down in a tub full of ice water was going to help me any, since it was ice cold water that had gotten me sick in the first place. I screamed and thrashed about in the water, but everybody seemed committed to keeping me in my place. "We got to get your fever to drop," explained the doctor. After that I didn't understand a word he said.

When I began to go numb, the doctor figured I'd had enough and gave me a reprieve. I asked Rose and Lizzy to turn away as I stripped out of my wet clothes and wrapped myself in a blanket. I jumped back into bed and pulled the mountain of covers over my head.

Doc Judd gave me two spoonfuls of his horrific tasting tonic and then listened to my heart and checked my wrist for blood flow. Doctor Judd remained at my bedside until he was satisfied my fever had dropped. He began to give Rose instructions, but Lizzy interrupted and volunteered to stay as my nurse. Rose said it wouldn't be necessary, but Lizzy insisted. Rose and Doctor Judd smiled at each other and then said it would be fine. From that moment forward, Lizzy poked and prodded me like a pin cushion and poured medicine down my throat every time I coughed or sneezed. Not that I wasn't grateful for the attention, but I couldn't help but notice that she was deriving a lot of pleasure from my suffering. No wonder she wanted to be a nurse.

Lizzy stayed with me on Christmas Eve while the rest of the family went to a special meeting at the South Union Church. Since food was scarce, everybody brought what they could, which in some cases wasn't much, but it became a feast when it all came together. The war had torn neighbors and families apart, so Reverend Parker felt that fellowship and a Christmas dinner would help to heal some of the travails that had beset so many in our neighborhood. Even during the toughest of times, people still found cause to give thanks and celebrate.

Lizzy's folks had gone to Newton to visit some relatives for the holidays and had allowed her to stay at our cabin and serve as my personal nurse. Sister Rose teased that she was my girlfriend, but I knew better. Lizzy was bound and determined to become a regiment nurse as soon as she was old enough and wasn't going to let anything or anybody get in her way. Some folks are said to have a calling for the ministry. Some are said to be born politicians, while others are born criminals. Lizzy Maxwell was destined to become a care taker. She was only truly content when nurturing or giving care to someone in need. It started when she watched her older sister, Sarah, die with yellow fever shortly before the outset of the war. Sarah writhed in pain for days, while Lizzy felt helpless to ease her agony. After her sister's passing, Lizzy swore an oath to never again sit idly by and watch another human suffer. The arrival of Doctor Judd from Ohio had given her the opportunity she needed. Judd had originally come to visit, but after seeing the need; decided to make South Union his new home. Lizzy's dedication and hunger to learn impressed him, so he agreed to apprentice her, in spite of her age. Judd went so far as to say that she was a born healer and would have made a fine physician, had she not been a member of the fairer sex. If it weren't for my fever and shortness of breath, she made having pneumonia a rather tolerable proposition.

Rose had left some chicken and dumplings along with a corn pone on the stove for us to eat along with candied sweet potatoes and a cherry pie. Unfortunately, Doctor Judd had left orders for me to eat nothing but broth until he returned on the next day. I begged and pleaded for a reprieve, but Lizzy stood firm; nothing but chicken broth and hot tea and apple cider. Out of compassion, Lizzy ate the same fare as me.

Once things quieted down, Lizzy unfolded the latest edition of the *Vincennes Sun* and began reading the news from the war. "It says here that Honest Abe Lincoln is gonna sign the Emancipation Proclamation on New Year's Day."

"What is the Emancifacation—" I asked.

"Emancipation Proclamation," she corrected. "It means that all the slaves in the secesh states are to be freed; Hallelujah! Lord be praised!"

"So I wonder…does that mean that the war is going to be over soon?" I pondered for a moment and then answered my own question. "I don't expect that the Rebs will be giving their niggers up without a fight."

"I spect not," Lizzy agreed. "The paper says: *the slaves from the border states of Kentucky and Missouri will not be affected by the new law in order to ensure their loyalty to the Union.* It says a peck of things I don't understand but I reckon it's all good news."

"I know slavery is wrong. Pa said no man has the right to own another man, but it seems like it is something that goes on a long way off. I just don't see why so many *Illinois Suckers* have to clean up somebody else's mess. Why did my Pa and your brothers have to go? It's not their fight."

"Slavery is more than wrong," Lizzy hissed like a cat. "It's a sin against this country and it's the duty of good Christian men to make things right. You know better than to say those things, Will."

"I guess so, but I feel so tired of everything. I'm tired of working so hard. I'm tired of looking over my shoulder to see if someone is going to kill me. I'm tired of being an orphan. I'm tired of all of the death and destruction. I'm just—tired"

Lizzy sighed and put the newspaper down at the foot of my bed. "I know you're tired and don't feel good, Will. You just need to rest up and things will start lookin' better, once you're on the mend." She went through her tattered bag and pulled out a dog-eared book with a threadbare cloth cover, stoked the fire and then positioned herself next to me on the bed. "As far as the sin of slavery goes—just lay there and listen." She opened the book to page one and began to read. *"Uncle Tom's Cabin or Life Among The Lowly,* by Harriet Beecher Stowe…"

As Lizzy read the pages, I closed my eyes and tried to imagine the slave girl, Eliza, crossing the ice-covered Ohio River to save her son from being sold down South. I wondered why Uncle Tom didn't do the same. The characters seemed to come alive with every turning page. For the first time in my life, I began to understand a little bit of what the world of a slave was like. I am ashamed to say, that I had never given the plight of the Negro much thought. I figured a slave had to work hard and couldn't do all of the things I took for granted, but I never considered the cruelty of a master selling a mama's baby right out of her arms. I thought about how much I missed Pa and how Tom's children must have felt the same. I got an uneasy feeling down in the pit of my stomach just thinking about it.

I fought to stay awake, but realized I was waging a losing battle. Lizzy agreed to resume the story tomorrow and poured some more of the putrid tonic into me. She wiped me down again and rubbed a mint and herb salve onto my chest. She tucked the quilt under my chin and kissed me softy on my forehead. "Good night, Will," she whispered and dimmed the lantern beside my bed. "Now get some sleep, I'll be in the rockin' chair watchin' over you."

I was sound asleep within minutes.

I felt a little stronger when I awakened on Christmas morning to the smell of flapjacks and maple syrup. Jaybird and Bub were sitting at the kitchen table with the business end of their forks pointed skyward, ready to attack Granny's first offerings from the griddle. Both brothers were wearing new red flannel night shirts that Ned's parents had sent from their mercantile in Marshall. Because of all of the hardships that had befallen our family, there wasn't going to be much money left for Christmas gifts. Apparently some of our friends and neighbors realized this and made sure my brothers had presents under the tree. Besides the two night shirts, Uncle Woody sent over a bag of rock candy, Reverend Parker carved a wooden top for every child in the congregation, and Doctor Judd gave a kaleidoscope to Bub and much to the mortification of my ears; a tin whistle to Jaybird. Granny knitted everyone a new pair of socks and Rose fitted us in Linsey-woolsey shirts.

When Rose learned that Lizzy would be spending the holidays, she frantically made her a shoulder bag out of some leftover material. She adorned it with a red needlework cross to identify it as a nurse's bag. Lizzy beamed with pride at being recognized as a nurse. She rushed over to show me, and adjusted my pillows so that I could sit up in bed and watch the festivities.

Granny served breakfast while Ned carefully positioned the Yule log in the fireplace. Granny passed out the hotcakes while Rose poured cider from a jug. Lizzy force fed me half of a pancake and nagged me to finish a mug of thick herb tea. I was beginning to feel better, but a trip to the outhouse was about all I could take. I was out of breath when I returned to my bed, which dictated another dose of salve on my chest and back. I became a spectator as everyone gathered around the tree to sing hymns and Christmas carols, accompanied by the squeak and squawk of Jaybird's newly acquired tin whistle. I was beginning to feel left out when Lizzy suggested that she resume reading Mrs. Stowe's novel.

Everyone seemed ready for an activity that didn't require Jaybird's musical talents, so her offer was gladly accepted.

Lizzy found her book in her new nurse's bag and took a seat at the foot of my bed. Jaybird crawled up next to her, but retreated to a spot on the floor next to the fireplace when he realized there weren't any pictures in the book. Bub sat next to Lizzy despite the lack of illustrations. Pappy lit his cob pipe and relaxed in his rocker and motioned for Granny to take her spot beside him. Rose waited until Ned took a seat on the floor, positioned a stool at his side and then began to peel a bowl of potatoes. Once Lizzy started, everyone quieted down and listened intently to the plight of poor Uncle Tom. Lizzy read with conviction for over two hours until Jaybird declared he would starve if dinner wasn't served right away.

Once the dishes had been washed and put away, Lizzy picked up the story where she left off. After a few minutes, her voice became strained and Rose began to read in her stead. I did my best to stay with them, but after a while, I dozed off to sleep. When I woke up after an undetermined amount of time, I found everybody in their same spot—quiet as a congregation of church mice.

Even Granny and Pappy, who had lived around slaves in the south for most of their lives, seemed to be moved by the story. Pappy blew his nose and Granny continually wiped her eyes as Simon Legree tortured poor Tom. Finally, sometime long after sunset, Sister Rose finished the last page and gently closed the book. We all sat quietly for several minutes without speaking.

Granny broke the silence. "I reckon there ain't no getting' around it. This blasted war had to be fought. The Good Lord just couldn't leave things as they was. All we can do is pray that it come to an end." Nothing else needed to be said.

Lizzy stayed on for another two days but once my fever broke, and I was on my way to recovery, she decided it was safe enough for her to go home. She still made the daily two mile trip to our cabin to make sure I took my tonic and poultice, but as I regained my strength, her visits grew shorter. Then one day, she didn't come at all.

I realized I no longer needed a nurse, but I missed her constant attention. When she didn't return for a second day, I began to think that I had done something to make her mad at me. On the third day, I began to worry about her, but then Reverend Parker arrived at our door with devastating news. On New Year's Day, the same day that Abraham Lincoln had signed the Emancipation Proclamation, a bloody battle had been waged at Murfreesboro, Tennessee on the Stones River. He said the newspapers reported there were over twenty five thousand casualties. He sighed and then nervously wiped his face with his handkerchief "One hundred of those casualties were soldiers from Crawford County," his voice began to crack. "Joe Maxwell, one of Lizzy's older brothers, was among the dead."

Chapter 24

I saw the plumes of dust on the road long before the lone horseman came into view. I could see by the new navy uniform, adorned with two rows of gold buttons, that he was a federal regular. I heaved the last of the corn into the crib and walked across the barnyard to meet the rider.

"Afternoon, boy—is the man of the house at home?" The soldier looked over my head to survey our farm. His tone dismissed me as not being worthy of his attention. His blondish white ringlets hung down to his shoulders, partially covering his Lieutenant's bars.

"It depends what you want," I answered with a portion of sass in my tone.

"Don't be impertinent with me," he barked. "I have orders to deal most severely with any Copperhead resistance I might encounter. Regardless of age—I might add."

It might have been that I was bone weary from working since dawn, or maybe it was the lieutenant's pompous demeanor; whatever the reason—I didn't like him. "Copperhead? You think that I'm a Copperhead?" I bent over, grabbed my knees and broke out in a fit of laughter. "That is the most ridiculous thing that I ever—" I felt the sting of his horse whip across my face before I could finish.

"Do you think this is some sort of joke, boy? I'll teach you to show some respect to your betters," The soldier flashed a devilish grin and his eyes burned red with hatred for me. I suddenly became aware that my freshness had not served me well. As I contemplated my next move, the tip of his whip popped my left ear lobe.

"What in the Hell are you doing?" I used my open hands to thwart his next blow. When he recoiled again I fell to the ground. I rolled up into a ball and used my arms to cover my face. "Stop it!" I cried. "Please stop hitting me!"

The louder I screamed, the harder he whipped me. I peeked through my fingers and saw his utter satisfaction with my plight. I was completely helpless. I began to whimper and my vision began to blur, when I heard the unmistakable blast of a shotgun.

"Drop that whip or the next one is gonna blow your head off." Ned unholstered his Colt 44 revolver and took aim at the lieutenant, while Pappy reloaded the shotgun. "I said—drop it!"

The lieutenant raised his hands above his head and let the whip fall to the ground. He smirked and motioned to the herd of blue jacketed horsemen who were thundering down the lane. "I'm afraid you white trash are all gonna regret this," promised the soldier as he backed away.

I staggered to the porch and stood beside Ned as he continued to hold the Colt on the young lieutenant. I began to survey the damage the whip had done to my flesh. I was trying to sort out the happenings in my mind. None of it seemed to make any sense.

"Lieutenant Jensen! What is the meaning of this?" demanded a burly middle aged man in a disheveled captain's uniform. There were at least a dozen mounted Union regulars behind him along with, much to my relief, Josiah Highsmith, Captain of the Honey Creek local guard.

"Looks like we found us a hot-blooded nest of Copperheads, Captain Weber," answered Jensen. "The boy started givin' me a hard way to go and then the one armed cripple drew down on me. It's a good thing you came along when you did or I might have been in a tough spot."

"You're a damn liar!" I crowed at the top of my lungs. "We aren't no damn Copperheads! He started whippin' me because I laughed at him."

"Keep your mouth shut, Will," Ned ordered. "I'll handle this," He lowered his revolver and took the shotgun away from Pappy. He placed the weapons on a bench on the porch and started walking toward the soldiers. "Captain, I have no idea what the lieutenant is talking about, but I can assure you— there are no Rebel sympathizers here. From what I observed, your lieutenant attacked the boy without provocation."

"Copperhead scum!" cried Lieutenant Jenson. "You aren't going to take the word of these traitors?" He removed his gauntlets and slapped them against his saddle.

"Be quiet, Jensen," Weber ordered. "And don't you dare get off that horse!"

"Mr. Highsmith, do you know this family?" Weber asked.

Josiah Highsmith spit tobacco juice at the feet of Jensen's horse. "This here farm belongs to Sam Farmer. He's a sergeant in the Illinois 49th. He's been missin' in action for over a year. Ned here—lost his arm at Pittsburg Landing. What was your regiment, Ned?"

"Illinois 21ˢᵗ Infantry," Ned replied.

"Thank you Ned," said Highsmith. "Ned was at death's door when he arrived last year. He's been on the mend ever since. I'd have to say he's pert near healed by now, seeing how he's just about to marry our local school marm. She lives here too. Her older sister was mother to the boy on the porch. She was killed during a Copperhead raid last summer. Her grave is over there behind the cabin. As far as the boy goes— Will Farmer is probably the best scout our home guard has. He can go places where a man can't go. Folks don't pay no attention to a kid. He's a born spy and the boy ain't afraid of nothin'. I would go so far to say that our boy, Will here, hates the Rebs, Copperheads and Knights of the Golden Circle more than any other soul in our neighborhood. He wants to fight the Rebs so bad—I'm half surprised he hasn't figured a way to join up yet."

"What a bunch of hogwash," Lieutenant Jensen mumbled.

"I'd advise you to keep silent, Lieutenant!" Weber barked.

"With all due respect," Jensen replied, "my source told me that this boy has been stealing horses to send down south."

"That's another damn lie, you son of a—" Ned turned around and shot me a look that made me stop before I said another word.

"Who is your source?" Weber asked Jensen.

"It was a big red headed boy by the name of Stubbs. He said he witnessed the crime himself."

Josiah Highsmith laughed out loud. "You're right about one thing, Lieutenant Jensen. I'll guarantee you that Burl Stubbs witnessed the crime, all right. His family is the biggest gang of horse thieves this side of the Wabash. The Stubbs boy has carried a grudge against Will ever since he whipped him in a fight a couple of years ago."

"Now I know you're lying," Jensen interrupted. "The Stubbs boy I talked to is twice the size of this boy. There is no way on earth he could have whipped him."

"I'd watch my tongue, young man," Highsmith warned him. "I don't take kindly to be called a liar. Besides, I'd reckon that boy would have given you all the fight you wanted, if you hadn't bushwhacked him."

"That'll be the day," the lieutenant smirked.

"Jensen!" Captain Weber exploded.

Highsmith raised his hand. "It's alright Captain Weber, but let me add one thing if you will."

Weber nodded for him to proceed.

"Lieutenant Jensen. Have you heard of a man that goes by the name of One Eye Skaggs?"

"Of course," Jensen replied. "Who hasn't?" Skaggs was being mentioned in the same breath as Champ Ferguson and William Quantrill.

"Our boy here blew off One Eye Skaggs's ear in a fair fight and took away his fancy Johnny Reb pistol, a LeMat grape shooter, as a trophy. Rumor has it that Skaggs has put a hundred dollar bounty on young Will's head. If he could take Ol' One Eye without any problems, I don't spect a wet behind the ears lieutenant from Minnesota would present much risk."

Jensen turned red.

Weber shook his head in disgust and jumped down from his mount. "Come here, son. Let's you and me have a talk."

Captain Weber was a squatty German with a round face with salt and pepper hair and neatly trimmed beard. He had a whiskey voice and a disarming smile that immediately put me at ease. "Let me take a look at those cuts, Will."

I winced as he carefully inspected each lash mark. Most were on my arms and shoulders, but the two or three that found my face and neck, hurt like the devil. He poured water from his canteen on to a white handkerchief and dabbed my wounds. I bit my lower lip in an attempt to hold back tears. "I'll send my surgeon over with some salve as soon as I get back. He'll have you back to as good as new before you know it."

"It's not necessary, sir. I'll be fine." For a reason I could not explain I broke into tears.

Captain Weber put his arm on my shoulder and guided me into the barn where the others couldn't see me cry. "That's alright son, let's get it out of our system." He wiped his eyes with his handkerchief and sounded like a bawling calf when he blew his nose. I knew he wasn't really crying and that he was just trying to make me feel better, but I sincerely appreciated his act of kindness.

I was able to regain my composure without losing too much dignity. "Thank you, Captain. I'll be fine now."

"I'm sure you will be," Weber replied. "You are a brave young man. I want you to know that Lieutenant Jensen will be severely reprimanded for his assault, but I'd like to hear what happened. I need you to tell me in your own words. Can you do that for me?"

I nodded.

"What did you say to him?" Weber asked.

"He rode up and asked if the man of the house was home, and I told him it depended on what he wanted. The reason that I answered that way was because when Pa went off to the war, he made me the man of the house. I have grown to realize over the past two years that my title doesn't hold much water with the grownups in the cabin. I can speak for the family on some minor issues, but anything important goes through Granny or Sister Rose. Now that Ned and Rose are married, Ned seems to do most of the talking for us. The lieutenant must have thought I was getting fresh with him, because he got awful mad real quick. He called me a Copperhead and I started laughing."

"What was so funny?" asked the captain.

"I'm as much a Copperhead as the Devil is a good angel."

"Then what happened?" Captain Weber smiled.

"That's when he started beating me with his horsewhip." I cringed at the thought of it. "He took me by surprise. He had me in a world of hurt before I knew what hit me. That's when Ned fired the shotgun and I got loose of him."

"And that's everything?"

"I'll swear on a Bible if you want me to," I said.

"That won't be necessary, Will. I believe you," he sighed.

"Thank you, sir." I realized that I liked the man. He treated me like I was a grown up.

Captain Weber took a short cigar from his jacket and stuck a match against the sole of his boot. "So you took One Eye Skaggs's LeMat away from him?"

"It was more like it fell to the ground when I shot him."

"Still, you were very brave. I doubt that one in a hundred could stand up to Skaggs and live to tell about."

"To be honest, Captain Weber, I was scared out of my mind. I was mighty lucky."

"Still, his LeMat is quite a trophy."

"I guess so," I said. "It's nice to look at, but jams up after the first shot. It really ain't much of a gun. I prefer Ned's Colt 44. It seems to be a peck more reliable."

"A Colt is a superior revolver." he agreed. "I have one myself. That gives me a marvelous idea." He enthusiastically slapped his hat against his thigh and walked out of the barn.

"Lieutenant Jensen! Present your sidearm!" Weber ordered.

"Sir?" Jensen looked puzzled.

"You heard me! Hand over your revolver!"

Jensen pursed his lips and presented his Colt 44, handle first.

Captain Weber inspected the weapon and nodded with approval. "Fine piece, sir. Fine piece indeed." He paused and manufactured a frown. "There is however, one minor problem!"

"What is that, Sir?" Jensen asked. He couldn't hide the agitation on his face.

"The engraving on the handle says: *Lieutenant Peter Jensen.* I'm afraid that won't do. Won't do at all, seeing how you now carry the rank of sergeant."

"Sergeant? That's outrageous!" Jensen exploded. "I protest!"

Weber remained calm. "You are right about one thing, Sergeant Jensen. Your behavior has been outrageous. You have assaulted a boy who is not only friendly, but one who is battle tested to boot. It doesn't take much of a man to horsewhip a boy!"

"But sir—"

"No buts, Jensen! You're lucky I don't have you bucked and gagged and thrown in the stockade for a couple of months. If there is one thing I despise more than an incompetent officer; it's an officer who is a coward and a bully."

"A coward?" Jensen roared as he jumped to the ground and threw his gauntlets to the dirt. "I'll be damned if I'm going to stand for this."

Weber cocked Jensen's revolver and pointed it directly at the former lieutenant's face. "Take one more step and I'll kill you with your own gun, Sergeant. There is a fine line between insubordination and outright mutiny. You, sir, are treading dangerously close to that line."

Peter Jensen immediately stopped in his tracks, realizing that Captain Weber was serious.

"Sergeant O' Hara!"

A round sergeant with a ruddy complexion and red bulbous nose sprang from a coal black mare and presented himself to Weber with an exaggerated salute. "Sir, yes sir!" He was much older than Jensen and spoke with a heavy Irish brogue.

"Escort Sergeant Jensen back to camp and notify the officer of the day that he is to be confined to his tent until my return."

"Sir, yes sir!" O'Hara saluted and clicked his heels. "Let's go, Peter darlin'. It's back to the nest with ya."

"My Colt!" Jensen snapped. "I'm not leaving without my revolver!"

"Oh, I'm afraid you will." Weber replied. "You see, Jensen, young Will Farmer has agreed not to press charges against you for assault on the condition that he receives an Army Colt 44 revolver as restitution. Under the circumstances, I think he is being more than generous with you."

"This is robbery and blackmail!" Jensen declared. "You'll not get away with this! My father will see to it! I swear he will."

Sergeant Finnegan O'Hara placed his beefy hand on Jensen's back and pushed him toward his horse. "Peter, Darlin'—what the Captain is givin' ya is called an order. It ain't called a request. Now be a good boy and jump up on your harse."

Jensen turned his glare toward me "This won't be the last you'll hear from me! You little…"

Captain Weber jumped in between us and stood with his face only inches away from Jensen's. "One more word from you, Jensen and I'll bust you to private. Now get on your damn horse and get out of here."

Peter Jensen jumped onto his saddle with a single athletic bound and sped away at breakneck speed. Sergeant O' Hara bounced on his mount and galloped away in pursuit of him.

Captain Weber walked over to me and presented me with Jensen's Army Colt 44 revolver. "I am extremely sorry for Jensen's behavior; please accept this sidearm along with my most inadequate apology. I promise you won't have to worry about him at any time in the future."

I was speechless. I wasn't sure what to do, until Ned motioned for me to take the pistol. "Thank you, sir, but I don't quite feel right about accepting this." The Colt was beautiful, but the rage on the demoted lieutenant's face told me that I hadn't seen the last of him. "What if Jensen decides he wants it back?"

"You leave him to me," Weber replied. "You have suffered an egregious assault through no fault of your own and it's the least I can do. We're going to be neighbors for a while and I can certainly use a resourceful young man such as you. I'll have my surgeon ride over to tend to your wounds this afternoon."

"It's not necessary," I told him.

"I won't have it any other way," he insisted. "Mr. Highsmith tells me you'd like to do some soldiering. Give me a few days to get settled in and then come over and see me at the camp. I'll put your skills to good use." Weber mounted his roan and ordered the soldiers to follow him back down the lane toward the Flat Rock Road.

—∞—

Chapter 25

Folks around South Union were beginning to lose their resolve. Any hope of the war ending soon had long since vanished. Almost everyone in the county knew someone who had been killed at Stones River. The Union Army enjoyed major victories at Vicksburg and Gettysburg during the summer, but The Army of the Potomac was once again bogged down in Northern Virginia and The Army of the Cumberland had been driven back to Chattanooga after being defeated at Chickamauga. Many Democrats, who had supported the war in order to keep the Union together, were not as enthusiastic as the Republicans, who were more concerned with abolishing slavery in the South. The Copperheads continued to harass South Union every chance they got. It became clear that the South more than likely couldn't win the war, so the Confederate strategy focused on prolonging the fighting as long as possible. Sooner or later Lincoln would lose popular support and have to negotiate a peace treaty. The Copperheads dished out their fair share of misery in the Wabash Valley. Besides burning houses and crops and stealing livestock, they constantly cut telegraph lines and derailed trains. Their tactics drastically raised the food prices to the point where only the wealthy ate well. The destruction of the local harvest along with a severe summer drought resulted in hunger that bordered on starvation. You could count the ribs on practically every child in our community. Yellow Fever, dysentery, malaria, and cholera ran rampant, taking a dozen lives in the month of July alone. Morale was low and patriotism was on the decline.

There was still no word from or about Pa. Uncle Woody Gogin wrote several letters on our behalf to the war department, but we never received a reply. I refused to admit he was dead, but I found my hope to be fading.

After healing from my bout with pneumonia, we received confirmation that One Eye Skaggs had put a hundred dollar bounty on my head. At first I took the threat as a badge of honor, but then we realized that the entire family was in danger. Josiah Highsmith organized a posse to go after Skaggs and I was sent to stay with the Gogins in Palestine until things quieted down. The posse got close to Skaggs on three separate occasions, but he managed to slip away every time. Even though Highsmith couldn't apprehend the guerilla leader, his relentless pursuit forced Skaggs's band of thugs to flee south of the Ohio River into Kentucky. Since Skaggs wasn't around to pay the bounty, I was able to return home before the end of February.

Rose reopened the schoolhouse during the months of March and April, but because of Copperhead threat, only eleven students enrolled for the spring semester.

As if we didn't have enough turmoil in the neighborhood, in March of 1863, Congress enacted the draft. It called for all men between the ages of eighteen and forty-five to be enrolled in local militias which could be called up into national service at any time. Since most of the men in South Union who were loyal to the Union had already enlisted at the beginning of the war, many of the draft notices were being served to men whose sympathies lay with the Confederacy. It wasn't long before a corporal with the Provost Marshall was fired upon while delivering a conscription notice to a man in Port Jackson.

In July, the army actually suspended the serving of draft notices when a mob of five hundred Copperheads surrounded the Provost Office in Olney and demanded that all the names on the draft rolls be turned over to be destroyed. Fortunately, a company clerk managed to sneak the list out the back door and fled to the safety of St. Louis.

One week later, one hundred Union Regulars arrived at South Union to serve draft notices and keep the peace. All Southern sympathizers in the area considered their deployment to be a declaration of war.

The one bright spot of the summer was Ned and Rose's wedding. Since a wedding was the sort of event that Copperheads liked to terrorize, Josiah Highsmith called out the entire Home Guard to provide security for the event. With such a show of force, over a hundred people felt safe enough to attend.

Rose added some lace and dried wildflowers to the dress that Ma wore when she married Pa. She added some pink silk ribbon to the hem, collar and sleeves for color. Aunt Eliza Gogin gave her a pair of Wabash River pearl earbobs and a pair of white slippers with three inch high heels. Rose practiced walking in wedding shoes, but up until the morning of the wedding, she still looked like a cow on a frozen pond when she tried to walk a straight line. Granny managed to produce a contraption called a whale-bone corset for the occasion. None of us had any notion as to its origin, and in my case, what it was used for. All I know is that Granny and Ned's mother shooed us out of the cabin, so as to give her privacy. After a chorus of groans and cries, Rose appeared three inches taller, with half as much waist and a much bigger bosom. Her hair was adorned with rag curls cut from one of my old night shirts. I didn't recognize her. She was a sight to see. Jaybird and Bub stood in shock with their mouths open wide enough to catch a horse fly. Pappy smiled and wiped a tear from the corner of his eye. My Sister Rose was a girl no more. She was absolutely beautiful.

Rose made a suit for Ned out of his dress blue army uniform. She sewed the sleeve closed over Ned's left arm stub instead of pinning it to his shoulder. She did a fine job on the sewing, but I was so used to seeing a pinned sleeve, her fancy needlework seemed to draw attention to his missing arm.

I remember when Ned first arrived in South Union. I am ashamed to say that I looked at him as less than a whole man. I couldn't help myself from staring at the one-armed soldier and thinking he was hideous or some kind of circus freak. He would be a burden for the rest of his life. I couldn't see Ned for what he was; a good, hard working and honest man. Once his wounds healed, he learned to do more with one arm than most could do with two. Last year, I bragged and moaned about how I had single-handedly worked the farm. This year, I could make no such claim. Ned had taken charge and I helped as much as I could.

Rose, on the other hand, loved Ned from the beginning. Where all I could see was Ned's missing arm—Rose saw the man she knew she was destined to marry.

Reverend Parker performed the wedding shortly before sunset in our front yard beneath a crimson maple. Jaybird, Bub and I stood next to Ned while the preacher said his *"do yas and don't yas.*" Ned's knees wobbled and his face turned red, while Rose shed a river of tears. I was starting to worry they weren't going to make it to the end of the ceremony, when Reverend Parker pronounced them *"husband and wife."*

The Widow Rush and the ladies auxiliary organized a pot luck carry in and dozens of *roastin' ears,* fresh from the field, were set to boil in cast iron kettles over open fires. It was a true bounty. There was more than enough for all, including the men in the militia. No less than a dozen fiddlers came armed with their rosin and bows, while Squire Logan declared he had rested his voice and was ready to call the square until dawn if necessary.

Despite protests from some of the women, there were several jugs of busthead and corn whiskey along with three barrels of beer hidden in the barn. Wash tubs were filled with sassafras tea and apple cider for the rest.

Some of my friends wanted to run and play games, but with all that had happened over the past few years; I felt I was too old for such foolishness. Even though I had not yet celebrated my thirteenth birthday—the days of my childhood were far behind me.

I was content to sit on a milk bucket and watch everyone sing and dance. It seemed that a lot of folks needed to let their hair down and cut loose a little, but not me. I had seen enough excitement over the past two years to last a lifetime. I was plum worn out. Still, it was good to celebrate. It was Sister Rose's big night and I didn't want to be a stick in the mud. When Rose asked me to dance a waltz with her, I agreed without hesitation.

Rose had long since kicked off her wedding shoes and hiked up her dress with the aid of some hairpins. Barefooted, we twirled around and stepped to the fiddle as we had done hundreds of times over the years. Despite her crippling shyness, Rose had always loved to dance and because I didn't know any better, I had always been her willing partner. It might not have been a *by the book waltz*, but it was spirited and well rehearsed. Halfway through the dance I realized that she wasn't my Rose anymore. When the music slowed to a romantic pace, Ned tapped me on the shoulder and I bowed out. She belonged to Ned. I decided I was okay with that.

The area between the front of the cabin and the front of the barn was decorated with dozens of lanterns and hundreds of tallow candles. It reminded me of one of the fairy tales that Ma used to read me when I was younger. I couldn't remember any of the details other than it was about a prince and a poor girl over in England.

I went back to my bucket to rest and watch the goings on. Pappy walked past holding a mug of beer in one hand and a mug of apple cider in the other. He handed me the beer and took several steps before realizing he had given me the wrong mug. He shrugged his shoulders and smiled at me. "Don't tell Granny where you got it."

I promised I wouldn't and guzzled the brew before anybody noticed. In reality, it wasn't my first beer. Pa would pour me a small cup during the holidays and I had tasted some wine from time to time, but it was the first time I finished an entire mug. After a few minutes went by, I decided that I liked the taste and took my empty mug in search of the keg.

It took some guile, but I managed to get my turn at the barrel during a lively square dance. To keep from making several trips, I found a milk pitcher in the cold house and filled it to the brim. I exchanged my fancy glass mug for a tin cup and hid my pitcher behind my stool. By the time six songs had been played, my pitcher was empty and I was in a festive mood.

I thought it might be a good idea to refill my pitcher, but as soon as I stood upright, I landed back down on the stool with a thud. My world started spinning like a top. I stood up again, but this time was able to grab hold of a rail fence and slow things down. I decided that it might be a good idea to walk around to the back of the barn and get some fresh air, but after three steps I realized that walking wasn't going to go all that well. I staggered back to the stool. I breathed a sigh of relief when I realized nobody was watching me. "Just rest a few minutes and try again," I mumbled to myself. I was starting to breathe a bit easier when Lizzy Maxwell appeared directly before me.

"I've been watching you, Will Farmer." She scolded me like a child. "You ought to be ashamed of yourself."

"I ain't done nothin' wrong." I felt like a little boy who just got caught with his hand in the cookie jar.

"If that's the case—then let's you and me walk over and see what your Granny and Reverend Parker have to say about your beer drinkin'."

I started to protest, but before I could say a word, everything started spinning again. "Oh Lizzy—I think I'm going to be sick."

"Oh come on, Will," she grabbed me by the arm and started pulling me toward the lane. "Let's get out of here so you can walk it off."

We walked down the lane toward Flat Rock and saw several men on horseback standing guard, so we cut across the pasture and stopped when we reached Honey Creek. Lizzy dampened her handkerchief in the stream and wiped my forehead. "I swear—there ain't a man nor boy in creation that has a lick of sense."

The ill effects of the beer were wearing off and I was beginning to feel normal again. "Simmer down, Lizzy. You just wanted to get me alone and all to yourself."

"Don't flatter yourself, Will Farmer. If'n I wanted a man, I could do a lot better than a tadpole like you. Besides, I know you're in love with that circus girl. What's her name? Cliffy?"

"How do you know about Cliffy?" I felt like I had been bushwhacked.

"It weren't that hard," she laughed. "You kept callin' her name that morning when I found you half frozen to death in your hidey hole. All I had to do was ask Rose about this Cliffy girl and she gave me the whole story."

"Rose told you about her? What a turncoat!"

"Oh keep your stallion in the corral, Will. I ain't gonna hold a school boy crush against you."

"A school boy crush?" I was offended. "I'll have you know that—"

"You'd have me know that you're a jackass? Why don't you just keep quiet and give me a kiss?"

I started to reply, but the words wouldn't come out of my mouth. I must of looked like a bluegill out of water.

"Well, what are you waiting for? You aren't scared are you?"

"I ain't scared of nothin'," I declared. I started to lean towards her, when she grabbed my face and pressed her lips against mine. I began to struggle but then realized that I was enjoying the moment. I lost track of time as the kiss seemed to last forever. Finally, Lizzy pulled away and took a deep breath and then sighed. "Tarnation! That's gonna last me quite a spell."

Between her kiss and the pitcher of beer, my head was spinning. As I leaned toward her for a second kiss, she pulled away. "What's wrong?" I asked.

"Ain't nothin' wrong. Things couldn't be better."

"Why'd you pull away? I thought that…"

"Will, you know I've got my heart set on bein' a nurse and I don't have time for no boyfriend. But all of the girls in the neighborhood are always talkin' about kissin' their beaus and I—well—I ain't never kissed nobody. With the wedding being all romantic and all, I decided I was going to get my first kiss tonight and you was going to be the kisser. I was watching you and hoping that you would ask me to dance, but you decided to drink beer instead. That's why I decided to save you from yourself before you got too drunk to be any use to me."

"So I'm not good enough to be your beau?"

"Oh heavens, yes!" She laughed. "You are plenty good enough, if'n I wanted one. But I don't. I am going to be a nurse and I'm not going to let anything or anybody keep me from that." She smiled and placed her fingertips against my cheek.

"But I desperately wanted a first kiss to remember for the rest of my life. I wanted you to be the one I'd be rememberin'."

Once again, I had nothing to say.

Lizzy grabbed me by the hand and pulled me back in the direction of the fiddle playing. "If you think you're up to it, Will Farmer, I think you owe me a dance."

—⟋⟍—

Chapter 26

I leaned back on the limestone rock and let the sun warm my face. The morning had been overcast and damp, so I welcomed the reprieve. The woods and underbrush along the Embarrass River were so thick, that very little light actually reached the ground as long as the leaves remained on the trees. It was the ideal spot to lay low if you were a Copperhead, horse thief or army deserter.

It was my job to be on the lookout for anyone who fell into those categories. Captain Weber figured that a boy with a fishing pole would have an easier time moving about the area than a posse of Federal troops on horseback. At first I told him I wasn't interested, but then he said he had the authority to hire me as a scout with a paid salary of nine dollars a month. Regular soldiers only made twenty dollars, so it was almost half pay. I'd been chomping at the bit to join the fight, so I figured this might be my best chance. Granny and Rose were against the idea of me joining up, but Captain Weber promised them I could quit at any time. Ned was more than able to handle all of the work around the farm, so I wouldn't be missed all that much.

At first, Weber had me grooming his horse, fetching his coffee, hauling his water and chopping his wood. I did everything he asked like a good soldier, but at the end of the first day, I thanked him for his offer and told him he would be better off to hire another boy to do his chores. I wasn't afraid of hard work, but if these were the duties of a scout, I would be of more use to my family scouting at home.

"Hold on a minute, Will," Captain Weber said. "Josiah Highsmith said you were full of pepper and I can see that he was telling the truth. Before I can trust a man in the field, I need to know that he can follow orders. Can you understand that?"

"Yes sir," I answered.

"I know you've been through a lot over the last few years, but I need to get a feel for what you can do and can't do. I cannot in good conscience send you into a potentially dangerous situation without being sure you can handle yourself accordingly. Lord knows I have reservations about using you at all because of your age, but I have the feeling your service could give us quite an advantage. So far you passed every test with flying colors. You are a capable young man."

"Thank you, sir." I realized I had acted like a spoiled little boy. "Captain Weber, I didn't mean to show you any disrespect. Forget what I said earlier. I'll be here bright and early tomorrow."

He smiled and lit his cigar. "I never doubted it for a minute."

Each day Captain Weber gave me a little more responsibility than the day before. It was a week later that he told me that I'd be going on a fishing trip.

It had been three weeks since I'd seen a familiar face. Weber thought it would be too dangerous for me to go back to the camp every night, so all contact was to be made by way of a note left in a metal box inside of a hollow tree. Weber sent somebody daily to check for messages and on every third day they would leave a bag filled with hardtack, beans, and some jerky or corn dodgers. With the army food, the fish I caught, along with the nuts, persimmons and paw paws I foraged, I managed to eat rather well. I'd go as far to say that I had the best duty in Uncle Sam's Army.

To that point, I had come across several men who could have been deserters, outlaws or just river rats. I was told to be friendly, but not to ask so many questions as to draw attention to myself. My job was to report who I saw and where they could be found. It was up to the army to bring them in if they wanted. By day, I carried my cane pole up and down the Embarrass from Port Jackson to Charlottesville, moving every couple of hours to cover more area. The winding turns of the river made it hard to judge distances, but I figured I fished nearly three miles of riverbank per day.

I was instructed to camp without a fire in the underbrush on the north side of the river in order to avoid any late night company. Any cooking was to be done in the daylight at riverside while I was fishing. I enjoyed the bluegill most of all. Bluegill meat is white and sweet, but they're such a small fish that it takes five or six to make a meal. If there wasn't enough bluegill or perch on the stringer, I could get by on a single catfish or buffalo. I suppose I would eat a carp to keep from starving to death, but fortunately, it hadn't come to that. Every afternoon I would cook up my mess in a small cast iron skillet over an open fire. I liked to char my fish until the skin was coal black. I wrapped the fish in a rag to save for a late dinner after sundown.

Rick Kelsheimer

I made myself a lean-to shelter in a heavy thicket next to a
hollowed out limestone boulder, a half mile north of the river.
I made sure that I was far enough away from any animal path,
so nobody would stumble on me by accident. After being in the
fresh autumn air all day, I slept like the dead at night for the
most part. There were times however, when my mind wouldn't
let me. Sometimes it was because I heard a panther or a wolf
howling in the distance. At other times, loneliness got the better
of me. Spending three weeks all alone was making me go a little
daffy.

I did talk to some of the men who I came across along the
river, but that was different. Since I was spying on them, I made
sure to go my way after a few minutes of small talk. Any man
on the Embarrass this time a year was either up to no good
or running away from something or somebody. Because I was
alone—Capitan Weber ordered me to keep an old squirrel
musket in plain sight for all to see. The musket was to act as a
deterrent, but in reality, it would be of little use if a competent
gunman meant me harm. It was strictly for show and to keep
an honest man honest. I was, however, issued a Spencer repeating rifle to use if I truly felt my life was in danger. The Spencer
was able to fire seven shots without reloading. Weber said that
since the Spencer was obviously U.S. Army issued, it would be a
dead give away to a deserter or Copperhead. I was to keep the
weapon nearby, but well hidden. I wrapped it in an old burlap
bag and then covered it in leaves. I made sure that it was never
more than twenty feet away. I did the same with Peter Jensen's
Colt 44 in the opposite direction. Anybody who meant to do
me wrong would be in for a big surprise.

Where I received a measure of comfort from my firearms,
as far as my safety was concerned, there was no such cure for

258

my loneliness. Some nights I fretted about Pa. Was he even alive? If so—why hadn't we heard anything?

Other nights I missed Ma—especially the days before the war when she was strong and full of life and love. Other nights I was just plain mad and full of hate for the Copperheads. Sometimes I was mad about Ma being sick and others I was mad at Pa for leaving us. I missed my family and carried a measure of guilt for not being there to help. I told myself that it wouldn't be that long before I went home and then things would get back to normal. After three years of war I had learned that most of the hostilities died down during the winter. It was hard enough for folks to survive during the long cold months of winter during peace time, let alone when they were trying to kill each other.

On certain quiet nights, my mind drifted in a different direction. I couldn't help but think about the time in Palestine with Cliffy. She was the most exciting and beautiful girl I had ever laid eyes on. I became shaky when I thought about her in her beaded circus costume or in the creek without a costume at all. Sometimes, my time with her seemed like a dream; as if she wasn't real. But then I remembered that bully circus manager, Sam Murphy, and cursed out loud. I realized that I would probably never see her again, but vowed that I would rescue her when I was older and had the opportunity to do so.

Other nights I spent a lot of time thinking about Lizzy. She was nothing like Cliffy, but her kiss at Rose's wedding was laying heavy on my mind. Lizzy wasn't beautiful like Cliffy, but she was pretty and had the kindest disposition of any girl I knew. We had grown close over the last year, but her brother's death had only solidified her desire to become a battlefield nurse. Even though I knew she liked me, nothing was going to stand in her way of putting on a nurse's bonnet. Granny told me that I was too young to be getting sweet on a girl. "It'll be several years before you start walking down that path. No need to grow up before your time," she told me. "Enjoy your childhood while you still can."

My childhood was long gone. Or at least that was how I felt. People treated me as if I was still a kid. I was carrying guns and spying on grown men. I had shot One Eye Skaggs's ear off for pity's sake. What kind of child does that? Why shouldn't I think of girls? I had been forced to grow up in a hurry; it was only right that I got to think grown up thoughts. On the nights when my mind went in this direction, I welcomed the first light of dawn.

There was one man on the river near Charlottesville who I suspected was quite harmless. He was a white-haired Negro, no wider than a buggy whip. He wore white cotton trousers and a loose fitting hunting shirt that looked like it was older than I was. He appeared every day about an hour before sundown to check his trotlines. He harvested his catch, baited his lines and disappeared within minutes. He always seemed to be in a hurry, but there was something about him that made me curious. He had a kind face and made it a point to smile or wave at me before he left, but never came near enough for us to speak. Since I was ordered to keep my distance, I didn't push the issue. But as the days went by, I felt drawn to say something. If for no other reason than I had never spoken to a Negro before. I wondered if he was a runaway slave. If he was, it didn't matter now that the Emancipation Proclamation was the law of the land. Despite my earnest intentions, I never did gather enough courage to start up a conversation.

Finally, he appeared one afternoon just as my cane pole bowed mightily from the pull of a whopper catfish. I pointed the tip of my pole directly at the fish to keep it from snapping it in half. I could tell from the fight that I had a big one on the line, but when the fish cleared the water with a mighty leap, I nearly dropped my pole into the river. It was the biggest fish I had ever seen in my life.

"Don't pull too strong!" the Negro shouted. "You'll lose him for sures!" He ran across the shallow channel and grabbed the end of my pole. He used his bare hands to gather my line and when the fish was close enough, he dove into the river after it. For thirty seconds, water flew everywhere. I had never seen anything like it. He and the fish were embroiled in a desperate wrestling match. Suddenly he stood up, proudly clutching the catfish tightly against his chest. "Good Lord's bounty from the deep!" he declared while trudging toward shore.

"It's as big as a hog!" The fish looked even bigger out of the water.

"Your people is gonna be eatin' good tonight," he shouted. "This feller is truly the king of the river,"

"He sure is," I agreed. "But it's more than I could eat in a month of Sundays. You can have him. I already have a mess of bluegill."

He looked puzzled. "You means—you don't want this lunker?" He threw the fish onto a patch of fescue and found a stick to push through his gill and mouth. Once the fish was centered on the stick, he hung it from the fork of a willow tree.

"Please take him. I have more than I can eat."

"Are you sure, son? He's likely to go at least twenty pounds. That's a fair piece of meat hanging in that tree."

"I'm sure," I insisted. "Most of it would only go to waste."

"Lord be praised!" he shouted. "The Misses is sure gonna be happy bout this. Yes indeed, she will!"

I had never heard a man speak like him. His words came out like a song at church. I couldn't help but like him. "Then it's settled. He's all yours."

"Bless you, son" he nodded. "Bless you indeed."

"T'ain't nothin'" I replied and held out my hand. "My name is Will Farmer. What's yours?

"Andy Johnson," he answered. He looked wearily at my hand.

"What's wrong?" I asked.

He grimaced, as he considered how to answer. Countless lines forged by hours of working in the sun, suddenly appeared on his face. "Most white folk won't take the hand of a nigger."

"I guess I ain't most folks."

A hint of a smile reappeared. "No—I spect you're not, Will Farmer." He gave my hand a vigorous shake.

Andy Johnson was given his freedom in 1840 by his master, a man named Mason Goff. Goff owned a large plantation in Kentucky and freed his slaves when he migrated to Illinois. Andy Johnson, who was Goff's foreman, along with most of his other slaves, followed their former master north of the Ohio River. Apparently, a freed slave in Kentucky stood a pretty fair chance of being kidnapped and being sold back into slavery. Goff's former slaves decided to settle near a Quaker settlement at Pinkstaff, Illinois. The Quakers had the reputation of being tolerant and always welcomed Negroes into their community with open arms. Before the war it was rumored that it was Quakers who moved fugitive slaves up the Wabash for the Underground Railroad.

Andy's wife and family, however, lived on a different plantation and were forced to remain in Kentucky as slaves. He came north with Goff and worked as a laborer with the condition that he was allowed to farm the corners of the fields, along with the areas next to the split rail fences for himself. Andy raised tobacco and was so successful, that Mason Goff went into a partnership with his former slave and started growing tobacco as a cash crop. Within two years, Andy earned thirteen hundred dollars, bought his family's freedom and moved them to Illinois. Twenty years later, he owned four hundred fifty acres on Allison Prairie.

Andy still worked from sun-up 'til sundown everyday and hoped to buy another two thousand acres for his children before he died. He said he had fished for his dinner ever since moving to Illinois and had taken quite a liking to the local catfish and carp. "Raised five boys and six girls with the fish out of this here river," he declared. "Ain't no better food store nowhere." Andy sat and talked with me for a half hour, which I learned was a lifetime for him. He reflected about his life as a slave and praised the name of *"Father Abraham Lincoln"* for freeing his people. He thanked me again for the catfish and promised that I had a friend in Andy Johnson for life.

I couldn't say what day it was when I got the message telling me to return to the camp first thing next morning. I was ready, I'd been living in the woods so long, I had forgotten what it was like to sleep in my own bed. My clothes smelled so bad they could stand up on their own. I was beginning to offend myself.

In the beginning, I felt like I was doing some good for the war effort, but as of late, I had my doubts. The days were growing shorter and the nights were getting colder. What had started out as an adventure had turned into pure drudgery. Without any news from the outside world, the war could have been over for all I knew.

It was late afternoon and I had already cooked enough fish for supper. I was packing up my guns for the night when I heard the sound of approaching hoof beats coming from upriver. I gathered my gear and took cover behind a fallen log on the top of a bluff.

I counted no less than a hundred horses along with a dozen riders thundering down the shallow river. As I began to speculate about who would be moving such a large herd, I recognized two familiar faces. Virgil Stubbs and his son Burl were at the front of the pack. There was no doubt about it—they were Copperheads.

—ɯ—

Chapter 27

"You aren't supposed to be back until tomorrow," Captain Weber didn't seem very pleased to see me.

"They'll be gone if we don't hurry." I had covered seven miles on the dead run and was ready to collapse. I had tracked the horses to a limestone canyon that was formed by one of the Embarrass's tributary creeks and was able to get close enough to overhear Virgil Stubbs's plans. "Stubbs is the leader of the gang," I explained. "He told the other men they would move out around midnight to meet a river boat at Shaw's Landing at dawn." Apparently Stubbs's gang had ambushed and killed a horse broker in Jasper County and intended to ship the animals down the Wabash River to Kentucky.

Weber patiently waited until I finished the story. "I need you to draw me a map to show us the way to the canyon."

"There isn't time for that," I told him. "Besides—you'll never find it on your own. I'll show you the way."

"I'm sorry, there's likely to be shooting," Weber explained. "Scouting's one thing, but I promised your grandmother that I wouldn't put you in harm's way."

I could feel the anger well up inside of me. I'd been left to fend for myself for the past two months and now he was worried about my safety! "I don't mean any disrespect, Captain, but I've been in shooting skirmishes before, Besides, I've been living in those woods, there ain't anybody that knows them better than me. I can show you a way to sneak up on them that will probably save somebody's life. Virgil Stubbs is a mean customer. If he hears you coming—somebody is likely to get hurt."

He removed his hat and ran his short plump fingers through his hair. "It's against my better judgment, but you do have a point. Can you ride a horse?"

"As good as any man in the neighborhood," I bragged. It wasn't close to being a true statement. I was at best, an average rider, but I gave him the answer he needed to hear to let me go on the raid.

Weber opened the tent flap "Corporal Schmidt!" he shouted.

A tall scrawny towhead with tobacco stained teeth appeared at the doorway and saluted. "Yes, Captain!"

"Corporal, find Mr. Farmer a saddle and a mount that's not too spirited and have him ready to ride in thirty minutes."

"I have just the right horse in mind for the boy," he answered. He saluted and disappeared. I bit my tongue. Who was he calling a boy? The corporal didn't look more than a year older than me.

"Will, I'll let you go along on the condition that you follow my orders explicitly." Weber spoke with a tone of authority.

"Yes sir. Anything you say."

"You will remain at my side at all times until you guide us to the gang's encampment. Once we get there and the shooting starts, you will remain in the rear with our surgeon. Are we clear on that?"

I took a deep breath and was about to protest when I remembered what Ned had told me about how a good soldier follows orders, no matter what. "Crystal clear, Captain."

The moon was so bright that we were able to ride through woods along the river without the aid of torches or lanterns. Unfortunately, the moonlight would make it all the easier for the horse thieves to see us coming. Weber ordered his fifty troopers to wait in a thicket, a mile upriver of the canyon, while he and Sergeant O'Hara went with me to get a closer look. We crossed to the south side of the Embarrass and made a sweeping loop to a limestone bluff directly above their hiding place. I motioned for them to be quiet as we were getting close.

We heard someone laughing directly below us. Weber sent O'Hara out to the ledge to get a better look and then motioned for us to join him. "Looks like we caught 'em with their pants down," O'Hara whispered. "Would ya just look at all of that horse flesh down there."

"How many men?" Weber asked

"I count fifteen, but they may have some lookouts." O'Hara paused, "Although any soldier worth his salt would have stationed a man up here."

Weber nodded in agreement. He turned toward me. "Is there any other way out of the canyon?"

"No, just back to the river," I told him.

Weber motioned for us to crawl back from the ledge. "We've got them trapped as long as they don't hear us coming."

"Why don't you let me take ten men downstream on foot to cut them off," O'Hara suggested. "Once we're in place—you can go chargin' in like Billy be damned. They'll be trapped like rats with nowhere to go."

"That will work as long as they don't see us coming," said Weber. "We're going to need to get a lookout up here."

O'Hara nodded in my direction. "Why not use the laddie, here, Captain? After all—its himself that's served up these scoundrels on a silver platter, such as it is."

Weber stared into the darkness, a hint of a grimace appeared on his face. "I could kick myself for not bringing another man with us," he muttered. "I guess we don't have any choice. Will, I need you to stay on this ledge and keep out of sight. Keep an eye on the gang and wait until we attack. If we catch them flat footed—you won't have to do a single thing. However, if they get wind of us coming and you see them setting up to ambush, I need you to take your Spencer and fire three shots into the air to warn us. After three shots, I want you to run like the blazes until the fighting stops. Can you do that, son?"

"Yes sir," I replied. "Stay out of sight, shoot three times and run like the blazes."

"I'm counting on you to stay out of sight. We should be ready to attack in thirty or forty minutes. So be on your toes."

I nodded and saluted as they disappeared down the backside of the bluff.

I belly crawled to the edge of the bluff and looked down into the canyon. The moon seemed to be getting brighter as it climbed the horizon, so I had to be careful my moon shadow didn't give me away. I could see a campfire at the other end of the canyon, along with puffs of steam coming from the nostrils of the horses. Other than that the occasional hoot of an owl or the distant bark of a dog, the night was eerily quiet. I could hear voices directly beneath me, but couldn't make out their words. Part of me was curious and wanted to get close enough to listen, but my horse sense told me to keep still. Men could get killed if I did anything wrong.

It was hard to judge how much time had passed, but it seemed to be longer than an hour. *What was taking so long?* After a few more minutes I began to worry that something had gone wrong. *They should have attacked by now!* I could feel my heart pounding harder with each passing moment. I couldn't stand to do nothing, so I decided to circle around the bluff and see if I could get a better look on the other side. Just as I was about to crawl away from the ledge, I heard the unmistakable click from the hammer of a gun.

"Make one more move and it'll be the last one you'll ever make." The voice was familiar. "Now keep your hands up away from that rifle," he demanded. "Nice and easy now."

I did what he said and then felt a rock hard thud against my skull. I saw a flash of white and then slowly everything faded to black.

I held my breath and struggled against the hand that held my head underwater against the shale creek bottom. The more I struggled, the harder he pushed. Frigid water burned my nostrils as it trickled into my lungs. Just when I was starting to worry about drowning, I felt myself being lifted into the air and then slammed to the ground with prejudice.

"I've dreamed about this day for the past two years and now you're gonna pay, Farmer!" Burl Stubbs drove the toe of his boot into my ribs. I winced in pain and tried to protect myself by rolling into a ball. I was able to block his next two kicks with my arms, so he stomped on my wrist instead. I gasped when I felt something break loose in my hand. I rolled over in agony. I was helpless and exposed. After countless shots to my midsection, my body went numb and my thoughts seemed to float away. I was somewhat aware of what was going on, however it was as if I were watching someone else take the beating.

"That's enough, Burl!" I heard someone shout from behind me. "You're gonna kill him."

"Damn right, I'm gonna kill him. One Eye Skaggs put a hundred dollars on his scalp and I plan to collect." He reared back and landed another kick to my stomach.

"I said that is enough!" Virgil Stubbs roared.

"But Pa!" Burl whined.

"He can't answer no questions if he's dead. Sometimes I swear you ain't got a brain in your head."

Burl mumbled something as the other men laughed at him. He reacted by stomping me one last time. I rolled over and went limp. I was still conscious, but decided to play possum. I knew Weber should be attacking at any moment, so I had to do whatever I could to buy some time.

I felt someone prod me with a stick. "He's out cold, Captain."

"Damn it, Burl—I told you to stop. Now we don't know what in the hell he was doin' out here." Virgil Stubbs paused. "Tie him to that tree over there, and we'll question him when he comes to."

Burl grabbed me by my collar and dragged me across the creek bottom, then threw me against the trunk of a tree. He returned a few seconds later, grabbed a handful of my hair and lifted me into a sitting position with my back against the tree. He took a short length of rope and tied my hands behind my back. He took a second piece and wrapped a loop around my neck and threw the other end over a low hanging branch. I struggled to remain limp as I felt the rope tighten around my throat. By holding my neck upright, I would give myself away, so I swayed aimlessly and tried to keep from gagging. I heard Burl stomp off into the night, cursing all the way.

I heard Burl yell at his father and then I heard Old Man Stubbs bark right back at him in no uncertain terms. It wasn't long before I heard Burl's profanity coming back towards me.

"Take that, you no good sombitch!" I jumped up from the ground when Burl threw a bucket of cold water in my face.

The noose pulled tight around my neck as I tried to shake the water from my eyes. I drew a deep breath and then pretended to lose consciousness once again. I knew I was leaving myself wide open for Burl to have his way with me. I figured that Weber should be attacking at any moment, so the longer I stalled the sooner I would be rescued.

Burl grabbed a handful of hair, slapped my face and then popped me on the side of my head with the back of his hand. He refilled his bucket from the creek and gave me a second drenching. Water went up my nose and into my lungs, causing me to hack and cough uncontrollably. "Time to wake up, Willy Boy."

"Go to hell, Burl," I barked back. Enough was enough. He was going to use me as his whipping post until I responded. I smiled at him to show him that he hadn't got the better of me.

I could tell by the look on his face that I might have got him a bit too riled up. My thoughts were confirmed when he slammed the bucket against my nose. "I don't care what Pa says! I'm gonna end this once and for all."

The rope pulled hard against my throat and I felt my feet lift off the ground. I strained to stand on my toes, but he heaved hard on the rope, causing me to sway in the air. "Make him swing," a man called out. "Give it to him, Burl," urged another. I tried to draw a breath, but couldn't force any air into my lungs. I could feel my neck stretching while my body tried to separate from my head. I kicked wildly, while desperately searching for something to stand on.

I had certainly made a mess of things. All I had to do was stay out of sight for a few minutes and things would have been fine. I had just resigned myself to my heavenly departure when help came from an unlikely source. Old Man Stubbs kicked Burl out of the way and grabbed the rope just above my head. Instead of letting me down gently, he pulled out a Bowie knife and, with a swipe of his hand, cut the rope, sending me to the ground with a thud.

Virgil Stubbs hurled obscenities at Burl with the speed of my Spencer Carbine. I heard some members of the gang moan, while others snickered at the tongue lashing. "I told you to leave him be until we can find out what he knows!" He walloped Burl's head causing his hat to go flying. "Now, see if you can go look after the horses without fouling things up." He pointed a finger at me. "Charlie, tie that boy to that tree and watch him until I'm ready to deal with him."

I rolled my neck muscles against the bite of the hemp rope. I hoped to work it loose enough to allow some air into my lungs, when I heard an explosion of rifle fire. Smoke and noise seemed to becoming from everywhere. I forgot about the rope and slithered next to the canyon wall. A bullet whizzed past my ear and ricocheted off my foot. I yelped and buried my head behind the hanging tree. I prayed that I wouldn't be mistaken for one of the horse thieves.

A commanding voice called down from the bluff after a brief, but furious exchange of gunfire. "Drop your weapons or you are all dead men!"

Everything went silent. The horse thieves were completely surrounded and caught in a crossfire. I cautiously peeked out from my hiding place and watched as two of the men placed their rifles on the ground and raised their hands over their heads. I could tell by the look in Burl Stubbs's eyes that he had no such notion. Burl inched his way over to a shadowy area beneath the bluff where he was out of sight of the Union rifles. I was the only one who could see what he was up to.

He waited until the soldiers started to climb down the bluff before taking aim. He had Sergeant O'Hara directly in his sights. I started to call out, but realized there wasn't enough time. With my hands still tied behind my back, I struggled to my feet and charged at Burl. I buried my shoulder into his ribs and we tumbled onto the ground, causing his rifle to discharge on impact. The shot echoed into the night. After a brief delay, I heard a man yelp. A few seconds later, a howling body landed on the canyon floor. In the process of saving Sergeant O'Hara, I apparently had redirected the lead ball from Burl's rifle to Sergeant Peter Jensen's backside.

Burl made it to his feet and tried to split my head open with the butt of his rifle. I rolled to the left, causing the gunstock to shatter on impact. He grabbed a knife from his sheath and reared back to strike. Just as he started to lunge in my direction, he was blown backward and disappeared in a plume of smoke. I thought for sure he was dead until he let out a howl in agony. "You shot my fingers off!"

"Lay still, Sonny Boy, or I'll not be so generous with my next shot," O'Hara barked. Burl did as he was told and was rounded up with the rest of the gang.

"Quite a fix you got yourself into, Master Famer," Captain Weber laughed.

"Sorry, Captain," I replied. "They snuck up on me from behind. I never saw 'em coming."

"Don't apologize, Will. You managed to keep the scoundrels occupied while we moved in. We captured thirteen Copperheads along with one hundred and thirty eight horses. With the exception of the bullet in Sergeant Jensen's ass, the operation was carried out without a single casualty. We couldn't have done it without you."

"Is Jensen still threatening to kill me?" I asked.

"He'll get over it," Weber assured me.

"You almost had another casualty," I told him. "I thought I was done for when I was hanging from the end of that noose." I showed him the rope burns around my neck. "It felt like my head was gonna pop clean off my shoulders."

"Sergeant O' Hara wanted to come in earlier, but I ordered him to wait until all of the other men were in place on the other side of the canyon. I knew you'd be fine as long as I could see you were still kicking. You were never in any real danger." Weber lit up a new cigar and walked away to inspect the newly acquired horse flesh.

I couldn't tell if he was being serious or just having some fun at my expense. Either way—I was ready to go home.

—⦿—

Chapter 28

It had been two weeks since the stolen horses had been recovered and I was still feeling the effects of the beating I had endured at the hands of Burl Stubbs. According to Doc Judd, I had suffered three cracked ribs, a broken wrist and severe rope burns on my neck. Fortunately the bullet that hit my foot was only a flesh wound. He said that none of the injuries were serious and in time I would heal as good as new. He told me that I would experience discomfort for the short term. That part of his diagnosis was true, if not understated. I felt like I had been trampled by the herd of horses in that canyon.

I stayed close to home during the first couple of weeks following the raid on the Stubbs Gang. Virgil and Burl Stubbs, along with the rest of the men, had been sent to Camp Butler Prison Camp in Springfield. It was said that conditions at the camp weren't fit for an animal, but at least they had a chance. At first, Captain Weber wanted to hang every last one of them, but because Burl was so young and many of the men had families in the area, he decided to turn them over to the Provost Marshall in Olney. He said it would help keep the peace in the neighborhood. After the beating I took—I wanted to see them swing from the end of a rope. As time went by, I could see the wisdom in Weber's decision.

After spending two months sleeping under the stars, it took me a while to get used to sleeping indoors. A new feather mattress did help ease my pain. Ned and Rose were given a barrel of feathers as a wedding present from Ned's parents. After stuffing their own mattress, they had enough left over to fill small pallets for my brothers and me. It was the first time I had slept on anything softer than corn shuckings. I prided myself on being tough, but a mattress of turkey feathers was a comfort that I would never again live without.

Captain Weber brought over a tall black gelding as a reward, courtesy of the family who owned the horses we recovered. He was a beautiful animal that stood fifteen hands tall, but it would be a while before I felt good enough to ride him. I did, however, walk and groom him daily. Other than Muddy, it was the only animal that I had ever owned. I named him Midnight in honor of his shiny black coat.

I tried to spend some time with Muddy, but in my absence, she had adopted Bub as her new playmate. She seemed glad to see me, but was more interested in looking out for my youngest brother. Ned kept Jaybird close and had managed to get him to do his chores without mischief or complaint. Granny and Rose ruled the cabin like a pair of queen bees, while Pappy seemed content to keep an eye on things from his rocker on the front porch.

Ned had cut and hewned enough lumber to build an extra bedroom on the back of the cabin to fulfill a promise he had made Rose. It was amazing to see how well he had learned to use an axe, saw and hammer with his one remaining arm. He was determined not to let his injury slow him down. I helped him frame a door, but for the most part he was too proud to accept any charity. Rose soon cured him of his prideful demeanor and like most married men; he quickly learned to be humble.

Even though we were in the midst of the war and despite our losses, bad crops and food shortages, the family seemed to be getting along fine without me. Everyone seemed happy to see me when I returned home, but I also realized I wasn't as important as I thought I was. It was a bitter pill to swallow. I decided to take it easy, heal up, and stay out of the way.

As a result of my injuries, Lizzy Maxwell felt compelled to visit me daily. She was convinced that nobody within two miles of South Union could possibly recover from an illness or injury without her assistance. To hear her talk, it wouldn't be long before Doc Judd would be taking lessons from her. I teased her about hanging around to collect a second kiss, but in all honesty, I enjoyed her company. She had a healing way about her. She wrapped my ribs and dressed my neck wounds with considerably more compassion than the army surgeon. She was well on her way to becoming a skilled nurse.

It was a cold rainy night in early December. The full moon that the Farmer's Almanac had promised was cloaked by layers of clouds which had blanketed our farm for the past two days. Granny and Rose were finishing the supper dishes while Lizzy cleaned the table. Lizzy was spending the week at our house while her folks visited relatives out of town. Jaybird and Bub took a spot on the floor at the foot of Pappy's rocker as he prepared to tell them a story about *Old Kaintuck*. Ned and I were setting up for a game of checkers when we heard the knock on the door. "Who in their right mind would be out on a night like this?" asked Granny. She wiped her hands on her apron and motioned for Ned to answer the door.

The man wore a long black coat along with the traditional black hat of the Quaker faith. His shoulder length snow white hair and matching beard were completely soaked. He stood straight as a statue. His face was plain and without emotion. "Good evening, friend. Would this be the farm of Samuel Farmer?"

"It is," Ned answered cautiously. "Is there something we can do for you?"

Granny stepped beside Ned and gave the stranger the once over.

He glanced back nervously at the covered wagon that was parked beside the front porch. He turned back and looked at Granny. "Art thou the mother of Samuel?"

"I am," she answered. "Why do you ask?" Her voice cracked with trepidation.

"My name is Eli Musgrave and I bring news of thy son."

Granny gasped and clutched her chest. "Please come inside out of the weather." She grabbed his hand and pulled him to an empty chair at the kitchen table. Once he was seated, Granny positioned her chair next to the Quaker. "Is—Sam alive?"

"I am not the one to whom the message was given." He spoke in the Friend's *Plain Talk*, which was common in the Quaker settlements in our area. "But to the best of my knowledge, thy son is alive."

"Praise Jesus!" Granny shouted. "Halleluiah!"

Pappy smacked the table with his hand and danced a jig toward the fireplace. Ned wrapped his arm around Rose as she began sobbing on his shoulder. Jaybird and Bub joined Pappy in dance while I struggled to hold back my tears. Lizzy must have noticed the look on my face and clutched my hand to give me strength.

"Where is he?" Granny asked.

"I am afraid you will have to ask the one to whom the message was given." The Quaker looked around the cabin. "Is the wife of Samuel at home?"

The house went quiet. "Sarah passed a year ago last summer."

"Of that I am sorry," Musgrave said. "The one who has the answers thou seeks is in the back of the wagon with my wife."

"Lord have mercy!" Granny declared. "Bring them in this minute! It ain't fit for man nor beast outside."

A sheepish look appeared on the strangers face. "Thee may wish the children to depart to their rooms beforehand."

Granny hesitated at first, but then nodded in agreement. "Bub! Jaybird! Up to your beds!" She glanced in my direction, but there was no way in blazes that I was going to miss this! She saw the look in my face and said nothing.

Both brothers pitched a fit, but did as they were told when Rose promised to bring two pieces of apple pie up to their room.

We all watched from the porch as Musgrave called into the wagon. A heavy set woman in an ankle length black dress and apron appeared and stepped gingerly from the wagon. Musgrave took her hands and guided her to the ground. She lifted her skirt to avoid the puddles and stepped up onto the porch. "This is my wife—Gretta," Musgrave said with a smile. He looked at Ned, then Pappy and then finally in my direction. "I will be needing your help with the next one," said the Quaker.

When I first saw her face peek out from the cover of the wagon, I felt my heart leap. She was the most beautiful woman I had ever seen in my life. When Musgrave helped her to the edge of the wagon, she smiled at me and extended her hand. A single ringlet of raven colored hair escaped from her gray flannel bonnet. Her skin was milky white, her lips were the color of roses and her eyes were emerald green. It wasn't until I wrapped my arm around her waist to help her to the ground that I realized that she was with child. I wasn't an expert on birthing, but it appeared to me that her baby could come at any moment.

By the look on their faces, Granny and Rose noticed her condition also. They pushed me out of the way and took charge of her as soon as she had her feet planted firmly on the porch. They tried to take her straight to bed, but she insisted on sitting on a wooden stool near the fireplace. "I am so cold," she whispered. Rose found a quilt and wrapped it around her shoulders.

Granny started to speak, but stopped when she noticed that everyone had crowded around our new guest. "Give the poor thing some room. As a matter of fact—you men get the horses out of the rain. We can handle this without you." It was apparent that Granny would not be hearing any debate on the subject.

We spent half an hour tending to the horses and wagon in the barn. The actual work only took half that time, but Pappy said we needed to give the women enough time to get things worked out. "I wonder what they're talking about?"

"I'd reckon they's talkin' about female business and it just ain't proper for a man to hear such things."

"Female business? What's that got to do with Pa being alive?" I asked.

Pappy looked at the Quaker man. "I spect we'll find out soon enough. Is there anything you can tell us, Mr. Musgrave?"

"I am afraid that I cannot tell thee anything. We just met the girl two days ago. We agreed to provide passage to this farm on our way to Michigan."

"Are you saying that she isn't with you," Ned asked.

"She is not," he replied. "As far as the female issues go, I too believe they are things a man should not hear nor speak of. I am sorry I cannot be of any help."

Mrs. Musgrave came to the barn carrying two plates of stew and a loaf of bread. She was a squarish woman and had a face that looked like she hadn't smiled in years. "My husband and I shall sleep in our wagon tonight. The women wish you to go back inside. You have much to talk about and we should not concern ourselves with your private affairs." Her husband started to speak, but she silenced him with a quick glare of her coal black eyes.

"We shall sleep in your barn if you have no objections," said Musgrave sheepishly.

The pregnant woman was sipping sassafras tea when we returned to the cabin. The plate of stew on the table in front of her had barely been touched. Granny motioned for everyone to gather around the table. I took a seat directly across from our guest. "You must be Will," she smiled, "although he never told me that you were so handsome."

"Pa is still alive?" I asked. "Where is he?"

"Calm down, Will," Granny jumped in, "the poor thing has been through a lot."

"It is fine," she said. "I feel stronger now. First, let me introduce myself. I am Genevieve Lefebvre. And to answer your question—yes your papa was still alive when I left him three

months ago. Who would these other handsome men be?" She
spoke with an accent that I had never heard before.

"This is my husband Ned Thompson," Rose told her in no
uncertain terms who he belonged to, "and this is Pappy John
Farmer. He is Sam's father."

Genevieve nodded. She seemed to recognize the jealousy
in Rose's voice. "Rose, why do you call your father Sam instead
of Papa?"

"His wife Sarah was my sister. Sam is actually my brother-
in-law."

Genevieve pursed her lips and nodded slowly with a puzzled look on her face. "That is strange."

"What is?" Rose asked.

"He talked about you all the time. He told me that you
came to live with the family at a young age. He told me how
beautiful and smart you were. He praised your loyalty and
kindness to the heavens. He said that one day you would make
a fine school teacher and wife. But he always referred to you
as his daughter, not once did he ever say that you were his
sister-in-law."

Rose covered her mouth with her hand. "He called me his
daughter?" she asked through a series of sobs.

"That he did, my sweet Rose. He loves you very much."

"What did he say about me?" I asked.

"Oh, he is proud of you too. He called you his little man."

When I heard that—I almost joined Rose in a crying party.

"Let's give the girl some room. There will be plenty of time
for catchin' up later," Granny said. "But, if you're feeling up to
it, I think we would all like to hear about what you know about
Samuel."

"I would be happy to tell you about your son, Mrs. Farmer."

"Call me Granny. Everybody else does."

"Granny it is," Genevieve agreed. "From what Sam told me, he was sent behind Confederate lines with the mission of getting the Negros to run away from their masters. He went from plantation to plantation and met with the slaves at night. He promised that there was freedom waiting for them on the other side of the Yankee lines. He tells them where to go and how to get there. *Sweet Jubilee* the people called it. Hundreds went north to Tennessee and Kentucky while others went west to New Orleans. Your Samuel is about as popular in Mississippi as Father Abraham Lincoln, himself." She looked at Rose and then me. "Folks round there call him Uncle Jubilo. Jubilo means *'sweet joy'*. That is what he has brought to the people in bondage; the sweet joy of freedom. Every now and then, the Yankees would send a man with news of the war and orders for Samuel. Sometimes they brought supplies and silver coins for food and bribes. Last summer, one of these messengers was captured and eventually hung."

"Lord have mercy!" Granny shouted.

"That's what they do to spies out of uniform in the South," she continued. "But first, they tortured the man until he told them where to find Samuel. He barely escaped and was shot twice. Once in the leg and another in his shoulder. That is when they brought him to me. I was hiding in a cabin in the swamp. He was a very sick man. He had lost bucketfuls of blood and was crazy with the fever. I was able to remove the bullets, but I was afraid that he was too late in arriving at my doorstep. I was so afraid he was going to die, that I didn't leave his side for two weeks. And then when I thought there was no hope, his fever broke. He had lost so much weight; you probably wouldn't have recognized him. At first, all he could keep down was broth. He had no appetite at all. But I would not take no for an answer and finally he was able to eat some eggs with bread. Eventually, he gained enough strength to stand up but he was still feeble. It took almost four months before he was able to walk for a few minutes without stopping. He needed another couple of months to heal completely, but word came to us in the middle of the night that soldiers were on the way. Some runaway slaves took him further south to a safe house. He was too weak to make the trip to the north. I wanted to go with him, but he knew I couldn't stand the thought of bringing my baby into the world as a fugitive. He wanted me to come here and let you know he is still alive. I slept in the woods and in the swamp during the day and followed the North Star at night. It took me six weeks before I reached the Yankee lines in Tennessee. Samuel wrote this pass for me to give to the first Yankee officer I found."

She reached into her dress and pulled a tattered piece a paper from her bosom area and placed it on the table. Granny took the letter and handed it to Rose. "Read it for us."

Rose opened the letter and began reading silently.

"Read it so we can hear," Granny snapped.

Rose fidgeted and then reluctantly began reading aloud.

"To whom it may concern,

This is a letter of introduction for the bearer of this letter. My name is Sergeant Samuel Farmer, formally of the Illinois 21st and 49th infantry. For the past two years I have been on a special assignment for General Grant behind enemy lines. Colonel Swanson or Captain Bartholomew from his staff can confirm this information if necessary. I am recovering from gunshot wounds and hopefully will begin to resume my assigned duties in Southern Mississippi. This woman before you is my wife, Jenny Farmer, who had come to my aid when she learned of my injuries. As you can see, she is in a delicate

*condition and needs to reach our home in Illinois before the birth of
our child. Any aid you could render would be greatly appreciated.*

Thank you in advance,

I remain,

Sergeant Samuel Farmer."

The cabin remained silent as she folded the paper and handed it back to Genevieve.

She told us that apparently Pa had learned about Ma's death from one of his contacts over a year ago. "He cried for her during those first few nights. He carried so much guilt about leaving her for the war. He misses you all very much. Because he spoke of you for hours on end—I feel I know each and every one of you. I know it is little consolation, but Samuel has sent hundreds of souls to the *Promised Land*. He may be Samuel or Papa to you, but to hundreds without any hope in Mississippi—he is *Uncle Jubilo*."

Granny sighed and took a deep breath. "So, you and Samuel... Are you married?"

Genevieve smiled shyly. "No we are not. I am in love with him, but there was no preacher in the swamp. All we could do was step over a broomstick. He wrote the letter for my safety for once I reached the north."

"And the baby...is it...?"

"No, Samuel is not the father," she looked at the floor as if searching for the words. "I was with child before I met Samuel."

"And the father?" Granny asked.

"He is the owner of a large plantation in Eastern Louisiana." Her eyes filled with tears and both of her fists clenched tightly against her chest. "He took me without my consent. That is why I had to run away."

Granny gasped as if she suddenly realized something. She covered her mouth with both hands. Rose seemed upset too. I wasn't sure why.

"I know things are different in the south," Ned added, "but I'm sure there are still laws for things like that. Couldn't you go to the local sheriff?"

Genevieve hesitated and cast her eyes downward.

Granny walked around the table, knelt beside Genevieve and took her hands in her own. She whispered something into Genevieve's ear. When Genevieve nodded yes, Granny kissed the side of her head. "It's alright child. You're safe now."

"What's going on?" Ned asked.

Granny looked again at Genevieve and waited for her approval.

"You can tell them," Genevieve replied softly.

"The reason she didn't go to the law was because she couldn't. The plantation owner didn't break any laws. He was her master."

"You're a slave?" I blurted. "How can that be? You aren't black!"

"Will! Hold your tongue!" Granny had fire in her eyes. I guess this was one of those occasions where I was expected to be seen and not heard.

Genevieve patted Granny's hand. "Don't scold him. His words do not offend me."

"You don't have to explain nothin," Granny said.

"I don't mind," Genevieve replied. "It is best that everyone knows." She looked at me with her green eyes and my heart melted. "I am what they call in the south an octoroon. My great grandmother was from Haiti, so one eighth of my blood is African. Down there, if you have a single drop of African blood in your body—you are nothing but a lowly nigger. My Grandmother was a free Creole, but when she died, my mama was sold as a slave to pay the family debts. I have been a slave since the day I was born."

"Those days are over," Granny assured her. "You're a free woman now."

"You're like Eliza in *Uncle Tom's Cabin,*" said Lizzy. "Except the Emancipation Proclamation made you free once you crossed the Union lines."

"I may have been freed, but from what I've seen so far—northern folks don't want freed slaves living next door." I could see the fear in Genevieve's eyes.

"It won't matter to folks around here," Lizzy assured her.

"No, Lizzy, she's right," Granny said. "Everybody ain't a fire breathin' abolitionist like you. A lot of folks has the devil in them, when it comes to matters of black and white."

The room went quiet. As much as I wanted to say something to make Genevieve feel better—in my heart, I knew what Granny said was true. Things would be mighty tough on her if folks found out she had been a slave. It didn't matter whether she was white or not. People could be heartless.

Granny's eyes said that she had come to a decision. "You said that you and Samuel stepped over the broomstick?"

"We did," Genevieve answered.

"Well, that's good enough for me. Many a mountain wedding has been sealed with a leap over a broom. This here letter from Samuel says that you are Jenny Farmer and that you are his wife." She got up and took the seat at the head of the table. "Pappy, go get the Bible from the mantle. Will, fetch me the ink and quill."

Granny went to the page in the front of the Bible that recorded the births, deaths and marriages for four generations of the Farmer family. She ran her finger down the list of names until she came to the blank line beneath Rose and Ned's entry. "We don't want your child to carry any shame, so I'll record your wedding day as February 25, 1863, if'n that's all right with you, Genevieve."

Genevieve nervously looked at everyone around the table and then nodded yes.

"Good!" Granny declared. "Now, if anyone here at this table has a problem with this arrangement; let 'em speak up now or forever hold their peace."

No one dared say a word.

"Then it's settled. Welcome to our family, Jenny Farmer."

Eight days later, Granny entered the name Samantha Genevieve Farmer into the very same Bible. Our family had grown by two souls.

—⁂—

Chapter 29

The Christmas of 1863 was truly a time of hope. Knowing that Pa was still alive made the hardships of the cold Wabash winter a little easier to endure. Having a baby girl in the house gave Granny and Rose hours on end of pure joy. They took turns feeding and rocking little Samantha while Genevieve recovered after the birth. Ned and I built them a new bed frame out of maple and we all donated feathers from our mattresses to fill a new one that Rose made out of an old quilt. Blankets were hung from the ceiling for her privacy at night and Ned promised to build a new bedroom as soon as the weather eased up in the spring.

As soon as Genevieve was strong enough to get out of bed she declared that from that day forward, she would go by the name of Jenny. "Samuel's letter says that his wife is named Jenny Farmer. God has seen fit to give me a new family, a new baby, and a new life. I think it is only fitting that I have a new name too. Genevieve Lefebvre is no more. As of this day; I am Jenny Farmer."

Jaybird and Bub took to Genevieve from the first day. Both brothers were so desperate for a mother's touch; they clung to her from the moment she arrived. It was Bub who first called her, *Ma Jenny.* She seemed to like it and the name stuck. Jenny treated the boys as if they were her own and when Samantha was born, they immediately became the protective big brothers. Granny and Rose seemed to accept Jenny's arrival without having their feathers ruffled. By allowing Jenny to become mother for the boys, it let Rose work at being Ned's wife and Granny was able to slow down, while still acting as head of the family.

Jenny seemed to realize that I was too old for her to suddenly become my mother. After all, I was almost thirteen and could pass for fifteen. She talked to me as if I were a younger brother, much in the same way Rose had always done. "I know I could never take the place of your mother," Jenny said, "I just want to do what I can to help. Your father truly loved her. She must have been a wonderful woman to bring three such wonderful boys into the world. I love your father with all of my heart and because he is a part of you; I love you too."

I knew she was blowing smoke when she referred to Jaybird as one of three wonderful boys, but she did make us feel loved.

Jenny was serious about her obligation to Ma. She prayed at her grave early each morning and promised to do right by her memory. It was hard not to love her. Because of the heavy snow on the ground, we were able to keep Jenny a secret for a few weeks, but when the weather broke, it was obvious people were going to find out that Pa had taken a southern bride.

Reverend Parker was the first person to learn about Jenny. He was understanding and kind to her, but suggested that we keep her African heritage a secret from the rest of the congregation. "Usually, I don't condone hiding the truth for any reason," he said, "but I fear people aren't as open minded as they should be. We are all equal in God's eyes and maybe one day in our lifetime people will see our Negro brothers and sisters as equals. Until then, for the sake of the mother and daughter, we should keep this to ourselves. Folks will whisper as it is…" Parker stopped himself to search for the right words. "… because of the circumstances surrounding her arrival."

"To hell with those people!" Granny roared. "We've taken Jenny into our family and it's nobody's damn business but our own how she got here!"

"Granny!" Rose scolded. "Not in front of Reverend Parker."

"I don't care who hears me." Granny replied. "There is more good in our Jenny than a hundred of the so-called Christian hypocrites who would judge her."

"It's alright," Jenny said and patted Granny's hand. "I have been a slave for my entire life. Mama used to say I was lucky to be born with the white skin. She said it would keep me out of the cotton fields. Any slave who could pass for white was always kept as a house nigger. As terrible as my life was, it was better than the souls who worked the fields. I will do as the reverend says. I couldn't stand it if I was to bring shame upon Samuel and his family. Reverend Parker is right. Words cannot hurt me, but it will be better for Samantha if nothing more is said. I can pass for white and nobody needs to know any different."

"It just ain't right," Granny fretted. "It ain't nobody's business but our own."

"This sacrifice is small," Jenny assured her. "I have crossed the Jordan River and found the Promised Land."

At first people were a bit standoffish to Jenny at church, but as soon as they got to know her, it wasn't long before she was accepted into the congregation. "She killed em with kindness!" Granny declared. "That girl could warm the heart of the devil, himself." Jenny was a ray of light in a world that was covered by the dark cloud of war.

The war had taken its toll on our community. In the beginning only the Republicans supported the war, but once the Rebels fired on Fort Sumter, most Democrats who were loyal to the Union became patriots. Men from both parties volunteered and went off to fight to save the Union. Everyone thought the war would be over in a few months and then life would get back to normal. Although the Union had won some important battles in the last year, the Army of the Potomac was bogged down in Virginia and the Army of the Cumberland was unable to push into Georgia.

Even though not a single official battle was fought in our neighborhood, South Union was severely scarred. With most loyal men in the county off fighting the war—the Copperheads and southern sympathizers were free to make mischief with little or no resistance. Most folks banded together to fight the local threat, but as time went on people were beginning to lose their resolve. The devastating loss of life at Stones River had made many people second guess the wisdom of waging such a costly war. Every month more and more bad news came our way. Local men were dying at Chattanooga, Chickamauga, Lookout Mountain, Nashville and Corinth. Word came that many had been captured and taken to the hell hole known as Andersonville Prison. Other men were dying from diseases in camps before they even got a chance to fight. Our county was missing an entire generation of men.

As the fighting went on, wounded men started to reappear. Countless men returned home having lost their arms or legs. Others had been blinded and maimed by Minie balls or shrapnel from cannon fire. Unlike Ned Thompson, many of these men couldn't or wouldn't recover enough to get on with their life. The woods were becoming filled with deserters who couldn't go home for fear of being imprisoned by the Provost Marshall.

Fuel was added to the fire when each township was given a quota of men to be conscripted. Just the act of serving the draft notice often ended in gunfire. It had gotten so bad that Captain Weber would send an entire company when delivering a conscription notice to someone who was believed to have southern sympathies.

People were tired of the war. Many who had supported the fight to save the Union in the beginning were losing their faith. Some were calling for Lincoln to negotiate a peace treaty and simply let the South go. Abraham Lincoln's name was being cursed everywhere from the barber shop to the blacksmith shop. "Abe the Orangutan! Nigger Abe! Abraham Africanus the First! Abe the Ape!" It seemed that only the Republicans and abolitionists still supported the war effort.

The Peace Democrats were growing bolder by the day in calling for President Lincoln to end the war and let the Confederate States go their separate way. Lincoln, however, was committed to saving the Union and ridding the land from the curse of slavery. Most around South Union seemed committed to stay the course, but many who lived south and east of the Flat Rock Spring leaned toward a negotiated peace. Posters and handbills started to appear on trees and fence posts around the neighborhood supporting General George McClellan for President. McClellan, who had been fired by Lincoln as Commander of the Army of the Potomac, promised to end the war as soon as he was elected. This message was gaining popularity with the war weary, but it boiled my blood.

If the South was allowed to secede; all of the death, destruction and suffering would have been for nothing. I may have been nothing but a dumb kid, but even I realized that to give up now was nothing short of cowardly. The war had taken Ma, along with Ned Thompson's arm and we had no idea if Pa was still alive or not. Several families in Honey Creek Township had suffered the same if not more hardship than us. After three years of fighting—we had to win.

So far, the disagreements about the presidential election had only resulted in a couple of fist fights around our neighborhood. Unless the Union Army showed signs of breaking the Rebels resolve, there looked to be trouble brewing on the home front. If things didn't change, Lincoln would surely lose the election in November. The thought of giving into Secesh demands made me sick at my stomach. Every night I got on my knees and prayed to God for the same three things. I asked him to bring Pa home, safe and sound. Secondly, I asked him to allow Abe Lincoln to be re-elected. Lastly, I begged him to strike down every last Johnny Reb south of the Mason Dixon line and send them straight to the furnace fires of Hell.

—⁂—

Chapter 30

It was late February when the Copperheads ended their hibernation. A gang of at least fifty men from Lawrence County rode across the countryside and either burned or destroyed almost every smokehouse and root cellar in our neighborhood. They quietly attacked between midnight and dawn and had disappeared before most folks knew they were there. At first light, Captain Weber sent his *Mounted Dutchmen*, which was the name that the locals had given to the soldiers from Minnesota, in pursuit of the raiders. By that time they were long gone.

It was a bit of a mixed blessing because nobody lost their life; but the result of the attacks was, never the less, devastating. Because food supplies run low in late winter anyway, the Copperheads calculated they could starve everybody by destroying the last of smoked meats and preserved vegetables, fruits and berries. More importantly, they hoped that by terrorizing the neighborhood, those who were on the fence about the war would join the Peace Democrats and demand a stop to the fighting at any cost.

The raiders managed to ransack every single house and farm, showing no prejudice toward rich or poor, young or old. It would be months before food from the gardens would be ready and the last of nuts and acorns had been scavenged by the varmints. Most farms had a few chickens for eggs and some flour or cornmeal in the cabin, but without smoked meats and canned goods it wouldn't be long before folks went hungry.

Amazingly, the raid on South Union had the opposite effect from what the Copperheads had intended. Instead of accepting defeat and clamoring for an end to the war, everybody's constitution only grew stronger. Folks pulled together and shared whatever they could to make sure everybody got by. People traded milk and eggs for a handful of potatoes or turnips. If a family received food from relatives from the North, they shared with as many neighbors as they could. Captain Weber gave me a case of bullets for my Spencer on the condition that after I hunted enough food for our family, I make sure others had meat on their table also. Normally I would only hunt for turkeys, rabbits and squirrels, but under those dire conditions, I shot at possums, coons, beavers, crows, owls and hawks. Any critter that had meat on its bones and was fit to eat was fair game.

After dropping off some meat at our cabin, I took the rest of my kill to the Widow Rush. On a good day I might have a harvest of as many as a dozen animals. To make sure that nobody ended up with a less desirable cut of meat, she along with another widow named Bertie Simons cut and seasoned the meat into small pieces and mixed it all together. After the meat was boiled, they added a few potatoes, turnips and a carrot or two along with some corn meal or flour to thicken it up to make a hearty stew. Once the stew was ready, Reverend Parker loaded the cast iron kettle into the back of his wagon. It took him over three hours to make his rounds, but he made sure that every child, widow, or anyone that couldn't fend for themselves had something to eat.

By gentleman's agreement—anyone who was fortunate to kill a deer would keep half for themselves and then take the second half to Josiah Highsmith's smokehouse. Men around the neighborhood took turns standing guard throughout the night. Once the venison was dried, it was given to anyone who needed it.

Hard tack, bacon fat, flour and dried beans were distributed around the neighborhood by the Army. Uncle Woody Gogin organized a food drive in Palestine and managed to raise two wagons filled with staples. I helped Reverend Parker deliver the goods to every family who had been paid a visit by the Copperheads. It was a tough spring, but when all was said and done, everybody helped each other and we all managed to get by.

Going to bed hungry only added fuel to my hatred for the Rebels. I couldn't stand waiting around. I wanted to fight and I didn't care how. I approached Captain Weber about joining the Mounted Dutchmen, but after the beating I took from Burl Stubbs last fall, he told me that I was too young to be placed in a combat situation. He said he could use me as a messenger or errand boy, but only if there wasn't any possibility of hostilities at the time. I persisted and he finally gave in. "If you're dead set and I put the emphasis on the words *'dead set'* to head south, you could try to pass for fifteen and enlist as a drummer boy."

It wasn't exactly what I had in mind, but it was better than nothing. "Great! When can I start?"

He disappeared for a few minutes and returned with a battered drum that looked like it was used for target practice and a leather-bound book of drum signals. "Learn this backwards and forwards and when you can pass a test at the Provost Marshall's office; you'll be cleared to go. That is—" Weber hesitated, "as long as you get permission from your grandmother." He winked slyly knowing that Granny would never sign the paper.

"I'll have it down in a week sir!" I promised. I was already trying to think of ways around the permission letter. Weber didn't know that I had a new step-mother. I didn't figure Jenny would sign either, but I would cross that road when I got to it.

"Take your time," he said, "It will be a month before the test will be given."

I was banished to the barn after my first day of practice. Apparently drumming was a language of its own. Instead of words, everything was written with musical lines and notes. The fact that I couldn't read music presented a bit of a problem. Determined not to let a lack of musical instruction prevent me from fighting the Johnny Rebs, I did my best to imitate the drummer at the army barracks. I knew that reveille was nothing more than a drum roll. I hoped it would be a likely place to start until I could get Lizzy Maxwell to come over and help me. She could play the piano at church, so I figured she had learned to read music somewhere along the line.

Beating the drum was harder than I had figured it to be. I moved my hands as fast as I could, but still couldn't produce a decent drum roll. After hours of practice I learned that by holding the drumsticks loosely in my hands, I could beat the drum like a champion. I could hold a roll for half a minute, and imitate several of the cadences that I had heard the camp drummer play. This was going to be a lot easier than I originally thought it would be. Jaybird and Bub marched in step and I played late into the evening. They strutted like peacocks at a spring dance.

Everything was fine until something happened that I still can't explain to this day. While I was in the middle of a perfect drum roll, Jaybird started to perform tricks like a circus acrobat. He executed somersaults, cartwheels, flips and even waddled like a duck. Then he ran inside and came back with Granny's umbrella. "Ladies and gentlemen," Jaybird hollered, "Feast your eyes on Jaybird the Great as he jumps from the hay-loft of death." I played a drum roll as Jaybird held the umbrella over his head and jumped safely into the haystack below.

"Do it again!" Bub cheered. "Do it again!"

Jaybird was never one who needed much encouragement to do something that he probably oughtn't. He climbed out of the haystack and started to climb back up to the loft, when I yelled out for him to jump from the roof of the barn instead.

Jaybird didn't think twice. He took a ladder from the hay-loft and climbed up into the barn rafters and then out through a hatch onto the roof. It was one thing for him to jump from the loft, which was only a few feet above the haystack, but the crown of the barn roof was twenty five feet above the ground.

"This looks dangerous," I told my brother. "Maybe you should come back down to the loft."

"I ain't no yellow belly," he shouted. "I'm Jaybird the Great. Now play that Drum!" He held the umbrella over his head and prepared to leap into the air.

Against my better judgment, I began the drum roll and silently prayed that this would end well.

"All hail Jaybird the Great!" He yelled one last time.

Just as Jaybird was about to attempt his death defying leap, Granny appeared on the front porch of the cabin. "Jaybird! Get down from there!" A rebel yell from a thousand Johnny Rebs running down hill, would not have been anymore frightful than Granny's voice at the moment.

You could tell by the look on Jaybird's face that he knew he was in trouble. He tried to stop himself, but he was committed to his fateful leap. As a result, he started to fall forward, but couldn't push off enough to reach the haystack. The umbrella, which was supposed to slow his fall and float him safely to the ground, turned inside out. It was over in split second, but that split second seemed to last forever. I realized that my prayers had gone for naught. This was not going to end well for the Farmer boys.

I stopped the drum roll and watched in horror as he fell from the sky. It was eerily quiet until he hit the hard clay ground in front of the barn. There was a sickish crack of bones as he slammed into the ground. Instead of staying down, he shot up and started running around in circles, dragging his broken foot behind him. Instead of crying, he yelped like a dog who had just taken a load of buckshot to his backside.

The commotion brought Ned, Pappy and even Jenny to the porch. All eyes looked at Jaybird in shock and then turned toward me. I felt like Cain right after he murdered his brother Abel. "Am I my brother's keeper?" I muttered to myself. Apparently I was.

Jaybird screamed bloody murder as Doc Judd set his foot and leg into a splint. "He made me do it!" He cried over and over while pointing an accusatorial finger at me. Even while suffering from what looked to be excruciating pain, Jaybird still managed to use the opportunity to put me in the doghouse.

I pleaded with Granny, to no avail. When she started after me with a broomstick, I hightailed it for the woods. I ran down the trail by the creek and took cover behind a briar bush. I was in trouble because of the "You're the oldest and ought to know better" rule. It was a stupid and unfair rule because it only applied to the oldest brother. Maybe it was appropriate in certain families, but having a younger brother as untamed as Jaybird kept me squarely in the gun sight whenever he acted out.

I stayed put for a couple of hours past sundown and then made my way back to the cabin at a snail's pace. I had hoped that staying out of sight might have given Granny enough time to calm down, but when I saw her broomstick sticking through the middle of my Union Army drum, I realized that any hope I had of being selected as a drummer boy was gone.

As spring turned into summer, the newspapers said that it would only be a matter of time before the Secessionists would have to surrender. Editors called for people to stay the course, and the Union would surely persevere. Uncle Billy Sherman was in Northern Georgia, just beginning his March to the sea, while Ulysses Grant and Robert E. Lee were still going toe to toe in Northern Virginia. Folks were used to hearing that the war would be over in a few months, so many weren't buying the message. In reality, the North was winning the war, but many people loyal to the Union were so sick and tired of the death and destruction; they simply didn't have the heart to fight anymore. The Copperheads knew that the South was barely hanging on, but they also believed that the war weary Yankees were ready to negotiate a peace to end the war; if things didn't change before the election.

Rick Kelsheimer

In the Wabash Valley, members of the Knights of the Golden Circle initiated a last desperate campaign of terror in hopes of eroding the support for the war. Bushwhackers from Kentucky joined the local troublemakers and descended on our *Egypt* like a plague sent on the Egypt of the Bible. They burned churches, derailed trains and blew up bridges. They shot anything that was unlucky enough to cross their path whether it was man or livestock. They randomly roamed from town to town and county to county, never sleeping in the same place twice. They avoided skirmishes with the local militia and seemed to know where Captain Weber's Mounted Dutchmen were at all times. Nobody knew where they were going to strike next. It was impossible to set a trap with the local militia because there was no pattern to their attacks. Everybody had to defend their own home the best that they could.

One night the bushwhackers set fire to a Hardshell Baptist Church just south of the Lawrence County line. Once the flames had taken hold, they waited in the cover of the woods until the nearby farmers came to fight the fire. Once the bucket brigade was fully engaged at the church, the arsonists methodically put the torch to every unprotected farm in the area. From that point on many of the locals refused to go to the aide of their neighbors for fear of losing their own farms.

Because of the Copperhead attacks and the fact that Jaybird was bedridden with the broken foot, I was forced to stay close to home. Ned and I took turns standing guard every night. Pappy would spell us for a few minutes every now and then, but his rheumatism was making it hard for him to get around.

Each night seemed to last forever as I gazed into the darkness waiting for the unseen enemy to appear. Every sound in the woods nearly made me jump out of my skin. There were rumors that One Eye Skaggs was back in the area and I was convinced he would come looking for his LeMat and revenge. I kept my Spencer loaded and with me at all times along with Peter Jensen's Colt 44. I was ready, but prayed for nobody to come.

If we came under attack, our plan was to open the barn door and let the livestock run into the woods. Hopefully we could find the animals in the morning. The alternative was to find their charred bodies in a burned out barn. Once the animals had left the barn, several packages of fire crackers would be set off in hopes of making the raiders think we had a barn full of militia. After that, whoever was in the barn would have to high tail it back into the cabin as best as they could. If you counted Pa's old fowler gun, we had seven firearms in the cabin. All were primed and loaded and ready to shoot. Ned made shutters out of hard maple to fit over the windows. We barred them at sundown making the cabin our last line of defense. Ned carved narrow slots in the doors and shutters, just wide enough to shoot through. We could shoot in all four directions, so it didn't matter which direction the attack came from. We practiced every day to make sure everyone knew what to do. Ned and I would cover the front and sides of the cabin. More than likely, that's where the attack would come from. Granny and Pappy would cover the back. Rose, Jenny and Jaybird would reload while Bub kept Baby Samantha entertained under a bed in the center of the cabin. Ned figured that they would try to burn us out, so every evening we poured buckets of water on the roof to make it harder to catch fire. Another bushwhacker trick was to send something burning down the chimney and then cover the chimney with a blanket. The cabin would fill with smoke, causing everybody to run outside to keep from suffocating. To guard against that, Ned had me slather a bucket's worth of axle grease on the shingles around the chimney. Hopefully, a would-be attacker would step in the goop and slide off the roof before any damage could be done. On the other hand, we prayed that a stray torch wouldn't find the grease and add fuel to the fire. I didn't know if Ned's precautions would work or not, but we rested easier knowing what to do in case we did come under attack.

Fighting the boredom was the hardest part of standing watch at night. Muddy and our sheepdog, King, would join me, but all they did was sleep once the sun went down. Jenny usually came with a biscuit or piece of pie after the boys had gone to bed. That was the best part of the night. She would sit with me for a while and tell stories about her life in the South. I could listen to her for hours. Her accent made her sound like she was reciting poetry. She told me that it was called Creole on account that most of her kinfolk spoke French in New Orleans. She talked about her life on the plantation. The house had rooms that were bigger than our entire cabin. There were floors of marble with ivory columns and stained glass windows. It was only some golden streets and a set of pearly gates shy of Revered Parker's description of Heaven.

But when I learned how it took hundreds of slaves to maintain these southern castles, I decided that these plantations were more fit as a lair for *Ol Scratch*, himself, instead of being used as a heavenly reward. "This cabin and little farm is more beautiful than a hundred plantations on the Natchez Trace," Jenny said as we watched the lightning bugs over the meadow. "Mama would have liked it too. That's all she ever wanted; a cabin of her own, with a garden in back, egg laying hens and a milk cow in the barn."

Jenny talked about her mama quite a bit. "She was a lot like your Granny. She would smother you with hugs and kisses one minute, then give you a swat with the business end of a broom the next. But there was never a night that you went to sleep without knowing that she loved you dearly."

I could see why Pa would love her. Besides being loving and kind, she was absolutely beautiful. It didn't matter if she was wearing her Sunday dress or an old apron and smock at the wash tub. There was something about her that came from within. It was because of her beauty that I had a hard time looking at her as my stepmother. A stepmother was supposed to be old and matronly, not someone who caused all of the boys to whisper in the back pew during the Sunday Meeting. Despite my reluctance to accept her as my new mother, I was beginning to trust her as a friend.

It was on one of those nights during one of our conversations, when I thought I heard a branch break in the woods. I signaled for her to be silent. We listened for several minutes without hearing anything else. "Must have been a varmint," I whispered. Just as I was about to speak again, I heard the definite whinny of a horse, not more than fifty yards away. I stepped back into the barn and motioned for Jenny to follow. I gave the Colt to Jenny and readied the Spencer for myself. I motioned for her to open the animal stalls while I lit the end of a hickory stick with a Lucifer stick. "Run for the cabin as soon as you hear the firecrackers," I whispered. She nodded yes and made her way to the barn door and waited for my signal.

I lit the first bundle and tossed it by the watering trough. There was a slight delay before the first *pop-pow* broke the silence. After that the rest of the firecrackers went off in unison.

Pop pop kapow... Jenny dashed for the cabin and the frightened animals ran out in the night to who knows where. I waited long enough to light four more bundles of the noise makers and then ran for the cabin as fast as I could.

Ned closed and barred the door as soon as I crossed the threshold. My heart was beating like a quick-time march. "We heard horses in the woods," I yelled and looked at Jenny to back me up. She nodded to confirm my statement.

We all took our places and waited for the attack. I glared out into the pitch black night, but couldn't see a thing through the smoke of the fire crackers. After five minutes of waiting— still nothing. After an hour of painful waiting, Ned looked at me with a less than assuring expression. "Are you sure you heard something?"

"I swear, Ned, I heard horses in the woods." I didn't blame him for questioning me. I would have probably done the same thing.

Before he could say another word, we heard the sound of gunfire in the not too distant west. "Sounds like it's at the Weger place," I said. The Weger farm was about a mile and a half to the west of our place. "Do you think we should go help?" I asked.

"As much as I'd like to," replied Ned, "We can't leave the women and young'uns undefended." We walked out onto the porch and saw the flashing red glow of a fire in the western horizon. "Besides, the Weger place is closer to the Army camp than it is to us. Weber can take care of things."

There were a few more rifle shots and then the night became silent again. The glow of the fire, however, lasted for hours.

It was hard for me to stay at home instead of helping our neighbors, but I knew Ned was right. We eventually went back inside, but slept on the floor near our firing positions just to be safe.

In the morning we managed to find every animal without any casualties. Once they were safe in the barn, Ned and I walked into the woods where I thought I had heard the horse. We were only a few feet away from our lane when we saw evidence that there had indeed been at least a dozen horses waiting last night. "I told you I heard something." I felt vindicated.

"Never doubted you for a second," Ned laughed. "It looks like our trick with the fireworks actually worked."

Later on that afternoon, we learned that the Copperheads had raided a dozen farms in our neighborhood during the night. Nine houses and seven barns had been burned to the ground. Norman Weger, a harmless sixty year old farmer died from a heart attack he suffered during the raid. We had been lucky.

Chapter 31

In September of 1864 Major General William Tecumseh Sherman captured Atlanta. After four years of death and destruction, it finally seemed like the end of the war was in sight. I should have been grateful, but deep inside I was disappointed that I wouldn't get a chance to fight in the war. We still hadn't heard any word from Pa, so fear and anxiety started to take hold again. "Was Pa still alive?" I asked myself. The more I thought about it; the angrier I became. At first I felt helpless because there was nothing I could do. Before long, helplessness turned to anger and bitterness. At least with anger, I could turn it on something else to keep from feeling powerless. My target, as usual, was anything to do with the South.

The summer had been mostly uneventful since the night of the Copperhead raid. We still stood watch every night, but most of the raids had moved south, closer to the Ohio River. Because most of our crops had been burned over the last three years, Ned and I only planted enough for our family. We had a big garden for greens and vegetables, but only planted four acres of corn, an acre of sorghum for molasses and a half acre of tobacco. We had also sown three acres of winter wheat, but it was just showing signs of sprouting. Once our small crop was harvested; I had plenty of time on my hands. I decided to see Captain Weber in hopes that he would let me fight the Copperheads before the war ended.

"I don't have enough work to keep my men busy as it is," Weber explained. "Any Copperhead on our conscription list has long since left the area. There are still dozens of deserters hiding in the woods, but those boys are too dangerous for you to mess with. We spend most of our time watching the homes of known southern sympathizers. Every now and then, we shake the tree and see what falls out."

"What do you mean when you say, shake the tree?" I asked.

Weber paused, obviously uncomfortable with the question. "We just ask some questions and see if it matches up with what we already know."

I started to ask another question about shaking the tree, but decided against it. "Isn't there anything I can do?"

He raised his eyebrows and then nodded his head. "You spent all that time on the Embarrass last year, maybe you can help."

"Anything would be fine," I replied.

"What can you tell me about a man named Mason Goff?"

I shrugged. "He owns a big farm east of Charlottesville. I've never met him, but I did get to know a black man who used to be Mason Goff's slave back in Kentucky. He followed Goff up here and still works on his farm. His name is Andy Johnson."

"So this darkie still works for his old master?" Weber asked. He seemed surprised.

"He seems to like him"

"Have you seen Albert—"

"Andy Johnson," I corrected him.

"Have you seen this Andy Johnson lately?"

"No," I replied. "But I know where you can find him. He checks his trotlines everyday about an hour before sunset."

"Interesting," a smile appeared on the Captain's face. "How did you get along with this Johnson boy?"

"Just fine," I replied. "He's a right nice fellow."

"Maybe there is something you can do for your Uncle Sam, after all." Captain Weber kicked his feet up onto his desk and flashed a smile that left me feeling a little nervous.

Captain Weber made me practice the questions until I could recite them backwards. If what he said was true, Mason Goff was nothing but a good for nothing Johnny Reb and needed to be punished. What didn't make sense was Andy Johnson remaining loyal to a man who worked to keep his people in bondage. Andy was nobody's fool, so why would he be faithful to the former slave owner? Hopefully, I would find out.

I saddled up Midnight and made my way down the Embarrass to one of my old fishing holes and found Andy's trotlines. Captain Weber wanted me there by noon so I wouldn't miss him, but I knew it would be several hours before he appeared.

The sun was just about to touch the tree tops on a western bluff when Andy arrived. "Well bless my soul—if'n it ain't Master Will, hisself! I plum give up hope of ever seein' you again."

"I haven't been able to stray very far from home this year because of all of the raids," I replied.

"It sure has been a devilish summer." He shook his head and looked at the ground. "My wife and young'uns has been sleepin' nights in a barn at the Quaker settlement when I ain't home. It ain't safe for a black man to be out after dark, so I've been staying in a shack at Master Mason's farm until the harvest is in."

"Why do you work for Mason Goff?" I asked. "Everybody says he is a Copperhead." I realized that Captain Weber's questions wouldn't work with Andy. He was far too smart and would know I was up to something if I used words that weren't my own.

"Who be tellin' you that?" Andy laughed. "Mason Goff ain't no more Copperhead than you or me. Don't get me wrong; he dearly loves the old days in the south. But them was the days before he married Missy Goff. Missy—she be what you call an abolitionist. She prays every day for a Yankee victory. Master Mason knows better than to say a cross word about ole Abe Lincoln. Cause if'n he did, he'd be sleepin' in the shack with me."

"But I hear people say he has twenty thousand dollars in Confederate gold buried in the back yard. They say he uses the money to help the Copperheads so they can keep the war going in the North."

Andy shook his head and started to laugh.

"What's so funny?" I asked.

"Folks has been trying to figure out where Master Mason's gold jar is hid for the last ten years."

"So he does have buried gold?

"Everybody within ten miles knows he's got gold coins buried somewhere on the farm. But it ain't twenty thousand worth and it for sure ain't being used to help the Johnny Rebs."

"I don't understand."

"It's simple. The reason Master Mason only keeps gold is that he can't read a lick. He can't tell the difference between a one dollar note and a twenty dollar note. He got himself cheated a couple of times and vowed never to let that happen again. He learned to count gold and silver by the size of the coin. So that's why he only does business with gold and silver coins."

"But why doesn't he keep his money in the bank?" I asked as I offered him some deer jerky and cornbread.

"Much obliged," he thanked me and took a bite of the meat. "He used to keep his money in a bank down in Vincennes, but it folded and Master Mason said he lost eight thousand dollars overnight. Ain't never gonna trust another man made bank again, he says. Only safe place for money is in the mattress next to a shotgun or squirreled away in the ground."

"So why do folks think he's helping the Copperheads?" I asked.

"Don't rightly know," Andy answered. "It might be that he sounds like a Johnny Reb. He was born and raised down in Dixieland. A man gets set in his ways of speakin' and ain't likely to change, just cause he moved north of the Ohio River."

I'd heard enough. As much as I wanted to catch a Southern spy, Andy convinced me that Mason Goff was not funding the Copperhead raids. We sat and talked for a few more minutes while enjoying the food Granny had packed for me.

"Have you heard anything from your Pa?" Andy asked in earnest.

"Last we heard—he was down in Mississippi." I paused to choose my words carefully. I didn't want to say anything that could be used against him or our family at home. Not everybody was in favor of freeing the slaves. "Pa is behind the rebel lines. He's helping the slaves get past the Union lines so they can be set free."

"You don't say! North to Jubilee!" Andy clapped his hands together and stomped on the ground." Your Pa's doing the Lord's work. He truly is! Hallelujah!"

"I know he got shot last year, but from what we know he's on the mend."

"I'll be prayin' for his healin' every night. I promise you that, Master Will. I truly do." His eyes glisten with tears. "Ain't many white men willin' to risk their neck for a black man."

I helped him work his trotlines, which were surprisingly full. "Why don't you take some of these lunkers home to your family. I know that you is partial to some catfish. I got more than enough for me and mine."

I hesitated, but Andy wouldn't take no for an answer. We shook hands and I promised to not wait so long to visit.

"You knows where to find me," he shouted as I rode away on Midnight.

It was too late to get to the army camp before sunset, so I rode straight home.

Granny battered the catfish in eggs and cornmeal and fried them in a skillet full of leftover bacon grease. She served them with a loaf of hot wheat bread and a pot full of fried candied apples. It was an unexpected feast and we all gave thanks for the Lord blessing Andy Johnson with a fishy abundance on that day.

After a breakfast of biscuits and chicory coffee, I saddled Midnight and rode directly to Captain Weber's tent. For some reason Weber refused to sleep in the barracks with the enlisted men. I asked him if he intended to sleep under the roof when the weather turned cold. "What you call winter down here in Illinois isn't anything more than a cloudy summer day up in Minnesota," he said with a smile. "I value my privacy and fresh air too much to be cooped up with sixty men under the same roof. The cold isn't anything an extra blanket won't cure."

He offered me a cup of real coffee and I gladly accepted and took a seat on the stool beside his desk. I started to speak, but Weber held up his hand to keep me from speaking.

"What is it Sergeant?" he asked. The soldier stepped into the tent, but paused before speaking.

I looked up and saw Sergeant Peter Jensen's eyes, full of wrath and hatred, staring in my direction. It was obvious he still blamed me for his demotion from lieutenant. Then I realized I was wearing his Colt 44 in my holster.

"What do you want, Jensen?" Weber asked sharply.

Jensen reluctantly broke eye contact with me and turned toward the captain. "Here is the report on last night's patrol." He presented a hand written form to the captain and waited quietly while he read the contents.

Weber removed his cap and ran his fingers through his hair. "It says here you completed a thorough search of the property, but you don't say what you were looking for or if you found anything."

Jensen seemed annoyed by the question. "We were looking for signs of cooperation with the enemy, sir and no, we did not find anything."

Weber pursed his lips and tossed the report on his desk. "You seem to be coming up empty on most of your searches, Sergeant. If things don't change, I may start to question your ability to gather intelligence."

"But sir, it's not my fault if there is no evidence on the property in the first place." Jensen's face turned an angry shade of scarlet. "These turncoats have taken precautions against our searches. Finding anything we can use would be like finding a needle in a haystack."

"I just hope you're looking for evidence and not lining your pockets."

"But sir!" Jensen interrupted. "I will not tolerate your accusations!"

Captain Weber bit his lip and looked at me. "Wait outside Jensen. We can continue our conversation after I finish my business with Mr. Farmer." Jensen stormed out of the tent without saluting the captain.

"So did you meet up with your darkie friend?" Weber asked.

"He told me all about Mason Goff's gold," I replied, "but Andy doesn't think he would help the Copperheads, on account of his wife being such a diehard abolitionist." I told him about Mason Goff not being able to read and about him losing all of his money in the Vincennes bank. "Andy said everybody in the county knows he has buried gold on the farm. He never tried to keep it a secret."

Captain Weber listened quietly until I finished. He reached into his desk and offered me a cigar. I declined. "Smoking is a bad habit, Will. I'm happy to see you don't partake," he said while he puffed on the stogie until it finally lit. "That was some mighty fine work, Will. It's a hell of a lot better than storming into a house and accusing them of giving aid to the enemy. I have the feeling some of my men have been trying to beat confessions out of innocent people. If we're not careful, we'll be tuning patriots into rebels." Weber spoke loud enough for the benefit of Jensen who was standing outside of the tent. "I honestly wish you were a couple of years older—you'd make a mighty fine soldier."

"Thank you, sir," I replied. I felt myself puff up with pride.

"Now, how can I repay you? How about a slab of bacon and a pound of coffee?" he asked.

"That's mighty generous of you sir," I said. "It's been so long since Granny has tasted real coffee, she might break into tears."

Weber filled out a voucher for the bacon and coffee and sent me to the quartermaster. As I left the captain's tent I couldn't help but walk directly past Peter Jensen. From the look on his face, it was obvious that he hated me and would do whatever he could to get even with me.

The smile on Granny's face made me forget about Peter Jensen. She closed her eyes and inhaled deeply as she opened the bag of coffee beans. "It smells like heaven," she declared. Granny had been utterly selfless over the past few years and never asked for anything in return. It felt good to do something nice for her for a change. This fireball of a woman with the surly disposition and heart of gold had single handedly kept our family together for the past few years. By her pure willpower we had survived sickness, death and heartache while she remained solid as a rock. Her hair had grown whiter and more lines had formed on her face with every passing month, but her resolve never wavered. The Farmer family would survive simply because Granny wouldn't have it any other way.

—∿—

Chapter 32

It was only a few days before Halloween and the news on the warfront was looking better by the day. Sherman was marching toward Savannah and there was nothing the Rebs could do to stop him. Grant had Lee surrounded in Virginia and Richmond seemed ready to fall at any moment. Abraham Lincoln, who only a few months before seemed to be on the verge of losing the election to George McClellan, was now predicted to win by a landslide. Since most of the soldiers were solid supporters of the President, Lincoln ordered that all soldiers who were not engaged in combat were to be given furlough so they could go home to vote in the election. More and more men wearing Yankee blue uniforms began to appear every day. For the first time in months, people could go about their business without fear of a Copperhead ambush.

Lizzy Maxwell was beside herself with excitement when her brothers, Bill and Archie, arrived home for the first time since the war started. Both brothers, who had been clean shaven when they left with the Illinois 21st, now sported chest length beards. Even though they had been only gone three and a half years, they both appeared to have aged fifteen. The most noticeable change was in their eyes. Before they left, their eyes were bright and full of life, but now there was a dull hardness to their gaze. There was a change in them that gave me an uneasy feeling. I was curious, but was afraid to ask about their battlefield experiences. Ned told me that a man is changed forever once he's seen the "elephant" on the battlefield. If looking at an elephant could change a fellow as much as it had done to the Maxwell brothers, I wasn't so sure I wanted to take a peek after all.

Having my own horse definitely made it easier to get around the neighborhood. Our other horses were used for working the fields or pulling wagons and didn't exactly take kindly to carrying passengers on their backs. Midnight was bred to be a cavalry horse and wouldn't know what to do in front of a plow. He was more spirited than any horse I had ever been around and at first I was a bit uneasy. But as I spent more time in the saddle, we began to trust each other and now riding the black gelding seemed second nature. Midnight needed to be ridden daily and got cantankerous if left in the barn too long. As a result I found myself touring the neighborhood on a regular basis.

I was approximately four miles south of home when I came upon Doc Judd and Lizzy. They had just forded Sugar Creek and Doc's buggy had lost a wheel. "Thank heavens," Doc exclaimed," Will, can you lend us a hand?"

The wagon had broken down on a steep incline making it difficult to raise the buggy's wheel. We managed to work the rig forward a few feet and moved it next to a round limestone boulder. I found a branch big enough to use as a lever and positioned it over the boulder. Once we got the axle high enough off the ground, I had Lizzy sit on the end of the branch while Doc and I mounted the spare.

"What are you doing way down here, Doc?" I asked.

"To be honest—at the present, we're lost," he admitted. "Harriet Warner sent for me. She said a band of Copperheads raided her parent's farm on the Embarrass last night. I guess they worked over the old couple and their hired Negro within an inch of their life. You don't happen to know where the Mason Goff farm is—do you?"

When I heard Mason Goff's name, I knew the hired Negro was Andy Johnson. "Follow me," I shouted. I snapped Midnight's reins and headed South at a dead run.

"They came for the gold, Master Will," he said. "But they didn't find it. No sir. Ol' Andy made sure of that." Andy's voice wasn't any louder than a whisper. Lizzy was cleaning the gash on the side of his head, while Doc Judd tended to the Goff's in the farmhouse. We found Andy lying on the front porch of the farmhouse when we arrived. His eyes were swollen shut and the right side of his head was bloodied from what appeared to be a pistol whipping. His right arm was broken at the elbow and worst of all—he was missing the two smallest fingers on his left hand.

"Damn Copperhead bastards," I growled. "Did you recognize any of the men?"

"They wasn't Copperheads," he said. "They was Yankee soldiers pretendin' to be bush whackers. I know so for a fact. I saw them change out of the uniforms down by the river. I was checkin' my lines at sunset when I first saw 'em. They didn't see me so I hid in a briar patch until they left. They said they was gonna beat Master Mason and the Missy until they tell 'em where the gold is buried. They was between me and the farm so I couldn't warn the master. So while they was in the house, I dug up the Bee Gum Bank and moved it to where them Yankees would never find it." Andy started to cry and Lizzy scowled at me to stop. She took a clean wet rag and gently wiped away his tears.

"You should try to rest now," Lizzy told him. "You can talk to Will later on when you're feeling better."

"Thank you kindly, Miss," a hint of a smile appeared on Andy's face, "but I needs to talk to Master Will first. My people should be comin' any minute to take me home."

Lizzy reluctantly nodded. "I understand, but please take it easy. You've lost a lot of blood."

"Did you recognize any of the soldiers?" I asked.

"No, can't say as I did, but I got something that probably will tell you who the Yankee in charge was." Andy paused to catch his breath.

"How is that?" I asked.

"After they changed clothes, I went back to the river and took the coat that belonged to their leader. I can't say for sure cause'n I can't read, but I think his name is sewed in the lining."

"Where is the coat now, Andy?"

"There is three haystacks just south of the big red barn. If you look in the middle stack about three feet from the ground on the east side—you'll find it there."

After digging around with a pitchfork, I found the jacket right where Andy said it would be. And just like he said, there was a name sewn into the lining of the navy blue overcoat. Soldiers often embroidered their names into their uniform jacket so that their bodies could be indentified in the event they were killed on the battlefield. In this instance, it would identify the man responsible for this raid on innocent civilians. The name on the jacket was Peter Jensen.

"I'm sorry, Will," the Captain explained, "I can't arrest a man on the word of a thirteen year old boy and a nigger field hand."

"We have proof!" I declared. "We have Jensen's jacket from when the men changed clothes at the river. I'm tellin' the truth, Captain. If you don't believe me; why don't you ask Jensen where his coat is?"

"Where is this jacket now?"

"Doctor Judd has it for safe keeping," I answered.

"I didn't say I wouldn't investigate," said Weber. I could tell he was feeling uneasy about the whole situation. "You're making a serious accusation. I'm talking a court martial and prison."

"They cut off two of Andy's fingers and beat Mason Goff and his wife to a pulp," I barked back. "I would imagine that the folks around here would consider that a serious matter."

"You need to watch your tone, young man," Weber warned me. "Rules and regulations need to be followed."

"I'm sorry sir." I regretted being disrespectful with the captain. He had always treated me fairly in the past. "It's just that Jensen was standing outside of your tent when I told you about the gold. He got his information from me; I feel like this is all my fault."

"Nonsense, Will!" His voice softened. "I asked you to do a job and you were only reporting your findings. You have nothing to feel guilty about. But now you have to let me do my job. You need to trust that I will see to it that justice is done in this matter. Now what I need from you is to go home and stay out of the way."

"But Captain—"

"But nothing," he interrupted. "All you can do is foul things up by staying. Go home! Now!"

He held out his hand to stop me when I started to speak. I nodded reluctantly and walked out of his tent.

I was almost home and had stopped at the creek to allow Midnight to drink. I was thoroughly disgusted that I didn't confront Peter Jensen. It wasn't fair. He was guilty as sin and Captain Weber acted as if he had done nothing worse than stealing a biscuit from the dinner table. It felt wrong to do nothing, but what could I do? I would have to trust Weber to do the right thing. Maybe if Doc Judd took Jensen's jacket to the camp in the morning; Weber would have to listen to him.

I was still mulling things over in my mind when I felt myself flying backwards from my horse. I had become so obsessed with Peter Jensen that I had failed to hear the men approach from the woods. I hit the ground with a thud and immediately lost my breath. I was struggling to force air into my lungs when I felt a boot smash into my ribs. I cried out in agony, but didn't have enough air to make any noise. One more shot like the last one would surely do me in.

"That's enough," said one of the men. "You don't want to kill him."

"Why not?" said the other. "He couldn't cause us no more trouble if'n we did."

"We're only supposed to give him the message."

I was just beginning to breathe again, but wasn't exactly sure what was going on. I was aware enough to hope that the man who wanted to keep me alive would win the argument. I felt one of the men pull me to my feet by my hair. Both men were wearing white bags over their heads with two holes cut for their eyes. The nights of the Golden Circle were known to wear masks during their raids, but these men weren't local raiders. I could tell by their boots that they were Union soldiers.

While one man lifted my feet off the ground, the other held a knife to my throat. He used enough pressure to let the cool blade dig into my skin. "You've been stickin' your nose where it don't belong boy. And as such I would just as soon slit your throat and be done with ya. I'm here to deliver a message. Are you listenin?"

I nodded yes.

"You'll not be makin' any statements or do any testifying about last night's raid. You've caused enough trouble as it is. What you'll be doing is runnin' away from home in the morning. Where you go doesn't matter, just as long as it's far away from here. You leave before dawn and leave a note sayin' you're goin' south to join the war."

"Do you understand?"

Again, I shook my head yes.

"Good. And just to make sure you don't get any smart ideas, I'm gonna let you know what'll happen if you don't do as you're told. We're gonna be real generous and let you live. But you'll be livin' your days knowin' that your chicanery cost the lives of every single soul in your family. We've been watching you for some time now. We'll kill your grand folks along with the two boys and the wee baby girl. Then we'll shoot the one armed man, but I think we'll have a little bit of sport with the two women before we set the blade to their throats. But in the long run—they'll all be dead. Every last one of 'em! Have I made myself clear?"

"Yes," I whispered.

"Good!" he said. "Make sure you leave a note. We don't want anybody to think that you're layin' dead in the ditch somewhere. Remember to be gone before sunup or they'll all be dead before sundown. That's a promise. We'll be watching."

As soon as he finished, the other man threw me back to the ground and kicked me in the stomach three more times for good measure. They disappeared into the woods and then I heard hoof beats running away to the west.

That night after everyone was asleep I packed a second set of clothes along with two blankets into a haversack. I filled a canteen with water, holstered the Colt and Spencer on my saddle and stuck the seven dollars and ninety cents from my pillow case into a tobacco bag that was secured to my belt. I wrapped a hunk of dried venison and a half dozen corn dodgers in a thin piece of cloth and tucked it inside one of my blankets. I filled a couple of bags with dried corn for Midnight and then sat down to write the letter. I did as I was told and said I was going south to fight the Rebs. I told them all that I loved them and asked for their prayers. Without saying goodbye, I mounted my black gelding and started riding east toward the sunrise. I had no idea where I was going.

—m—

Chapter 33

The sun had just risen above the tree tops when I reached the Vincennes Trace. South would take me to Vincennes. I had never been to Vincennes, but I knew it took two days to get there. Folks from South Union talked about going to the stores and markets there, so more than likely, Vincennes wouldn't be far enough. To the north was Palestine, which would be a nice place to live, but I would have to lie to Uncle Woody Gogin about why I left home. Eventually he would surely visit my family and the truth would come out. I couldn't take a chance. There wasn't any doubt in my mind that Peter Jensen's masked henchmen wouldn't hesitate to make good on their threat to kill the family. I would have to go further to disappear. I remembered that *the trace* went to Marshall, Paris, Danville and then finally Chicago. I was just about ready to head north when a handbill that was nailed to a dead oak tree caught my eye.

ROBINSON & LAKE CIRCUS

Vincennes Indiana

Last Performance of the Year

OCTOBER 31 thru NOVEMBER 6

"Cliffy!" I spoke out loud. I would go to Vincennes.

The morning sunshine soon gave way to a drizzle. By afternoon, the drizzle turned into a downpour and a cold wind was blowing out of the west. The road turned to slop as I made my way through Purgatory Swamp. Purgatory Swamp was the ugliest, most inhospitable piece of Earth I had ever encountered. I would have stopped to take cover beneath a tree if there had been a tree. There was nothing but briar patches, sink holes, quick sand and scrub brush. What few trees I could see in the distance were on the far side of the swamp with no way of getting to them. Water was rising on both sides of the trace turning it into a path no more than six feet in width. The wheel ruts were filling with water and Midnight was beginning to get anxious about the treacherous footing. I had passed a northbound rider who told me that Russellville was less than two miles south, but it seemed like I had traveled double that distance and still—there were no signs of a town. The rain came harder and I was beginning to panic when I finally saw a split rail fence. The cabin had a no trespassing sign on the door, but at least there were signs of life. Ten minutes later I found a livery stable at the edge of the muddy village of Russellville.

The owner was an old toothless man by the name of John Henry Tracy. I asked him if he knew where I could find a dry place to camp.

"Might as well ask how to fly to the moon on a day like this," he chuckled. He had big red lips and his mouth was full of tobacco which made him look like a quacking duck when he laughed. "You can board your horse overnight and sleep in the loft for four bits if you're interested. Two bits if'n you clean out the stalls in the morning."

I thought it was a might expensive, but I was cold and tired. "I'll clean the stalls," I said and handed him the money.

"I need the other two bits up front," he growled. "Not that I don't trust ya, Sonny Boy, but I wouldn't want you riding out before sunup without doin' your chores. I'll give the money back when your work is done."

I dug into my bag and handed over a second quarter. All I wanted to do was go to sleep, but Midnight was covered in mud. I drew a bucket of clean water from a well and washed the mud away under the lean-to and then dried him off when I got him into a stall. Since oats were included in the livery price, I saved the dried corn to use later. After climbing into the hayloft, I made quick work of a corn dodger and a strip of venison. I made a mattress out of hay and spread my blanket on top. I was exhausted. I hadn't slept for over two days. I was out cold within minutes.

A screech from a barn owl jarred me out of a dream. I had no idea how long I'd been sleeping. The rain was still tapping a steady tune on the roof and the temperature had dropped considerably. I rolled up in the blanket, but my mind wouldn't let me get back to sleep. My thoughts turned to my family at South Union. I wondered what they were thinking of me. The fact that I had run away to keep them safe didn't help any. I wanted to be at home. As the crow flies, I was only fifteen miles from home, but to me, that stable in Russellville felt like it was on the other side of the world. I was alone. I don't know how long it took, but eventually, I cried myself back to sleep.

Besides shoveling out the stalls, John Henry Tracy gave me a dozen extra chores before refunding my quarter. If I would have known the amount of work involved, I would have gladly forfeited the two bits. It was mid morning before I left Russellville and I smelled like a pile of road apples.

The rain had eased to a drizzle and the trace was a sloppy mess. The southern end of Purgatory Swamp was less hospitable than the section north of Russellville. The trail grew more treacherous by the hour as the Wabash River started to climb out of its banks. The rising water would soon cover the road entirely. When the rain once again started to fall, I had no choice but to keep going forward. It took all day, but, I finally reached the ferry at Westport. I paid eight cents to the ferry-man and crossed the Wabash into Indiana.

Palestine was the biggest town that I had ever been to but, compared to Vincennes, it was nothing more than a bump in the road. The first building I saw as I walked Midnight up the hill from the riverside was a massive red brick Catholic Church. Its shining white steeple made it the tallest building that I had ever seen. There were dozens of riverboats lined along the docks. Rugged looking black men, who I assumed had to be freed slaves, were loading corn, wheat, whiskey, hogs and horses onto the boats to send south to support the war.

There were enough Union soldiers on furlough for the election to defend the city against a siege. The mood of Vincennes was definitely pro-Lincoln, so if there were any Copperheads around, they more than likely would be keeping their thoughts to themselves.

Campaign posters adorned every fence post and tree. 'Re-Elect Honest Abe' and 'Four More Years for the Rail Splitter' dominated the landscape. Posters with Maj. Gen George B. McClellan in uniform promising Liberty, Union, and Constitution came in a distant second place. There were several smaller bills announcing that General John "Black Jack" Logan would be speaking on Sunday at the Vincennes Commons on behalf of President Lincoln.

The corner of Main and Second Streets was packed with people who were listening to a tall white haired man standing on a stump. He ranted and raved like a preacher while condemning the peculiar institution of slavery. Half of the crowd cheered while the other half booed and jeered the old man. Two and three story buildings went in both directions as far as I could see. I wish I could have stayed to watch and listen all night, but I had a circus to find.

After being twice sent in the wrong direction, I found The Robinson and Lake Circus at a meadow on the southern outskirts of town. As I approached the makeshift city of brightly colored wagons and tents, I began to lose my courage and began to question the wisdom of my plan. What if Cliffy didn't remember me? What if she had left the circus? There were a lot of 'what ifs' that I hadn't given any thought to.

My mind was going in circles when I recognized the familiar painted wagon with the words: 'Maya the Magnificent', printed on the side. I tied Midnight's reins to a tree and warily approached the wagon. I held my breath and listened at the door. I could hear movement inside. I took a deep breath and gently tapped on the door three times.

"It's open," a voice called from inside.

Cliffy had her back turned away from me and was rummaging through a chest of clothes as I stepped through the door. She was wearing a red satin robe with some kind of frilly yellow trim around the cuffs and collars. "I thought I told you to come in an hour. I wasn't expecting you so—" She stopped in mid sentence as soon as she turned around. "Will? Is that you?"

"Hello Cliffy."

"I almost didn't recognize you—you've grown so much."

"It's been two and a half years," I said. Cliffy looked older too. She was still beautiful, but there was something different about her. She looked tired and her eyes seemed to be hiding something.

"Don't just stand there!" She extended her arms. "What on earth are you doing here?"

"I had to leave home and I didn't have anywhere else to go." As soon as I felt her embrace, I lost control of my emotions and broke into tears. I had come with the intention of proving that I had become a man since we last saw each other. Instead, I found myself crying like a baby. I couldn't have acted more unmanly if I had tried. I was ashamed of myself, but the tears kept coming.

Once I finally gathered my wits, I told Cliffy everything; from Ma's death to the masked men's threats to massacre my entire family if I testified against Peter Jensen. She listened intently for over an hour without uttering a word. I told her about Ned and Rose getting married, and my run-ins with One Eye Skaggs and Virgil Stubbs. I described Peter Jensen's torture of Andy Johnson and the Goff Family. I even told her about Lizzy Maxwell's kiss at Rose's wedding. "Don't you see, Cliffy, I had to leave. I didn't have any choice."

"It's alright, Will," she assured me. "You're safe now."

I was still in her arms when the door banged open. "Who the hell is in here?" A giant of a man with a barrel chest and long black beard stormed into the wagon. The beating I took from the circus manager, Sam Murphy, in Palestine suddenly came to mind. But this man wasn't Sam Murphy. He was double Murphy's size and was in a nasty disposition.

"Simmer down, Clay Boerwinkle!" Cliffy scolded him and pulled my head hard against her bosom. "It's just Will. He's come to me for help."

"Who's Will?" he asked in a slightly softer tone.

"Will is an old friend. He's been like a brother to me. Don't tell me you're jealous of a twelve year old boy!" Part of me wanted to object and state that I would be fourteen in three months, but I saw the wisdom in pretending to be twelve.

Clay Boerwinkle was immediately disarmed. "Well—I just thought that—well—I heard voices and I just thought…"

"I swear, Clay, If you don't start treatin' me with some respect, I'm gonna have to lock my door to you!"

"I'm sorry, Cliffy," he apologized. "I didn't know."

"Oh, you are always sorry! Just come in and shut the door behind you."

Cliffy had me retell my story to Clay. I realized that a man of his size would make a much better friend than enemy, so I did everything in my power to convince him that I was telling the truth.

Cliffy waited until I finished before she spoke. "Clay, you're so good when dealing with this type of thing—what do you think Will should do?"

Boerwinkle, who obviously was enjoying being put into the position of expert, sat down on a stool that was much too short for his long legs. He paused and rolled his eyes up toward Heaven as if to show he was giving my problem some serious thought. "Son, it sounds like you got yourself between the proverbial rock and the hard place."

"Tell me something, I don't know," I grunted.

"Yessiree Bob, Sonny Boy," he ignored my comment. "You've certainly gotten yourself into a pickle. I'm going to have to give this matter some thought."

"In the mean time, Will is going to be staying with me," Cliffy spoke in a way that suggested there wouldn't be any further discussion on the matter, "and he's gonna need a job. Do you think you can help him with that, Clay?"

"Well, I guess so, but…"

"Good! It's settled," Cliffy declared.

"But what about our date?" Clay asked.

Cliffy smiled and patted my hand. "Wait right here, Will, while I speak to Clay outside." I nodded yes as she took him by the hand and led him back outside. I couldn't hear what they were saying through the closed door, but I could tell by the tone of Clay Boerwinkle's voice that he was not a happy man. The conversation went on for a few minutes, but then the voices softened and Cliffy returned to the wagon by herself.

"Great! All I need is someone else who wants to kill me," I said half jokingly.

"Don't worry about Clay," she assured me. "He's harmless."

"He doesn't look harmless. He's as big as a barn. What do you see in a guy like that?" I asked.

"All I see is protection in Clay. As long as I let him steal a kiss every now and then, he stays satisfied. If it weren't for him I'd be fair game for every huckster and cutthroat around. Clay is big enough to scare them away."

"What happened to Sam Murphy?" I asked.

"Sam got his throat slit in a card game," she replied without a hint of remorse.

"So you're free from your bond?"

"I'm free from Murphy, but I still need a protector," she sighed. "Sam wasn't cold in the ground for more than a few hours when men started coming out of the woodwork. Most were the kind who didn't want to take no for an answer. They think that just because I wear a skimpy costume in my act, I am the sort of girl who will show them a good time. But I'm not like that. I've done what I've had to do to survive, but I'm not going to be like those women who are all used up by the time they reach thirty."

"Why don't you leave the circus?" I asked.

"Where could I go?" she replied. "The world isn't a safe place as long as the war keeps going. Girls like me can disappear and end up dead without anybody noticing or caring. I don't know where my family is, and even if I did, life wasn't any better with them than it was with Sam Murphy."

"You could get married," I suggested.

"I'm sure I could marry if I wanted, but the type of man who would be willing to marry a circus girl, most likely would be the kind that wouldn't think twice about cheatin' on her either. I have men offer me fancy clothes and jewelry, but what I really want is a simple life with my own house and yard. I would like to have two children, a fat house cat and a black wrought iron fence. I'd like my husband to love me and other men to ignore me when I walked down the sidewalk."

"I'm sure you could have that, except the part about men ignoring you," I said. "You're much too beautiful for any man to keep his eyes to himself."

Cliffy turned a bright shade of crimson and then playfully messed my hair. "Oh Will, I wish you were just a couple years older; I truly do. You would surely be the man of my dreams.

But for now, the circus is the safest place for me. I am valuable to Mr. Robinson and Mr. Lake as long as people pay money to see Maya the Magnificent. Are you hungry? I'm starved"

We ate pork roast and dressing along with fresh green beans, collard greens and creamed onion soup in a downtown restaurant. "Do you always eat this well?" I asked.

"Only when I'm with someone special," she smiled. "By the way, Will, How old are you now?"

"I'm fourteen," I replied.

She nodded slowly with a look of doubt in her eyes and then started counting with her fingers. "How old?" she asked again.

"Well, I'll be fourteen in February," I admitted. "Why?"

"Just wondering…"

"About what?" I asked.

She shook her head. "It's nothing."

"You're lying."

She scratched the tip of her nose before speaking. "It's just that you are in such a hurry to grow up and leave your childhood behind. I would give anything to have a second chance at mine. It was taken away before I even got the chance."

"I don't understand," I replied.

"I've been lying about my age for years." A serious look fell on her face. "I'm only sixteen. I'm only two and a half years older than you, Will. That's why I said I wish you were only a couple of years older or I was a couple younger. I would give anything to live in your world. I pretend to be a woman of the world, but everything I know is the life of a circus girl and a bonded slave."

"So you were only ten when your Pa sold you to Sam Murphy?"

She nodded, yes, as a single tear formed in the corner of her eye. I thought about wiping it away, but changed my mind. It was the first time that I ever saw Cliffy for who she was. In spite of the bangles and sequins on her costumes and her brassy way of talking to men, she was nothing but a frightened young girl, doing whatever it took to survive. "It was the worst day of my life. My father traded me to that sick bastard, Sam Murphy, for a mule and saddle. I was just a little girl! What kind of man does that to his own daughter?"

I didn't know what to say. I took her hand in mine and looked into her eyes as she gazed into the candlelight. She was hurting and there wasn't anything I could do about it.

After the dinner we walked hand in hand back to her wagon. I had intended to sleep on the floor on the opposite side from her bed, but she asked me to hold her for a while. She sobbed for a few minutes and then went to sleep with her face buried against my chest. I rested my chin on the crown of her head and inhaled the perfumed fragrance of her raven hair. I prayed for that moment to last forever. I fought as long as possible, but finally gave in to the need for sleep. Neither one of us let loose of the embrace. I don't know which one of us needed the other the most.

The morning sun came all too soon. Cliffy woke up and kissed me on the forehead. The broken little girl was gone and Maya the Magnificent, once again, had taken her place.

Chapter 34

Clay Boerwinkle was true to his word. He found gainful employment for me at a job known as *the circus dungman*. During all of my years, I had never encountered the word dung. So therefore, I didn't have any idea of what a *dungman* did. Within the first few minutes on the job, everything became painfully clear. A circus dungman shovels shit. Not just your run of the mill cow, horse, and pig shit, but monkey, lion, tiger, zebra, camel and worst of all—elephant shit!

The livestock manager, a round Scotsman by the name of McQueen, informed me that an African elephant produces three hundred pounds of dung per day. The circus owned ten elephants, so even with my limited ciphering skill, I realized that I would be shoveling three thousand pounds of droppings from those giant beasts alone.

It was bad enough to handle the manure once, but after the pens had been shoveled clean, I had to load the stinking payload into dozens of wagons for use as fertilizer. I had never worked so hard at a more miserable job in my life. I kept my mouth shut and did what I was told for a wage of twenty cents a day. By the time my work was finished, every muscle in my body ached and I smelled so bad, my own stomach was turning.

Cliffy was waiting for me when I checked out for the day. "Do you feel as bad as you look?" she laughed.

"Worse," I answered.

"Shewwee! We need to get you cleaned up!"

I was embarrassed as she took me to the showers. "I'll take your clothes to the laundry woman and get your other set from the wagon while you wash up," she told me.

It took quite a bit of scrubbing, but eventually I felt clean again. It was hard to believe how much my life had changed over the past few days. I was torn apart on the inside. I wanted to stay with Cliffy, but somehow things just didn't feel right. It was like I was running away from my duty to my family.

After I slipped into my clean clothes, Cliffy and I strolled along the shore of the Wabash toward downtown.

"How was your day," I asked.

"Better than yours," she laughed. "I practiced on the rope for a couple of hours and then took it easy for the rest of the afternoon."

"Must be nice," I replied.

"Oh, I'll be plenty busy in a couple of days when the show starts. Two performances a day and for the most part I'll be confined to my wagon until we leave town."

"Why is that?" I asked.

"The reason we can walk through town now is because nobody around here has seen my act," she said. "Right now, I'm just a girl walking with a handsome man."

"Stop teasing," I laughed and playfully punched her arm.

"Ouch! You hurt me!" she cried half heartedly before smiling again. "I'm serious. As long as I'm with you; nobody will give me a second look. But after they see a performance of me flying through the air in my skimpy costume, I become some sort of trophy that men seem to be willing to do almost anything to get their hands on. After that, the only way I can walk out in public is with somebody as big as Clay Boerwinkle. He's big enough to discourage most of the dogs to keep their distance, but there are still some who try to get past Clay anyway."

"What does he do then?" I asked.

"It ain't pretty," she admitted. "Mostly he just cracks their heads a little; just enough to scare them away."

"Do you think he wants to crack my head?"

"Don't worry about it," she assured me. "He doesn't see you as a threat. He looks at you like you're an orphan. I think he feels sorry for you and actually wants to help."

"That's good—I think?"

"It is." She answered. "Scamps like us need all the friends we can get in this world."

Instead of finding a restaurant, Cliffy bought two bowls of something called Jambalaya from a Negro woman on the river dock. It was a stew with meat, fish, peppers and rice. I had heard of rice, but never had tasted it before. Ma used to say that rice was a *slave crop of the South;* not fit for a God-fearin' Christian.

It took me a while to get used to the flavor and the heat. The spices almost burnt a hole in the roof of my mouth, but after a few bites, I decided I liked it. It was amazing to me how different the world was thirty miles from home.

Cliffy and I walked and talked on the streets of Vincennes for the next two nights. Mostly she wanted to know about my family and our life at South Union. She wanted to know everything about everybody. "Rose sounds like a wonderful girl, but I think your Granny would scare me a little," she said.

"She might be rough as a cob on the outside, but she's really got a tender heart. She'd like you," I assured her.

"I doubt that she'd like me if I showed up on her doorstep with you. People tend to look on girls like me differently. She'd think I wasn't good enough for you."

"Don't say that Cliffy! Don't you ever say that again." I could feel my temper flaring up inside of me. "You are the best person I know. I'm the one who's not good enough for you."

"I was just teasing, Will," she said while wrapping her arms around me. "I didn't mean to get you upset."

"You don't understand." I could feel my throat tightening with every word. "I love you, Cliffy. I love you more than anything in the world." Once the words were spoken, I began to cry.

"Oh honey, don't cry." She put her hand on my face and pulled me close, so we were looking eye to eye. "I love you too, Will. I truly do…"

Her hesitation cut me like a knife. "But…?"

"There ain't no happy ending for a girl like me." I could hear the hurt in her voice. "No matter how much I want it, people are never gonna look at me like a respectable woman. I'll always be a circus girl and to most people, that ain't no different from being a whore."

"But you're not!"

"You and I know that," she said, "but it's what everybody else thinks that counts."

"I'll kill anybody who calls you that!" I declared.

"And that's the problem, Will," she calmly patted my hand. "Things might go well for a while, but then we'd run into someone who knew what I did. They would say something and you would want to do something about it. Before long you'd be in trouble. I could never live with myself if something ever happened to you."

"It wouldn't be that way," I protested. "Look at Jenny. A few months ago, she was a slave in Mississippi, She met my Pa and now she's a member of our family, and nobody thinks anything about it."

"So all of you Farmer men go around the country and rescue girls in trouble?"

"Don't joke about it! I'm being serious." I was feeling a little hurt.

"It's different with your Pa and Jenny, they're both older."

"And I'm just a kid."

"That's not what I meant," she hesitated. "But it does make a difference. I'm old enough to marry, but you're only thirteen."

"I'm almost fourteen!" I protested.

"Alright, you're almost fourteen," she agreed. "It would be over two years before we could get married. Two years is a long time with a war going on, who knows what can happen."

"We could run away where nobody knows us," I suggested.

"And do what?"

"I could get a job," I told her.

"Doing what?" she asked.

"I can work as hard as any man."

"Oh honey, I'm not selling you short. Clay says you're the best shit shoveler he's ever hired. He said if you stay on he'd move you up to a better job, but the circus life ain't right for you. You are better than this. You have a family who loves you and a life to go back to."

"But they'll kill them if I go back!"

"Those men won't be there forever. It won't be that long until you can go back and things will be like they were before. It doesn't sound like the war is going to last much longer anyway.

Just stay with me until the circus leaves town and then you can go home. I'm sure things will have calmed down by then."

"And if they haven't?" I asked defiantly.

"Well then, you come back to your shovel." She smiled bravely. "I think the elephants love you as much as I do."

I laughed at her joke even though I didn't feel like it. "I don't understand, Cliffy. You say I'm too good for the circus, but what about you? If this is such a bad life why don't you leave?"

She paused and gazed into the sky as if searching for the answer. "I have no place to go. I have no family. The circus is the only thing I have. Besides, it's the only life I know."

"You do have someplace to go. You can go with me back to South Union."

Cliffy was right, once the performances started, things got hectic in a hurry. I shoveled mounds of manure by day and watched Cliffy perform at night. She was wonderful. She had the crowds eating out of her hands with her high flying acrobatics. She walked the high wire and twirled like a dancer from a rope at the top of the tent without a safety net below her. She had them all on the edge of their seats when she dove into the barrel of water from the platform. They feared for her safety as she remained underwater for far too long in the barrel before making her escape. Maya the Magnificent was the star of the show.

The more I watched, the more I realized that Cliffy only seemed happy when she was performing. She hated the life she was living, but something came over her when she stepped upon that platform amidst the wires and riggings. It was as if she was a bird that was set free from her cage. The applause fueled her confidence making her want to fly higher every night. She seemed so natural as she executed her stunts that I tried to ignore the danger she was in during each and every performance. One slip of the hand and she could be gone forever in an instant. I tried not to think about what could happen, but it was always in the back of my mind.

After the shows, Cliffy and I would eat a late supper in the circus chow tent and then walk for a few minutes along the riverside before returning to her wagon for the night. We slept in each other's arms, but we never talked about her leaving with me again. Down deep, I knew I would be leaving soon and tried to ignore that painful thought as long as possible.

I could tell she was dealing with things in her own way too. She disappeared with her thoughts for several minutes at a time, but would never share what those thoughts were. She just smiled and whispered "happy thoughts" and kissed me lovingly on the forehead or tip of my nose.

I wondered how she really felt about me. How could she have feelings for me, when there were so many men vying for her attention? I didn't have anything to offer her other than my heart. I finally decided that in reality, she probably felt sorry for me and was too nice to tell me the truth. She had managed to keep Clay Boerwinkle away, but I think the new circus boss was growing weary of me moving in on his star performer. If I stayed much longer, there was certain to be trouble on that front. I decided to enjoy her company as long as I could.

I was standing at the edge of the bleachers waiting for Cliffy to make her appearance when I thought I heard somebody call my name. "Will Farmer!" I heard it again and then felt someone grasp my elbow and twirl me around. It was Bill Maxwell,

Lizzy's older brother, in his navy Union uniform. "Where in the hell have you been?" he growled. "The whole county has been out looking for you. Your poor Granny is beside herself with worry. She's afraid one of those Minnesota boys had done killed you."

We walked outside of the tent where we could hear each other. "I had to go. They said they'd kill my whole family if I didn't leave."

"Everybody knows all about it. Doc Judd went to see the Dutch Captain, what's his name?"

"Weber," I replied.

"The doc went to Captain Weber with that Jensen feller's jacket and told him the same story you did. Weber went over to Mason Goff's and talked to your colored friend. Weber took one look at the boy's missing fingers and rode back to the camp hell-bent for retribution. He roughed up Jensen a little and made him confess about the raid. Then when you turned up missing, everybody was afraid they killed you to keep you quiet."

"I didn't feel like I had a choice," I told him, "They said they'd kill everybody, even the women, if I wasn't gone before sunrise."

"Your Captain Weber beat on Jensen a little more and he gave up the dirt on a couple of his cronies. They slapped 'em in irons and sent them down to the hooskow in Olney at the Provost Marshall. You don't have to worry about those boys anymore."

"Glad to hear that," I sighed deeply. "How did you find me?" I asked.

"Lizzy had mentioned that you were sweet on a circus girl. Me and some boys from my regiment were comin' down here to listen to Black Jack Logan's speech when I saw the circus posters on the trace. I put two and two together and thought I'd come down and take a look-see. And here you are."

"Guilty as charged," I admitted.

"So where is this circus girl?" he asked.

I motioned for him to follow me. Cliffy's act had already started. She was twirling like a dervish, thirty feet above the ground, holding onto the rope with a single hand. When we reached the performance ring, I calmly pointed upward.

"That's your girl?" he asked. His jaw dropped.

"It is," I nodded.

"Lord have mercy," he muttered.

He watched her entire act without saying another word. As soon as she reappeared from her five minutes in the barrel, he motioned for me to follow him outside. "I don't know what lucky clover you found, but if you want to ride home with us— we'll be at the Westport Ferry at noon tomorrow." He shook his head in disbelief. "Listen, Will, I don't know how you ever got hooked up with this girl, but your family misses you real bad. After seein' her performance there, I'll understand if you decide not to go. I'll make sure to tell em you're alright, but it'll break their hearts if you ain't with us. So you do what you have to do. I'll understand either way. I'm sure you've got some thinkin' to do. Either way—we'll be leaving on the ferry at high noon."

"You have to go," Cliffy whispered. "There is no other decision to be made. Your family is safe and they need you."

"But Cliffy—I love you."

"I love you too, Will," she began to sob. "You'll never know how much I do. And always will…" For the first time since we'd been together she kissed my lips in a way that didn't make me feel like we were just friends. She began breathing heavily and pushed me against the wall of her wagon. She held me tight and pressed her body hard against mine. "I'll love you, Will Farmer, until the day I die."

I dressed and left early in the morning while she was still asleep. Leaving was hard enough without saying goodbye. I knew that I could never leave if she asked me to stay, but deep inside, I knew she wouldn't. She wanted out of this life, but she couldn't let go because of the guilt and shame she carried. I told her that I didn't care and neither would my family. I told her this might be her last chance to get away. She cried and told me it was already too late.

Bill Maxwell looked surprised as I rode down the ramp to the ferry on Midnight. "I'd just about given up on you," he smiled. "Although, I wouldn't have blamed you if you stayed." He patted me on the back and didn't say a word about the tears I had to wipe away. "Let's go home, Will."

—ᴍ—

Chapter 35

I tried to keep my distance behind the others as we made our way through Purgatory Swamp. Bill Maxwell and his brother Arch rode in front while a pair of privates from Robinson named Pratt and Rainwater followed right behind them. The four soldiers, all dressed in their Union blue uniforms, were all in a good mood and hadn't stopped talking since we left Vincennes. They tried to draw me into the conversation with a little good natured ribbing, but I couldn't force myself to speak. Before long they were singing *John Brown's Body* and *When Johnny Comes Marching Home*

Going home was the right thing to do, but leaving Cliffy was almost more than I could bear. I wondered what she was doing at that very moment. Did she miss me as much as I missed her? I knew one person who would be happy to see me gone; Clay Boerwinkle. Clay was probably turning summersaults by now. It was obvious that he was having doubts about Cliffy looking at me as a little brother. At his size, he would have made short work of me if he wanted to.

Purgatory Swamp was much dryer than the previous week, so they decided to follow a trail through the middle of the swamp instead of following the *Vincennes Trace*. Apparently it was a more direct route and would knock several miles off the trip. I really didn't care one way or another. It would be nice to get home again, but there would be countless questions to be answered and I didn't feel like talking.

It was middle to late afternoon and a hint of sunshine peeked through the clouds as we left the swamp for the cover of the hardwood forest. I had no idea where we were, but the Maxwell brothers obviously did. The road wasn't much wider than a deer path. The woods were so thick that even the most expert of pioneers would be lost if he ventured far from the trail. We rode single file for a couple of miles when Bill Maxwell motioned for us to stop and keep quiet. I could hear voices up ahead, but couldn't make out what they were saying.

"Copperhead meeting," he whispered. "Follow my lead."

Before I realized what was going on, the others started to sing at the top of their lungs

"Glory, glory, Hallelujah,
Glory, glory, Hallelujah,
Glory, glory, Hallelujah,
His truth goes marching on."

Within seconds we were in a clearing that encircled a small log hewn Hardshell Baptist Church. There were at least a couple dozen men milling around the chapel door. At first glance, most of the men seemed to resemble hardened criminals instead of your run of the mill church goers. Our sudden appearance had apparently caught them by surprise.

"How-dee-do," Bill Maxwell greeted them with a tip of his cap. "Come to hear some preachin', boys?"

"We've come to get away from the gospel you Yankee boys have been preachin'; that's for damn sure," shouted a man from the top church step. "If you blue bellies know what's good for you; you'll keep on a movin'."

Bill Maxwell stopped in his tracks. "What did you say?"

"Uh-oh," whispered Rainwater. "Get ready."

"Ready for what?" I asked. I was just beginning to pay attention to the situation.

"To fight or run," he replied. "Or maybe both."

The fact that we were outnumbered eighteen to four didn't seem to bother Bill Maxwell. After all, he'd seen the elephant so many times down south, he wasn't about to let a gang of Southern Illinois Copperheads get the best on him. "We've spent the last two years taking Braxton Bragg's best shot, so I don't 'spect a motley gang of Johnny Reb wannabes are gonna get us to move one way or another. Besides, you boys are ridin' a dead horse. Uncle Billy Sherman is damn near to Savannah and Sam Grant has Granny Lee bottled up in Virginia. It's only a matter of weeks before the war is over."

My Colt and my Spencer were wrapped in my blankets. Any move on my part would probably make matters worse, so I carefully worked Midnight around the others and prepared to ride hard.

"Jeff Davis ain't done yet; just you wait and see," said the man who had issued the warning. He unbuttoned his duster and put his hand on a short barreled shotgun. The rest of the Copperheads followed his lead and started to go for their guns.

"Jeff Davis can go to hell," Maxwell shouted. He pulled out his side arm and shot the ringleader in the hand that held the shotgun. "Let's go boys," he shouted and spurred his horse up the trail at a breakneck pace.

The other soldiers took off behind him leaving me to bring up the rear. I slapped Midnight's flank and headed north in a hail of bullets. We didn't look back to see if they were following until we were five miles closer to home. The four soldiers laughed as if the skirmish was some kind of game. The sound of the bullets whizzing past my head had made me forget about Cliffy for the moment. My stomach, which was in knots to begin with, was now wrenching and heaving after the close call. As soon as we stopped at a small creek to rest and water the horses, I ran into the woods and became violently sick.

They chuckled at me when I returned, but stopped short of giving me a hard time. Bill thought it might be too dangerous to camp out that night, just in case the Copperheads were following us, so we kept on riding after dark.

It must have been midnight by the time we reached the Maxwell's two story clapboard farmhouse. I was thoroughly exhausted, so when Bill said I should spend the night in the barn, I didn't argue. Besides, it would create a lot less commotion by not waking everybody up in the middle of the night. The reunion was going to be hard enough anyway. A few more hours wouldn't matter.

I gave Midnight a quick wipe down and then threw my blankets onto a short mound of hay in the loft. I felt guilty for putting him away damp after a hard twenty five mile ride, but just didn't have it in me. I had just fallen asleep when I felt the pressure of a boney finger poking me in the ribs.

"Don't you dare go to sleep without speaking to me!" I couldn't tell if Lizzy was mad or just playing with me. By the time I gathered my wits about me, I decided it was a little of both. "I was worried sick about you, Will. Where have you been?"

"It's a long story, Lizzy. Can't it wait til tomorrow?" I begged her.

"No it can't!" she insisted. "I want to know where you've been."

"I was in Vincennes," I told her.

"What were you doing down there?"

"I was shoveling elephant shit at the circus. That's what I was doing!"

"Oh," she said with the sound of hurt in her voice.

I had no reason to be cross with her, I felt ashamed of myself. "I'm sorry Lizzy. I had no right to talk to you that way."

"It's alright," she said. "I know you're tired." She hesitated before speaking again. "Did you see Cliffy?"

I nodded yes and then looked away. It was too painful to talk about it.

Lizzy wrapped her arms around me from behind while I silently sobbed. A few minutes later, just as I was dozing back to sleep, I felt her gently kiss the back of my head. "We can talk about it in the morning," she whispered.

The frantic barking of John Maxwell's hound dogs shook me from a deep sleep just as the first of the pre-dawn light appeared in the east. I rolled over and tried to grab a few more winks, when the barking became even more earnest. I sat up and let my eyes adjust to the darkness.

"Who's out there?" shouted John Maxwell as he walked out on to the front porch of his house.

I hurried to the door and peeked outside. There looked to be at least twenty armed men standing in the front yard. On further inspection, they looked to be the same men from our skirmish at the church.

"We've come to arrest Bill Maxwell and we ain't leavin' till you send him out," shouted a man from the crowd.

"Let me see the writ," said Mr. Maxwell.

After a long pause the man finally answered. "We don't have no damn warrant and we don't need one neither!"

"Then I don't reckon we'll be sendin' the boy out to you until you come back with the sheriff and a writ. I suggest you boys get off my property before someone gets hurt." John Maxwell turned around and started walking back toward his front porch.

"Then I'll be damned if I won't burn your house down instead," shouted the man. An explosion of gunfire suddenly ensued. The noise was deafening. When a bullet ricocheted off of the door, I dove back into the pile of hay. I found my Colt and checked the percussion caps, but was unsure of what to do. Everyone was shooting at the house. To shoot into the mob would do nothing but get me killed. I crawled back into the hayloft and peeked out the door. Bill Maxwell had stepped out onto the second story balcony and while dressed only in his long underwear, began firing into the crowd while screaming at the top of his lungs. I saw two of the Copperheads fall in agony. One was shot in the shoulder; the other one in the knee.

Bill Maxwell awkwardly fell to one knee. A spot of crimson began to grow around his thigh. He limped back through the window into the upstairs bedroom while a pair of rifles began blasting from the lower part of the house. There was a sudden lull in the action when I heard a loud piercing cry from somewhere in the house.

"Lizzy's shot!" Mrs. Maxwell cried. "Oh' my God—they shot Lizzy!"

"Hold your fire!" Someone yelled from the inside of the house. "There's women and children inside."

The Copperheads drew back to the cover of some trees to tend their wounded. A grimy man with a tobacco stained shirt and beard stepped forward. "You can send the women and young'uns out. We'll give 'em safe passage until they're clear of the shooting."

"The girl's hurt too bad," John Maxwell shouted from his front porch. "She can't be moved."

"Then we'll settle for your son," he replied. "Send Bill Maxwell out and we'll be on our way."

"Not without a writ and a sheriff," he replied. "We'll come peacefully if I see an arrest warrant."

There was a long silence. "We'll be back later," said the man. "Go ahead and send for the doctor. We got wounded of our own to tend to."

Arch Maxwell immediately ran to the barn. I offered to go for Doc Judd, but Arch said he would be quicker and he also intended to round up some militia and give the Copperheads their comeuppance. I helped him with his saddle and then made a dash toward the house with my rifle and pistol in hand.

Private Rainwater was wrapping a bandage around Bill Maxwell's bloody thigh. Jon Maxwell and Pratt were standing guard at the front windows. "Can't see them scoundrels, but I know they's still out there,"

"How's Lizzy?" I asked frantically.

Mr. Maxwell started to say something, but became too choked up to speak. He nodded for me to go upstairs and then peered back through the window, eager to shoot any bush-whacker brave enough to show his face.

I followed Lizzy's cries of agony as I climbed the stairs to her second story bedroom. I stopped in my tracks as soon as I walked through the door. Her night dress was covered in blood. Lizzy's mother and another woman, who I later learned to be her cousin Bess, were holding her down on the bed as she writhed side to side in pain.

"Will!" Lizzy cried out. "It hurts so bad!"

I didn't know what to do. Bess gave me a look that said I should leave the room. I stepped backwards toward the stairs. "Please don't leave me, Will!" Lizzy cried. "Help me!"

Lizzy's mother nodded and motioned for me to come help. Lizzy latched onto my hand and dug into my skin with her fingernails. She rolled her eyes and clenched her jaw as the pain seemed to come in waves.

"Hold her shoulders down against the bed," instructed Mrs. Maxwell. "I've got to stop the bleeding."

I wrapped my arms around her shoulders while Bess spread her weight across Lizzy's knees. Mrs. Maxwell took two folded towels and pressed down hard against Lizzy's lower stomach.

"Ohhh!" Lizzy cried. "Please don't. It hurts too bad!"

"Be strong child!" Her mother spoke with an amazing amount of calmness to her voice. "I've got to keep pressure on the wounds until the doctor gets here. Be strong and pray to Jesus!"

I made the mistake of looking down at the wounds. There were two bullet holes that had burst her bowels wide open. I had to force down what I was feeling inside. *Be strong for Lizzy's sake,* I told myself. "Look at me, Lizzy. I need you to hang on! Doc Judd's gonna be here any minute."

"I'm tryin' as hard as I can, Will." Her eyes seemed to beg me for a sign of encouragement. I did the best that I could, but I'm sure that she could see right through me. I didn't know the first thing about medicine, but it didn't take a doctor to see that things were bad.

I held her hand and kept her talking until Doc Judd came through the door. "Go downstairs. Boil some water and tear some sheets into small pieces, Will." Doc did a double take. "Will! You're back!" He sighed. "I just wish it were under better circumstances. Now, go boil some water"

When I came back with the water and bandages, Lizzy's mother told me it was best if I stayed outside. From the tone of Lizzy's cries, I didn't need much convincing. I went back downstairs where all of the men were still standing watch at each window. Bill Maxwell's leg was oozing blood through the bandage, but the burly soldier showed no signs of letting his injury slow him down. The Copperheads had retreated far enough to stay out of rifle range, so everything had slowed to a waiting game. Seconds seemed to pass like minutes until Arch Maxwell returned with some local men with blood in their eyes. They seemed more than ready to take the fight to the Copperheads when Captain Weber and his *Mounted Dutchmen* arrived from the west. The Union troops took a position directly between the two opposing sides. Weber walked into the house and sent a lieutenant to parlay with the leader of the mob.

Weber met with Bill Maxwell and his father while I sat by myself at the kitchen table. I tried to listen to their conversation while keeping an ear opened toward the commotion upstairs. Lizzy had quieted down during the past few minutes, but I wasn't sure if that was good news or not. So much had happened during the past couple of days, that I was having trouble sorting it out in my mind. As much as I wanted it all to be a dream; this was all real and all bad.

I was staring out the back window when Captain Weber sat down next to me. "You seem to have a nose for finding your way to the middle of all the trouble in the neighborhood, Mr. Farmer."

"I was sleeping in the barn, when it all broke loose," I told him. "I was going to head on home at daylight. I guess that's what I get for oversleeping."

"Maxwell told me everything. He said you had joined up with a circus in Vincennes when he found you."

I shrugged.

"I want to apologize to you for putting you in that situation in the first place. I shouldn't have doubted you. I just couldn't believe that Jensen would stoop so low. I've known his family for years. He had always been spoiled rotten as a child, but to actually torture those people like he did—I'm flabbergasted."

"What do you want me to say, Captain?"

He waited several seconds before answering. "I don't want you to say anything, son. I just wanted you to know that Jensen and his accomplices won't be a threat to you or your family anymore. They'll all be going to prison for quite a while." He turned and walked back toward the front door.

"Captain Weber!" I shouted before he went outside.

He stopped and turned at the threshold. "Yes?"

"Thank you, sir." I replied.

He smiled and offered me a friendly salute. "You're a good soldier, Mr. Farmer. Damn good soldier, indeed."

When the Lawrence County Sheriff finally arrived, it became clear that there had not been a warrant issued for Bill Maxwell's arrest. But by using his wounded hand as evidence, the man who was shot at the church, signed a complaint against Bill. The Sherriff arrested Bill Maxwell for attempted murder and took him directly to the Lawrenceville jail. To insure that nothing happened on the way, John and Arch Maxwell along with Privates Pratt and Rainwater escorted them. Realizing that the Copperheads seemed hell bent on lynching Maxwell, Captain Weber sent two dozen troopers with the posse just to make sure the prisoner arrived safely. Once Bill was secured in the Lawrence County jail, Weber ordered a small detail to remain on duty in Lawrenceville until the trial.

I waited several hours in the kitchen until Doc Judd finally came downstairs. He looked utterly exhausted.

"How is she?" I asked.

"She's resting now." He spoke softly without looking me in the eyes. "I gave her enough laudanum to make her sleep through the night."

"But will she live?" I asked emphatically.

"It doesn't look good, Will. The bullets did quite a bit of damage. To be honest, I don't know how she's lasted this long."

"Can I see her?" I asked.

"Let her rest, "Doc replied. "Maybe tomorrow—if she's up to it."

"But what if—"

"She's in the Lord's hands now, Will," he interrupted. "There's nothing we can do now except pray." He removed his spectacles and cleaned them with his handkerchief. He was fighting to hold back the tears. "Everyone has been worried sick about you. Why don't you let me take you home?"

Chapter 36

Sister Rose and Granny showered me with hugs, kisses and a bucketful of tears. "I thought you were dead," Rose cried. "We thought those soldiers had killed you."

"Why didn't you come to us?" Granny added.

"They said that they would kill you all, if I didn't leave. I thought I was doing the right thing. I'm sorry, Granny."

"Oh, it don't matter none. We're just glad to have you back." She ushered me to the kitchen table, "You must be starving. Sit on down and let me cook you something to eat."

"I'm not really hungry, Granny. I'd just as soon get some sleep if you don't mind."

"That don't sound like you. Are you feeling alright?" she asked.

Doc Judd stepped in and told them about the shootout at the Maxwell place. The jubilation over my return quickly turned to silence.

"Is Lizzy going to make it?" Rose asked.

"I'm afraid the wound is mortal," he admitted.

"Mortal?" I shouted. "You didn't say she was going to die!"

"I didn't lie to you, Will," he replied. "I told you it was in the Lord's hands now; and it is. The best thing we can do for Lizzy and her family is pray for them."

"It won't do any good," I yelled back. "God doesn't care!"

"Will Farmer!" Granny gasped. "Don't you ever talk like that!"

"It's true!" I shouted back. "If he cared, he wouldn't let all of the bad things happen. Lizzy never hurt a person in her life. Neither did Andy Johnson! Neither did Ma!"

"Stop it, Will!" Rose lashed out. "You don't know what you're saying."

"You should know better than anybody. Your husband lost his arm at Shiloh! What about your parents? What kind of God makes you an orphan?" I had totally lost control of myself.

"Oh—Will." Rose broke into tears and I instantly felt lower than dirt.

"I should have stayed in Vincennes," I muttered as I ran out the door and headed straight for the barn. I started to throw a saddle on Midnight, but stopped myself. Muddy grunted from her pen, looking for some affection or perhaps, in her own way, looking to comfort me. I ignored her completely.

Why had I opened my big mouth? I don't know why I said the things I did. It wasn't their fault. It really wasn't my fault either. It seemed like the whole world had gone to hell. I couldn't see how my life could possibly get any worse. I didn't want to leave home again, but I missed Cliffy so much my chest ached. But most of all, the thought of Lizzy dying had my stomach wrapped in knots. She had wanted to talk to me last night, but I had been rude and sent her away. I promised to talk to her in the morning, but God, in all of his wisdom had other plans.

By my way of thinking—God was an easy target. What had I done that made him go out of his way to punish me? I didn't consider myself a bad person, but he had seen fit to punish me like the worst of sinners. Blaming God was the only way to make any sense out of my life.

Suddenly, I realized I was feeling sorry for myself, while Lizzy was fighting for her life. *What sort of selfish person was I?* I was mad at the world and ashamed of myself. Not knowing what to do, I dropped down in a mound of straw and began to punch the ground until my knuckles became bloody and numb. I was completely and hopelessly lost.

I don't know how much time had passed by when Jenny appeared at the barn door. "May I come in?" she asked.

I reluctantly nodded yes. I wonder if she had been there long enough to witness my tantrum. Jenny was wrapped in a dark gray shawl and wearing a coal black dress. With her long black hair pulled tight into a bonnet, she looked almost matronly.

"I don't need any—"

"Shhh," she interrupted and placed her forefinger in front of her lips. "You don't have to say a word." She continued to walk toward me.

"I'm sorry for—"

"Shhh—not a word." She took a seat next to me on the straw mound. "Sometimes a boy just needs his mother."

"But, you're not—"

"Shhh—I know I'm not, but I'm what God has sent you." She wrapped her arms around me and brought my head to her chest.

Without uttering another word, I broke into tears. It was as if years of pain and frustration poured out of me. Once I started, I couldn't have stopped the deluge if I had wanted. I wasn't crying over anything or anyone in particular. Not Lizzy, not Cliffy. Not Ma or Pa either. For the past few years, I had kept everything bottled up inside of me. I had worked so hard to be the man of the house that Pa wanted me to be. And now it was falling apart. I was a fraud. I was no more a man than Jaybird or Bub. I had been pretending to be something I wasn't. I was nothing but a stupid kid crying like a baby on his mama's lap.

I don't know how long Jenny held me in the barn that afternoon. Apparently she did know what I needed. We didn't speak more than a dozen words that day. "There will be plenty of time to talk," she assured me. "Just not today." It was well after dark when she walked me back to the cabin. I went straight to my bed in the loft and was sound asleep within minutes. I came down for breakfast the next morning and ate a biscuit and a couple of eggs. I finished a small mug of milk and then went back to bed. I slept like the dead until the next morning.

Everything seemed different when I finally got out of bed to stay. Maybe it was like the soldiers seeing the elephant for the first time. Maybe I had finally witnessed enough of life's cruelties to realize that the world is a cold dark place and there are no happy endings.

After breakfast, I brought the family up to date on what had happened over the last week and a half. Oddly, they didn't seem surprised. Apparently Doc Judd had learned about my adventures in Vincennes from his frequent visits to the Maxwell house. Everyone remained silent until I finished.

Granny asked me if I had anything else to say before she spoke her piece. I didn't. "I know you thought you was doing right, but you can't fight this war all by yourself, Will. You ain't the only one sufferin'. We've all been through hell these past few years and we still don't know how things are gonna turn out. The reason we have persevered this far is because we stuck together as a family. We might not all be of the same flesh and blood, but that don't mean we ain't a family; and a strong family at that. You've been asked to carry a burden that no boy your age should have to endure. And yet you've accounted yourself as good as any man. But there are some things you can't do alone. This thing with that no good soldier over at the barracks concerned the whole family and that's how it should've been dealt with. That being said—it's all water under the bridge now. We need you, Will. It might not seem that way all the time—but we do. I need your word that you won't be runnin' away no more."

"I won't," I told her. "I promise."

The women all made over me, while Pappy slapped my back and Ned playfully punched my shoulder. Jaybird and Bub ran outside to play as if nothing had happened. I was back in everybody's good graces again. I would be a good soldier and do what was expected of me.

Everybody had gone about their business when Rose pulled me off to the side. "Lizzy's been asking for you."

"How is she doing?" I asked

Rose began to choke up. "She's in a heap of pain, Will. I've never seen anything so pitiful, but she's being brave. Doc Judd has her on a healthy dose of laudanum, so she sleeps a good part of the time."

"Do you think I should ride over there?" I asked.

"I'll go with you."

I waited downstairs for over an hour while Rose helped Doc Judd change Lizzy's bandages. Neighbor women from around South Union took turns sitting with Lizzy, since her wounds were still open and they required around the clock care. I didn't quite understand all of the details, but the nature of her injuries made it inappropriate for any member of the male species to assist in the vigil.

The tic of a grandfather clock seemed to make each minute pass like ten. I had no other choice, but to sit and wait. Lizzy's mother poured a mug of sassafras tea and placed it on the table in front of me. She offered me a piece of pie, but I declined. I watched Mrs. Maxwell clean every inch of the kitchen three times over without stopping. Her jaw was clenched and her face was expressionless. I wanted to say something to make her feel better, but the proper words never came to mind. I sipped my tea in silence. Finally, I heard footsteps coming down the stairs. "You can see her now," said Doc Judd. "Just make sure she stays calm."

I nodded and then slowly climbed the stairs to her bedroom. Visions of Lizzy covered in blood while crying in agony came to mind. Even then, I knew I would never be able to erase that memory for as long as I lived. There was a roaring fire in the fireplace and a heavy aroma of balm, herbs and salve. There was also a smell of sickness and decay that was all too familiar to anyone who had witnessed death on the frontier. I didn't know what to expect as I neared her bedside. I tried to prepare myself for the worst, but I wasn't ready for what I saw.

Lizzy seemed to have shriveled to half her normal size. Her skin had become a shade of ashen gray that is usually reserved for bodies on display in pine boxes. Her eyes were dull. Only a faint flicker of the spark was still there. She managed a hapless smile as soon as she saw me. "There's my boy." Her voice was barely louder than a whisper.

"How are you doing, Lizzy?" I tried to produce an honest smile.

"I'm dying, I'm afraid to say." She made the statement with the same conviction one might say, "It sure is nice weather we're having," or "it looks like rain."

"Don't say that, Lizzy. It's not funny."

"Calm down, Will," she scolded me. "I'm not a little girl anymore. Besides, there's no reason to pretend otherwise. I've spent the last few years studying to be a nurse. I know what's going on. Doctor Judd has been honest with me. He says it's only a matter of time."

"But Lizzy," I protested. "You gotta believe you'll get better. You can't give up."

"There's a war going on, Will—people die." She hesitated and coughed. "It's just my time."

"I refuse to believe you're not going to live through this."

"You don't have any choice." She placed her hand over mine. "Reverend Parker said that I'm bound for glory and I'm ready."

"Does it hurt bad?"

"Something fearful to be honest," she admitted. "The laudanum makes me sleep, but I can't get through the day without it."

"Is there anything I can do for you?"

"Just talk to me," she replied.

"I'll come every day," I promised.

"I'm afraid that won't be possible," she told me. "Things are going to get pretty rough and I don't want you to see me that way."

"But Lizzy—"

"It's okay. I'm feeling better today—so we can visit for a while, but today is going to have to be—goodbye."

"I don't know what to say."

"Why don't you tell me what you did in Vincennes?"

"I joined the circus."

"Did you walk the high wire or tame the lions?"

"I shoveled elephant shit," I answered.

Lizzy laughed so hard she went into a coughing fit. I got worried and started to go for help, but she stopped me. "Don't leave. I just got tickled. Just give me a second and I'll be fine." She took a couple of deep breaths and motioned for me to sit back down at her side. "Just elephants or were there other animals involved?"

"I shoveled for the lions, tigers, zebras, horses and monkeys, but compared to those elephants—their shit ain't shit."

I waited through a second laughing fit. "Please promise me; no more poop jokes!"

"I promise. What else would you like to talk about?"

"Tell me about your circus girl," she answered. "Tell me about Cliffy."

"Nothing to tell," I told her.

"Don't you dare lie to me, Will Farmer. I don't have time for any lies."

It was uncomfortable, but I told her everything.

"You've got it bad." She shook her head in mock disgust.

"What do you mean?"

"You're in love with that girl," she answered. "Head over heels and lovesick."

"I think I am." I could feel my face turning red.

"I thought it was just some kind of school boy crush. Rose made it sound like she was much older than you. I didn't know she was so young."

"She does what she has to do to survive." I told her.

"I suppose if things were different, I'd be jealous." She had a faraway look on her face. "Oh well," she sighed.

"I'm sorry, Lizzy. I didn't mean to make you feel bad."

"Don't be silly, Will. I never gave any thought about getting married. All I ever wanted to do was be a nurse. It's just that I won't ever know what it feels like to be a wife or mother. I'm never gonna be any older than fourteen." She pursed her lips and tried to hold back the tears. She couldn't. She held my hand against her cheek and turned away. I remained silent while she sobbed.

I waited until she was still before speaking again. "Is there any news from Bill?" I asked.

"He's supposed to go before something called a grand jury next week in Lawrenceville. His lawyer said there ain't nothing to worry about, on account of that there won't be any Copperheads on the jury. He says nobody is gonna take the word of a southern sympathizer over the word of a Yankee soldier."

"How is his leg?" I asked.

"The bullet went all the way through, but Doc said it isn't healing quick enough to suit him."

"Any word on who shot..." I wished I hadn't asked the question.

"Who shot me? No. The sheriff said since it was a mob, it couldn't be proved who the shooter was."

"So, your brother is in jail for winging one of those Copperhead bastards and they get away scot-free after ..."

"...killing me." She finished my sentence for me. "No, it doesn't seem fair, but God has other plans for me. I've forgiven the man, whoever he is, for shooting me. Reverend Parker said it's important that I don't dwell on it. You need to do the same, Will."

"I don't know if I can, Lizzy. I'll try, but I'm not promising anything." I didn't want to let it show, but I felt a ball of hell-fire anger rise up inside of me.

"I want you to promise me that you'll let this go."

"I said I will try."

"Not good enough," she snapped.

"Okay—I promise."

"You're a good person, Will Farmer, but you carry a lot of hatred inside of you. You hate anything and everything to do with the South. You might feel that you have justification, but all you're doing is hurting yourself. You need to let all of this anger and spite go. You need to do something good with your life."

"Like what?" I asked.

"Well—you could be a preacher or maybe a doctor."

"A preacher? Reverend Will Farmer?" I almost choked on the words. "Are you joking?"

"A girl in my position doesn't joke." She was somber and serious. "This war has taken so much already. It breaks my heart to think it's gonna take you too. I see you get all worked up for revenge and I know nothing good is gonna come from it. You might feel better for a while, but then you'd have to live with yourself. You'll look in the mirror and end up hating the face looking back at you."

"I haven't done anything yet and you're making me feel guilty."

"Good," she said. "I want you to feel guilty and see my face on my deathbed anytime you get a bad thought in that head of yours."

"Yeah, but me a preacher?"

"Maybe that is asking a little too much of you," she laughed. "I guess I'll have to settle for Doctor Will Farmer."

"Lizzy, you know I'm not smart enough to be a doctor."

"Don't give me any of your guff. You're plenty smart. You just have to put your mind to it. You have to take all of your hatred toward the Johnny Rebs and turn it into something good. It don't matter what it is as long as it's good. Besides, since I won't get to be a nurse, you could practice medicine on my behalf."

"That's quite a bit of guilt you're heaping on me."

"I'll haunt you if you don't do what I say." she warned.

I realized I wasn't going to leave without promising that I wouldn't take revenge on anything or anybody. I think the part about me becoming a doctor was a bit of a stretch. I went ahead and promised and she said she would have to take my word on it.

We talked about friends and family for a few more minutes. I could see that she was struggling more by the minute until finally she winced in pain. She recovered and gave me a slight smile and then moaned loudly from a sharper pain.

"Should I go get some help?" I started to get up.

She clutched my wrist. "Give me a minute until this passes."

Rose poked her head through the doorway, but Lizzy motioned for her to wait outside. Rose reluctantly stepped back into the hallway.

It was hard to watch her deal with the pain. I could tell she wanted to scream out in agony, but fought hard to hold it in for my benefit. I looked the other way until her breathing slowed and the spasm began to ease. "Is it like this all the time?"

"Pretty much so," she admitted.

"I'm so sorry. Is there anything I can do for you?"

She took a deep breath and looked as if she was struggling to find the right words. Suddenly she began to sob and hid her face beneath the blanket.

"What is it Lizzy?" I asked.

She said something, but the combination of her sobbing and the covers muffling her voice, made it impossible to understand. I pulled the blanket away and then took her hands in mine. "Please tell me," I whispered.

She nodded. I used the edge of the blanket to dry her tears. "Do you remember when we kissed at Rose's wedding?"

"Sure, I remember." Now I was beginning to feel a little uneasy.

"I'm embarrassed to say that was the only time anybody has ever kissed me. So, as things turn out, you are the love of my life. I know we're just friends—"

"—best friends," I interrupted.

"Alright, best friends, but who knows what would've happened, a couple of years from now?"

"What are you saying?" I asked.

"I was just thinking of what could have been. Is it impossible to think that you and I might have been married and had a houseful of kids together?"

The thought of me having children scared me witless, but I realized what she was asking. "Sure Lizzy—you'd make a wonderful wife and mother!" I could see by the smile on her face, that I had used the right words.

"Then could you do me one last favor?" she asked.

"Anything," I replied.

"I know I must look awful, but could you kiss me one last time?"

"Of course." I brushed the hair from her eyes with my fingers as she gently pulled my face toward hers. I closed my eyes as our lips touched. I allowed her as much time as she needed. It was as if she put a life's worth of love into that moment in time. Our goodbye moment. I hoped she could sense my feelings for her too.

She pulled away as her muscles wrenched violently.

"What is it, Lizzy?" I asked frantically.

"Time to go, Will," she groaned.

"What can I do?" I begged her.

"I'll love you till the day I die, but you've got to go now." She turned her head to the left and called out for Rose.

Rose was already halfway to the bed. "Do what she says, Will," Rose said as she pushed me away. There were tears in her eyes, so I figured she was eavesdropping on our conversation.

"Not like this," I protested.

"She doesn't want you to see her like this. Tell her goodbye and leave."

"I love you too, Lizzy." Rose pushed me out of the room before I could say another word.

Chapter 37

Nobody expected Lizzy to live until Thanksgiving. She did. Even though her condition continued to worsen, she amazingly clung to life. Doc Judd couldn't explain it. "By all intent she should have passed away several days ago," he explained. "Unfortunately, her extra days haven't brought her any comfort. The most humane thing would be to ask for the Lord to take her home."

Rose continued to spend every other day at Lizzy's bedside. She, along with several neighborhood women, cared for Lizzy in shifts. Lizzy's mother had worked herself sick and had actually collapsed from exhaustion. Apparently Lizzy's pain was relentless and without relief.

"She doesn't get a minute of peace," Rose told us. "Everyone tries to comfort her, but I don't know if we're doing her any good. I've never seen anyone suffer so much."

I felt totally helpless. I know when Lizzy told me goodbye; she didn't expect to live more than a day or two. I was certain that she would want to see me, but neither Rose nor any of the other women would let me near her. They all said it was better that I remember her how she was. I pleaded with them, but they all stood firm. No meant no.

It made me angry when they implied I would think less of her. She was my friend and nothing was ever going to change that. I'd want a friend at my side if I was in her place. But I kept my mouth shut for Lizzy's sake. I would try to be the good person she wanted me to be.

A foot of snow fell on Thanksgiving morning. On the previous afternoon I had the good fortune of spotting a tom turkey in the top of a maple tree, so we were able to have a simple traditional feast. Sweet potatoes, beans, pickled beets, corn pone and blackberry pie were served along with mugs of real coffee that Uncle Woody Gogin had sent for the holidays. The price of coffee was so high that we hadn't seen anything but chicory water for the past year. We didn't ask how or where he had acquired the fresh roasted beans. "Just give thanks like the holiday says and don't ask no questions," said Granny when we received the gift.

After dinner, Ned and Jaybird popped corn in the fireplace, while Pappy and I cracked open hickory nuts on the kitchen table. Bub sat beside Jenny as she sang a sad song about a chariot takin' her home. Rose tried to coax Baby Samantha into walking across the room. Samantha had just taken her first steps a few days earlier and was about as sure footed as a newborn calf. Granny rocked in the old bentwood chair while smoking her cob pipe with a look of contentment on her face.

The news from the war was good. Sherman had split the South in half and was only a few miles away from the Atlantic Ocean. Abraham Lincoln had won re-election by a landslide, although he lost Crawford County by a wide margin. Grant seemed to have Lee trapped in Virginia and all of the newspapers said the war couldn't go on much longer.

We still hadn't heard anything from Pa, but everyone seemed content to believe he was still alive. I tried to stay optimistic, but if I had learned anything over the previous months; it was to expect the worst. I was careful to keep my mouth shut and not ruin the holiday for the others. As much as I tried, I just couldn't relax. I often thought of Cliffy, I wondered what she was doing, or who she was with at the time. I longed to be in her arms in her wagon. Everybody said it was puppy love, but I knew better.

After daydreaming about Cliffy, my mind would be drawn to the reality of Lizzy's situation and I would be consumed with guilt. *I should be able to do something for her,* I thought. But I couldn't even get close to her. I felt like running out into the woods and screaming at the top of my lungs. I was helpless. For the time being, smashing hickory nuts with a mallet would have to do.

Two weeks later, Lizzy was still clinging to life. "The Lord must have a reason," was all Doc Judd would say. I could tell from the look on Rose's face, that it was getting harder for her to go to her bedside. I asked her for details, but all she could do was shake her head and cry. I decided to stop asking.

Bill Maxwell was acquitted by a grand jury in Lawrenceville and sent home. Apparently his leg was ulcerated from the gunshot wound, so he stayed at home to recuperate instead of rejoining his unit in Tennessee. There were rumors circulating around the neighborhood that a man from Russellville was bragging that he used poison laced bullets when firing at the Maxwell house. Doc Judd said it might be the reason neither Lizzy's or Bill's wounds were healing, but there was no way of knowing for sure.

I couldn't understand why nobody was going after the man who shot Lizzy. There was a rumor that Josiah Highsmith was getting a secret posse together to pay a visit to Russellville, but Captain Weber got wind of it and threatened to jail the vigilantes as if they were Copperheads. He said to leave things to the United States Army and the Lawrence County Sheriff. That's when I realized that nothing would ever get done.

It was five days before Christmas and Lizzy was still alive. Rose said she was growing weaker by the day and the end could come at any moment. I begged to see her one last time, but once again was turned away.

It was late in the afternoon and I had just finished feeding the animals. Snow had begun falling around noon and it looked like the storm could be setting in to stay. Granny had been cooking all day while Jenny tended to the children. Ned sat at the kitchen table and read the latest news aloud from the Robinson newspaper while Pappy seemed to hang on every word. "Sherman took Savannah without firing a bullet," he reported. "It says here that the town fathers came out to meet him with open arms. It sounds like the Johnny Rebs have lost the will to fight. It won't be long until it's all over."

"Hallelujah!" Granny shouted. "Sam will be marching through that door any day now. I can feel it in my bones."

"I pray yours bones speak the truth," Jenny added.

"They ain't lied to me yet," she laughed. "My boy is comin' home. Mark my words."

"Here's something that ought to be of interest to you, Will." Ned sat upright as if he had found something important. "The rebel outlaw known as, One Eye Skaggs, was found dead outside of Paducah, Kentucky last week. It was reported that he was hung from a hackberry tree on the banks of the Ohio River. A vigilante group known as the Regulators of Northern Kentucky is suspected of bringing the notorious outlaw to his just reward, but it has not yet been confirmed." Ned carefully folded the paper. "Looks like nobody will be coming to collect that reward he put on your head after all."

"I wasn't scared," I bragged. "I already whipped him once, but I have to admit, I'll sleep better with him not around." Everybody laughed, but I was actually grateful. Every time I heard a noise in the dark, part of me always worried that it was One Eye Skaggs coming to even the score.

We were still laughing when the blowing wind and snow whooshed into the cabin as Rose opened the door. Her face was chapped and her cheeks had turned a dark shade of pink from the cold. Her coat and scarf were covered in white powder. "It's turning into a blizzard out there," she cried as she made her way to the fireplace. She had just finished her shift with Lizzy.

"Where's Doc Judd?" Ned asked.

"He's going to spend the night with Lizzy. It's been a rough day for her. Mr. Maxwell offered to bring me home, but he's suffering mightily too, so I decided it would be better if I just walked."

"You could have caught yourself a death of a cold," Granny scolded her.

"I'm fine," Rose assured her. "I'm just going to warm up a bit and run this medicine over to the Widow Rush. Doc says it's important that she gets it tonight."

"Horse feathers!" Granny howled. "You ain't going back out in that storm. Will can ride over there on horseback and be back in a few minutes."

"But I told Doc Judd that I would do it," Rose protested.

"You look chilled to the bone," Granny overruled her. "Besides, Will don't mind at all. Do ya, Will?"

Everybody looked in my direction, so I just smiled. I knew good and well that I didn't have a choice in the matter. I grabbed my coat and hat and in honor of the recently departed One Eye Skaggs, grabbed the LeMat pistol as weapon of choice for the trip.

Midnight didn't want to go out into the blizzard any more than I did. He was skittish and snapped at me when I put the bit to his mouth. Muddy on the other hand was anxious to get out of her pen. Muddy seemed to have a calming effect on the horse so I decided to let her tail along with us.

The wind was blowing so hard that it was almost impossible to tell the difference between falling and drifting snow. I wrapped the scarf around my neck and urged my reluctant horse to head north. Visibility was only a few feet, so our pace was so slow, I would have made better progress on foot. Muddy seemed to lose interest in the excursion at the halfway point and turned back toward the farm. She had been free to forage the woods for years, so I wasn't worried about her getting lost. It took over an hour to cover the mile and a half to the Widow Rush's cabin. She was grateful for the tonic and gave me a steaming mug of sassafras tea to warm me up. She wanted me to stay until the storm died down, but I assured her I would make it home just fine. I thanked her for the tea and headed back into the cold.

The road was completely drifted over by the time I started back. I knew the way from memory so I wasn't worried. I was more concerned with Midnight's behavior. He had been in the snow before and had never acted this way. Something had him spooked. His ears perked up, but I didn't hear anything.

I pulled back on the reins until we came to a complete stop. I still didn't hear anything.

Then I heard a deep devilish growl just as I nudged Midnight forward. He cried out and reared back on his hind legs. I went flying backwards and hit the ground with my leg awkwardly bent beneath me. I felt a flash of pain shoot up my leg as something snapped in my ankle. I rolled over in time to see the black tail-end of my horse running toward home.

I cried out from the pain, but instantly remembered the sound that caused Midnight to light out on the dead run. It was a wolf. I spun around in a circle and didn't see anything. I reached inside of my jacket and pulled the LeMat from my belt. It was loaded. I reached into my bag, found a percussion cap and placed it on the nipple with my shaking hands. I still didn't see anything, but I thought I heard the growl again. The sound was coming from directly in front of me. The blowing snow was so thick, the wolf could be ten feet away and I still wouldn't be able to see it.

Suddenly, it leapt out of the blizzard and was on me. I managed to get a shot off before it reached me. There was a quick yelp, but it kept on coming. My pistol went flying as it locked onto my arm and violently shook its head. The thickness of my coat offered some protection, but before long, I could feel its teeth tear into my skin. I tried to push it away, but it snapped at me and then went for my throat. I punched at it as it tried to gnaw through my scarf. The wolf was much too fast and strong for me to defend myself. I was losing the battle when a giant black blur smashed into us. I was stunned, but still half conscious. It took a few seconds for me to shake away the cobwebs. It was Muddy. She had attacked the wolf and knocked it ten feet into the woods.

Both animals were locked in fierce combat; each tearing and biting at each other at a feverish pace. I limped around looking for my pistol. Amazingly, I found it in a clump of snow covered briars. I somehow managed to get a cap in place and moved as close as I dared. Muddy and the wolf were covered in blood, but neither showed signs of slowing down. I steadied my hand and tried to get an open shot, but I had as much chance of hitting Muddy as I did the wolf. Finally, Muddy tore away at the wolf's throat; causing it to yelp wildly in pain.

It staggered a few feet away before collapsing. I limped to the animal and saw that it was still panting. It growled and snapped in my direction, but could not make it to its feet. My hands were shaking uncontrollably. I used my left hand to steady my right. I bit my lower lip as I slowly squeezed the trigger. The wolf went silent. I fell to the ground and breathed a sigh of relief. I looked over and for some reason decided to study the bloodied animal. *Why did you want to kill me so bad? Look at what it got you!* This lump of fur, teeth and bones, that only a moment ago wanted to kill me, was now as lifeless as a rock. It didn't make sense. Nothing in my life made sense.

I couldn't feel the pain in my ankle anymore. I didn't feel the cold in the air either. I probably would have sat there until I was frozen, if the thought of Muddy suffering hadn't come to mind.

Muddy tried to stand up when she saw me coming, but fell back into the snow. The wolf had ripped her to shreds. Most of her skin was ripped away, exposing her muscles and tendons. She was covered in blood along with a white foamy ooze. She whimpered and her breathing was shallow. "Don't try to get up," I told her. "I'll go get the wagon and get you home." I took three steps and realized I would never make it. I hopped back and sat beside her. I looked at her again and saw how much she was suffering. I looked into her eyes and couldn't believe what I saw. She wanted me to praise her for doing a good job. I wrapped my arms around her neck and ran my hand from her forehead to the end of her snout. "Good job, Muddy. Good job, girl." A look of contentment came over her for a moment. I'd heard farmers say that an animal didn't have a soul. A pig has no concept of life and death. I knew this wasn't the case with Muddy. Her eyes testified that she knew that she was dying. Then she shrieked and squealed in pain and began to violently shiver.

"Never let an animal suffer if you can do something about it." I had heard Pa speak those words dozens of times. This is exactly what he was talking about. Muddy was going to die and in the meantime, she was in misery. She was suffering needlessly. I knew what I had to do.

I found the LeMat in a snowdrift next to the wolf. I checked the ball and readied a cap and limped back to Muddy's side. I could see the pain in her eyes. Even through her misery, I could see the soulful look that had made her different from other animals. She had been a playmate and friend for as long as I could remember. How could I kill her?

I looked at her one last time and realized that I had to end her suffering. It was the right thing to do. It was the only thing to do. She closed her eyes as I pointed the pistol at her head. "I'm sorry, girl," I muttered as I pulled the trigger. Nothing. The LeMat had jammed. I didn't know whether to curse or give thanks. I threw the pistol into the snow and crawled to her side. I tried to comfort her as best as I could. A few minutes later, my childhood companion, the little piglet that Jaybird had plucked from the mud, took her last breath. Once she was gone, I broke down and began to cry. Everything that had been bottled up inside of me came pouring out like a river. I crawled over and leaned against a tree that was big enough to shelter me against the wind. I continued to cry until there were no more tears left. Not long after that, I began to go numb. I could no longer feel any pain in my leg. I couldn't feel anything. I knew it was dangerous, but I didn't care. A few minutes later, I drifted off to sleep.

I had no idea where I was or how much time had passed when I opened my eyes. I was covered in blankets and the room was completely dark with the exception of a single candle. "Muddy!" I cried out. "Where's Muddy?"

"Shhh! I'm here, Will." Jenny took my hand and raked the hair out of my eyes. "You're safe now."

I looked around the room and realized that I was in bed next to the fireplace at our cabin. "How did I get here?" I asked.

"We were worried sick when your horse came home without you. Ned, Rose and I went looking for you in the wagon. We almost missed you, but Rose saw your pistol. You were almost completely covered with snow by the time we found you."

"Ouch!" I felt a sharp pain in my ankle as I rolled over.

"Does your leg hurt?" she asked.

"You could say that," I yelped.

"Dr. Judd left you a tonic for the pain. He said to give you three spoonfuls as soon as you woke up." She had the first spoonful of the awful tasting syrup in my mouth before I could argue.

A few minutes later, my pain started to ease. "I need to get Muddy," I told her. "I can't leave her out there like that."

"Shhh…"she whispered. "Ned took care of it."

"She saved my life. That wolf would have killed me, if Muddy wouldn't have…" The medicine hit me like a brick. I tried to finish the thought, but couldn't. Everything slowly went dark as I drifted back to sleep.

For the next few days, I floated in and out of sleep. I don't know if it was the pain or the medicine or if I was just exhausted. Whatever the cause; I couldn't have gotten out of bed if I wanted. I slightly remembered conversations but couldn't tell you what was said. It wasn't until Rose came to my bedside on Christmas Eve and told me that Lizzy had passed away, that I finally got out of bed. I asked about going to the graveyard service, but Rose said they had buried her that morning so folks could spend their Christmas Day with their families.

"I missed it? How could you let me miss her funeral?" I was angry and heartbroken at the same time.

"Doc Judd said to keep you in bed," she said. "You were in no shape to go. Besides, the Maxwell's didn't want a big to do. Only family and a few friends were there. I went on behalf of our family. Everybody knows you would have been there if you could."

I didn't know what to say. Lizzy was gone and buried and life went on. Surprisingly, I didn't shed any tears. I began to feel guilty. I cried bucketfuls over a pet pig, but had nothing for Lizzy. She had been my best friend. What kind of horrible person had I become?

I finally got out of bed and ate dinner with the family. It was a venison and potato stew. It was usually one of my favorites, but on that day nothing tasted good. After dinner Jenny helped Samantha and the boys decorate the tree, while Rose and Granny cleaned up the kitchen. Pappy puffed his evening pipe in his rocker. Ned was away on some errand, but I never asked what it was. I sat on the stool and looked out the window as the sun faded in the southwest. I wasn't looking at anything in particular, but I kept watch until it was pitch black outside. The night was crystal clear without a hint of wind. The frozen snow sparkled like thousands of gemstones beneath a white full moon. I suppose it was beautiful, but I could find no beauty in the world. Not in a world that lets an innocent girl like Lizzy suffer such a horrible death while her killer stays free to joke about his poison bullet.

Bub came over to see what I had been looking at for the past hour. "Look, Granny!" he shouted. "It's the Christmas Star!"

Everybody crowded around to see the star. "It sure is Bub," she assured him. "That's the same star the led the three wise men to the *Baby Jesus.*"

"Down South, we call that the *Miracle Star,*" Jenny added. "Pray a miracle to Jesus on that star and it will come true."

"There's no such things as miracles," I told them and stormed out the door. I'd seen enough over the past few years to know there weren't any happy endings. Life wasn't fair and God didn't care about anybody in South Union. I stood on the porch and stared at the damn star and couldn't bring myself to ask for a miracle. It would be just another disappointment.

Jenny stepped onto the porch holding my jacket and scarf. "Put these on before you get sick again." I was cold and did as she said. After I was bundled up, she stood next to me and took my hand in hers. "Now, how can anything that beautiful not be called *The Miracle Star?*"

"God doesn't care about anybody," I declared. "If he did, he wouldn't let all of these bad things happen to good people."

"Bite your tongue, Will Farmer!" She scolded me. "Who are you to question the mind of the Almighty?"

"I'm sorry, Jenny. It's just the way I feel about things. Can you blame me?"

"Yes I can. Do you think that you are the only boy who ever had something bad happen to him? God gives us the ability to rise up out of the pain and heartache. He gives us the ability to overcome. Do you believe that your pig laid its life down to save you?"

"She did!" I declared. "I wouldn't be here if it wasn't for Muddy."

"Then why can't you believe that God sent his own Son down to Earth to do the same thing? That's the reason the Lord Jesus hung on that cross. He did it for you. Can you see what I'm telling you?"

"I guess so." I answered.

"God sent that star as a sign to tell the world that the *Baby Jesus* was born in Bethlehem. That's why they call it the *Miracle Star*. It's up to you whether you ask for a miracle or not. You can't get nothing, if you don't ask." She patted my shoulder and walked back inside of the cabin.

I stood on the porch for a while longer, but I just couldn't make myself ask for the miracle. As much as I tried, I couldn't make myself believe that anything would come of it. As I wrestled with the subject of my faith, the silhouette of a solitary soldier on horseback appeared on the horizon. "Oh God, please let it be good news," I whispered without thinking.

As he came closer, I recognized the soldier to be Captain Weber. "Good evening, Mr. Farmer. I heard you gave your family quite the scare."

"The wolf? It wasn't that bad. I banged my leg up when I fell off of my horse. Other than that—I'm fine."

"Glad to hear that," he chuckled . "I guess it takes more than a big bad wolf to get the better of Will Farmer."

"I reckon," I was embarrassed for tooting my own horn.

"Is your family inside?" he asked. "I've got a telegram for them. I didn't want it to wait until tomorrow."

I was afraid to ask, so I just led him into the cabin.

You could have cut the tension with a knife as we gathered around the table. Weber handed the telegram to Granny but she signaled for the Captain to read it instead. He smiled and for the first time, it looked like it was going to be good news.

Weber adjusted his gold rimmed spectacles and cleared his throat. "This wire is coming from a Lieutenant Samuel Farmer from New Orleans. *Dear Family, Have reached safe haven in New Orleans and will work processing freed slaves into Union Army. I am safe now and should be home in two months. Hope this finds you all well, with all my love, Samuel.*"

The cabin erupted in cheers of joy. Pa was alive and would be home soon. All three of the women began crying. Pappy slapped the table and the boys began to dance around the Christmas tree.

Captain Weber raised his hand to get our attention. "There is a post script that requires an answer," he said.

"What is it?" asked Granny.

"He wants to know if a woman by the name of Genevieve Lefebvre is residing at the cabin."

A hush fell over the room. Granny pursed her lips. "You tell Sam that there is nobody by that name a livin' here. But make sure you tell him that Jenny Farmer and his baby girl, Samantha, can't wait to see him."

Jenny covered her face to hide her tears, while the Captain scribbled down the return message. Granny tried to feed him, but he kindly refused. He did, however, accept a snort of Christmas cheer from Pappy's jug. He stopped at the door and wished us a Merry Christmas. He had no idea how much his gift of the telegram meant to us all.

We ate Christmas sweets and apple cider to celebrate the news. With all that had happened, it was nice to finally get some good news.

I looked out the window to see if the star was still there. It was. Jenny must have sensed my thoughts. "What do you think of that *Miracle Star* now?" she asked.

"I guess there might be something to it after all," I admitted.

"You better believe it!" she playfully elbowed my ribs. "Did you make your wish yet?" she asked. "I have the feeling there might be another miracle left tonight."

"I don't know," I shook my head, "I don't think it will work for me."

"Nonsense!" she scolded me. "You aren't no better or worse than anybody else." She grabbed my shirt sleeve and pushed me out the door. "You go out there and make that wish or I'll not let you back inside. Don't tell anybody what you wished for, or it won't come true."

I did what she said and then banged on the door.

"Did you make the wish?" she asked from the other side of the door.

"Yes! Now let me in. It's freezing out here."

Jenny opened the door with a devilish smile on her face. "Was that so hard?"

"No," I admitted. Everybody was smiling at me as if they all knew something that I didn't. "What's going on around here?"

"Nothing," Rose answered. "We're just having a little fun with you."

"It's been a long night for everybody," Granny shouted. "Time for bed."

Bub and Jaybird complained, but didn't argue when Granny shooed them upstairs with her broom. "Christmas morning is going to be here before you know it."

Rose force fed me three spoonfuls of Doc Judd's syrup. Without question, I would be sleeping well that night. Within minutes, I started to get drowsy. "When's Ned getting back?" I yawned.

"He'll be back before morning," she assured me.

"Where did he go?" I asked

"He went to get some Christmas presents. Now you get some sleep." Rose tucked the blankets under my chin and lovingly kissed my forehead.

"Good night, Sister Rose," I whispered. I was asleep before she could answer back.

I heard Ned arrive in the middle of the night, but being under the influence of Doc Judd's pain elixir, I didn't have the strength to get out of bed. Later on, I became aware of activity in the back of the cabin. *What could be going on at this hour?* I was curious, but still couldn't find the pepper to see what the fuss was about. Everything would have to wait until morning.

The voices of Jaybird and Bub begging to open their presents and the smell of bacon on the griddle jolted me from my sleep. "Merry Christmas, sleepyhead!" Rose shouted when she saw my eyes open. "We were afraid you were going to sleep the day away."

"I think you gave me too much of Doc's tonic," I told her. "I feel like an elephant landed on my head." I staggered to the table and sat down next to Ned. Granny poured me a mug of cider and then smiled like a cat that ate the church mouse.

"What are you smiling at?" I asked.

"Merry Christmas, Will." She continued smiling at me. It got to the point that I began to feel uneasy.

I looked around the cabin and everybody had the same silly grin on their face. "What are you looking at?"

Nobody answered. The room was full of smiles but none of them would tell me what was going on.

"What is wrong with you people," I demanded. "This isn't funny!"

Jenny finally broke the silence. "Did you make a wish on the star?"

"What are you talking about?"

"Did you make your wish on the *Miracle Star*?" she asked again.

"I did. Why do you ask?"

Jenny took me by the hand and led me to her room in the back of the cabin. I felt a little silly, but I went with her. She knocked on the door. "Can we come in?" she asked.

I heard a muffled 'yes' and Jenny opened the door. I didn't know what to expect, but when I saw who it was—I couldn't believe my eyes! It was Cliffy!

"What are you doing here?" She was sitting up in bed, with both of her legs splinted and braced.

"Aren't you going to come over here and give me a hug?"

I was careful to stay clear of her legs as I made my way to her bedside. "I've missed you," I whispered as I wrapped my arms around her.

"You'll never know how much I've missed you," she told me. "I thought I'd never see you again." She started sobbing and buried her head on my shoulder. I remained silent and was happy to let her cry as much as she wanted. I looked around and saw my entire family watching us. I didn't care. Cliffy was in my arms.

After our tearful reunion, we moved her bed next to the fireplace, so she could participate in the Christmas festivities. We all sat around and listened as she explained to me how she had been injured. "It was the last show in Vincennes. You had left that morning and I had spent the day crying in my wagon. I had no business performing that night. I was walking on the high wire and I started thinking of you. I lost my balance and then everything went blank. When I woke up three days later, I found myself in a second rate boarding house on the river. The circus had left town. My room had been paid up until Christmas. The doctor who had set my legs told Clay Boerwinkle that I would be bed ridden for at least three months and that I would never be able to perform again. Boerwinkle had taken all of my money and left me with a five dollar gold piece. I had no place to go and then I thought about you. You had told me so much about your family; I felt like I actually knew them all. The more I thought about it, the more South Union sounded like Heaven. That's when I decided to write the letter."

"What letter?" I asked "I didn't get any letter."

"That's because it was addressed to me," Granny said.

I looked at Cliffy. "I don't understand."

Cliffy patted my hand. "Will, I know you'd let me move in without asking questions, but the decision wasn't yours to make. I wouldn't dare do anything that would come between you and your family. I told your Granny how I feel about you and that I knew we were too young to get married. I asked her if she knew of a place near you where I might be of some help. I told her I was willing to do anything."

"It turns out, Doc Logan needs a nurse and the Widow Rush has an extra bed," said Rose. "Cliffy can move in with her after her legs heal. In the meantime she's going to stay here while she's on the mend."

I looked at everyone around the fireplace. "And everybody knew about this except me?"

"Every one of us," declared Bub.

"And that's where Ned has been the past couple of days?" I asked.

"We wanted it to be a Merry Christmas for you and Cliffy," Ned explained.

"A Merry Christmas for everybody!" shouted Bub. "Now let's open our presents!"

The cabin erupted in laughter and Rose began pouring apple cider for everyone. That's when I saw Cliffy take Granny by the hand. "I can't thank you enough for taking me into your home, Mrs. Farmer."

"Just call me Granny. Everyone does."

"Okay—Granny it is, I never believed that I would ever get a second chance at being a part of a real family."

Granny smiled and moved a stray curl away from Cliffy's eyes. "Stay around here long enough and there's no tellin' what you might see. If there's one thing that I've learned; this cabin is a place of second chances for everyone who walks through that door. Welcome home, child."

Later that night after the sun had long since settled beyond the horizon, I walked outside and searched for the star in the east. The *Miracle Star* seemed even bigger and brighter than before. I suddenly felt small and humble. My wish had come true. In a world that had been ravaged by war, *The Creator* had seen fit to answer the prayer of a lowly boy in a place called South Union. I looked up at the star and smiled. "I'm sorry. I never should have doubted you." And that's when I realized that He was truly the God of second chances.

—⁓—

Epilogue

Christmas 1885

I had just set fire to the Yule log in the fireplace in our den and was watching my wife, Mae, decorate our Christmas tree with our two daughters. Mae was wearing a traditional red satin dress, adorned with black ribbons and a festive mother of pearl brooch that was carved into the shape of a candy cane. Our girls, Rebecca and Anna, were adorned in matching black velvet dresses trimmed in white lace. They handled every ornament as if it was a treasure from the Orient.

Mae was a wonderful wife and mother and made sure the holidays were a special time for all us. From day one, nothing was more important than her family. Because Mae's youth had been cut short by poverty and abuse, she was determined to leave our girls with memories of an enchanted upbringing. She managed to walk a fine line between making sure that the girls had everything they needed without spoiling them.

Mae and I were married the day after I graduated from the Cincinnati School of Medicine. It was the happiest day of my life. It was also the same day that Cliffphilia Willow Maya McGee became Mrs. Mae Farmer. She wanted a new name for her new life.

After working with Doc Judd for a couple of years, we moved to Terre Haute, where I opened a practice of my own. We have lived in our two-story brick home on Sixth Street ever since.

I had just placed the star atop the tree when Rebecca started screaming. "Look everybody! It's the miracle star!"

We all went to the window and there it was—just above the eastern horizon. My mind instantly took me back to the Christmas of 1864 and the first time that I wished on the Miracle Star. Looking back, it was the exact moment I started on the path to get to where I am today.

It has been twenty years since the war ended, but hardly a day goes by that I don't think about those days in South Union. It was a time of sadness and hardship, but out of that devastation, I discovered my faith. During a war that had consumed an entire nation, God still performed tender mercies for those who believed and sought His face. In my case, He showed favor for a boy who didn't deserve His Amazing Grace.

—⁓—

A Note from the Author

Approximately two miles west of Flat Rock, Illinois and a quarter mile north of Maxwell Corner is a manicured dirt lane that will take you to Seceder Cemetery. Beneath the shade of a dozen ancient conifers is a modest headstone that marks the final resting place for Elizabeth "Lizzy" Maxwell. It was at Lizzy's gravesite that I conceived the idea for this book. By all accounts, Lizzy was a quiet unassuming fourteen year old girl who was shot and killed because her family decided to fight against the peculiar institution of slavery. Lizzy suffered in agony for seven weeks before succumbing on Christmas Eve in 1864. Most historians agree that the American Civil War had to be fought to remove the blight of slavery from our land. Scholars study the great battles and legendary generals, along with the issue of state's right and the politics that led to the war in the first place. Battlefield strategy is broken down and second guessed. The sheer number of casualties is overwhelming. Nearly 620,000 men lost their lives in the line of duty during the Civil War. That represented two percent of the nation's population at the time. The equivalent in today's population would be 6,000,000 deaths. What seems to be overlooked is that children were the most innocent and forgotten of all of the victims of the American Civil War.

Lizzy Maxwell's tombstone stands as a silent reminder of that fact.

I'd like to offer a special thanks to my Irish bride, Angela. Without her hours of help and support; this book would not have been possible.

I'd also like to thank Becky Nidey, Kyle Howe and John "Bub" Kelsheimer for their editorial help. It's a thankless job but somebody has got to do it.

I'd like to thank David Foote along with the gang at the Susie Wesley Memorial Library for their help with the local research.

I would also like to thank my family's historian, my lovely aunt, Sharon Oreskovich, for inspiring me to study the past in search of a story.

Most of all, I would like to thank my loyal readers. Without you, I would have quit a long time ago.

Rick Kelsheimer

15 August 2013

Made in the USA
Middletown, DE
18 November 2022